Towards Improved Retirement Savings Outcomes for Women

OECD
BETTER POLICIES FOR BETTER LIVES

Please cite this publication as:
OECD (2021), *Towards Improved Retirement Savings Outcomes for Women*, OECD Publishing, Paris, *https://doi.org/10.1787/f7b48808-en*.

ISBN 978-92-64-33453-3 (print)
ISBN 978-92-64-43307-6 (pdf)

Photo credits: Cover © Radoman Durkovic/iStock/Getty Images.

Corrigenda to publications may be found on line at: *www.oecd.org/about/publishing/corrigenda.htm*.

Foreword

The gender pension gap, or the fact that women tend to live on a lower income in retirement than men, is well-known and is usually measured by combining all sources of pension income, whether public or private, pay-as-you-go or funded. However, little is known about the specific contribution of funded and private retirement savings arrangements to this gap. Given the growing weight of retirement savings arrangements in the provision of retirement income around the world, understanding how they may contribute to the gap today and into the future is of paramount importance.

Towards Improved Retirement Savings Outcomes for Women examines the contribution of retirement savings arrangements to the gap in retirement income between men and women. It provides governments with solutions to ensure that the design of these arrangements does not disadvantage women more than existing gender gaps already do, in particular in the labour market. It first analyses why the gender pension gap exists and sheds light on some of the labour market, behavioural and cultural factors that contribute to income inequalities in retirement. The study also examines how differences between men and women arise during the accumulation phase, using country case studies to assess how demographics, labour markets and other factors may affect gaps in pension plan participation, assets and entitlements. The study then explores the extent to which the design of retirement savings plans affects men and women differently. Finally, it provides policy options to improve retirement savings outcomes for women and to help close the gender pension gap.

This publication is the work of the pension team from the Consumer Finance, Insurance and Pensions Division of the OECD Directorate for Financial and Enterprise Affairs. It uses data from the Eurosystem Household Finance and Consumption Survey (HFCS), the Luxembourg Income Study (LIS) and the Luxembourg Wealth Study (LWS) databases, among other sources. It has greatly benefitted from the comments of national government delegates of the OECD Working Party on Private Pensions (WPPP). This international body brings together policy makers, regulators and private sector representatives from close to 40 countries to discuss issues related to the operation and regulation of funded retirement income systems. Delegates assisted in verifying the accuracy of the information corresponding to their respective countries. Any remaining errors are solely the responsibility of the authors.

The editorial team for this publication was led by Pablo Antolín. Chapter 1 was prepared by Romain Despalins; Chapter 2 by Elsa Favre-Baron; Chapter 3 by Diana Hourani; Chapter 4 by Stéphanie Payet; and Chapter 5 by Jessica Mosher. Pamela Duffin and Edward Smiley provided editorial and communication support.

Table of contents

Tables

Figures

Boxes

Editorial

Mathilde Mesnard
Deputy Director, OECD Directorate for Financial and Entreprise Affairs

The gender pension gap, or the difference in retirement income that men and women receive, remains substantial at 26 per cent on average in the OECD. It is a clear result and signal of gender inequalities along the life cycle, despite the significant progress made to reduce them in pension systems over the last decades. Retirement savings arrangements are playing a growing role in this gender pension gap.

Closing the gender pension gap for retirement savings arrangements poses a particular challenge, given that the income from these arrangements is closely linked to employment and income patterns. This link means that gender differences with respect to labour market participation and gender wage gaps, which are reinforced by women's disproportionate role as caretakers, will directly contribute to the gender pension gap. These labour market differences affect every stage of preparing financially for retirement, from access to and participation in retirement savings arrangements, to the level of contributions made throughout one's career, through to the level of income received in retirement. The design of retirement savings arrangements alone cannot correct for all labour market differences. Nevertheless, it should strive to reduce the impact that these factors will have on the retirement income of women, or at least ensure that inequalities are not exacerbated.

There has been progress over the last two decades in reducing the gender differences that have been driving the gender pension gap. Women have joined the labour force in increasing numbers and the gender pay gap has decreased by 5 percentage points. These trends have been aided by more and more women completing higher education and by changing societal attitudes about the role of women as homemakers and caretakers. Increased employment and higher wages have flowed directly through to improved retirement savings and entitlements for women.

Nevertheless, there is still a long way to go to achieve gender parity, and the ongoing COVID-19 crisis is threatening this progress, particularly given the pandemic's adverse impact on women. Women are more likely to be employed in the most heavily impacted sectors, such as hospitality, tourism and retail. They are also more likely to hold part-time work, positions which are more vulnerable to lay-offs. Furthermore, women have shouldered the brunt of children's education following school closures, as well as other caretaker responsibilities. These responsibilities have led many women to reduce their working hours or withdraw from employment, thereby reducing their ability to contribute to their retirement savings plans. Women's retirement income is also more likely to be negatively impacted by the indirect effects of the pandemic, such as the potential increase in divorce rates following lockdown measures or policies that have allowed individuals to withdraw their retirement savings in response to the pandemic.

It is therefore even more urgent that policy makers take measures to address the gender pension gap and ensure that we do not reverse the progress made. While the situation calls for measures beyond the pension system to help women overcome barriers to working and address pay gaps, attention still needs to be paid to the design of retirement savings arrangements to ensure that it is not exacerbating gender inequalities in retirement. This report sheds some light on the drivers of the gender pension gap and provides concrete policy options that governments can consider for the design of retirement savings arrangements to help continue the progress made in reducing the gender pension gap.

Executive summary

The gender pension gap observed today is mainly the result of past work history differences between men and women. Differences in labour market participation, part-time employment, wages, and career length translate into different pension outcomes down the road. The transmission mechanism from the labour market to the pension system is direct with retirement savings arrangements, which depend upon putting aside part of individuals' total earnings to finance their retirement. Given the growing importance of these arrangements in the provision of retirement income, policy settings should at least ensure that their design does not increase the gap, putting women at a further disadvantage.

This publication provides governments with guidelines to ensure that retirement savings arrangements do not further exacerbate inequalities between men and women stemming from labour market or other factors. This study first presents evidence of the gender pension gap in retirement savings arrangements in selected OECD countries. It then explores the literature to shed light on some of the behavioural and cultural factors that contribute to these inequalities. Country case studies then look into the question of what explains the gender gap in pension coverage, assets and entitlements in some OECD countries, with a focus on unpacking drivers other than labour market factors. The study then analyses the rules and parameters of retirement savings arrangements using a gender lens. Finally, it provides policy options to improve retirement savings outcomes for women and to help close the gender pension gap.

Key findings

- On average in the OECD, combining public and private sources, women aged 65 and older receive 26% less income than men from the pension system.
- Part of this gap originates from retirement savings arrangements, as women participate less in retirement savings plans and build up lower pension assets and entitlements, in particular from the ages of 25 to 44, which may correspond to the impact of the first career break for parenting.
- Beyond labour market drivers, behavioural and cultural elements, as well as societal interactions, may influence the decisions taken by men and women in a way that contributes to the gender gap in retirement savings arrangements. Compared to men, women are often found to be more risk averse and have lower levels of financial literacy overall, which may influence their attitude towards savings. Marital choices may also affect retirement incomes, as couples may be able to mutualise their pension savings. Gender stereotyping could also encourage women to opt for solutions that are more conservative than what their actual risk preferences imply. Moreover, communication campaigns may fail to take into account certain needs specific to women, such as how to compensate for the decrease in salary and contributions during parental leave.
- Country case studies demonstrate that while labour market inequalities are important drivers of the gender pension gap, aspects related to the design of retirement savings arrangements also explain much of the gap. They show that factors such as pension eligibility rules can lead to significant differences in pension plan coverage from workplaces. The studies also exhibit evidence of

behavioural biases, particularly when it comes to personal pension plans that may lead women to save less than men.

- The design of retirement savings plans is not always gender neutral. Women are disadvantaged compared to men when:
  - eligibility criteria based on working hours or earnings restrict plan access;
  - contributions or pension right accruals stop during periods of maternity and parental leave;
  - conservative investment strategies are used for the default option;
  - pension rights and assets are not split automatically between ex-spouses upon separation;
  - retirement benefits are not indexed;
  - pay-out options with survivor benefits are not available.

Policy guidelines

There are ways to design retirement savings arrangements that mitigate their effects on the gender pension gap. While it cannot address the drivers themselves in all cases, particularly those stemming from the labour market, the design of these arrangements should at least account for and accommodate gender differences that can lead to lower eligibility, lower participation, lower and less frequent contributions, lower returns, lower individual rights, and lower retirement income. As such, retirement savings arrangements should aim to be gender neutral. The following policy guidelines would contribute to reducing the gender pension gap:

- **Promote women's access to retirement saving arrangements** by increasing the availability of such arrangements in industries predominantly employing women and relaxing eligibility requirements.
- **Encourage women's participation in retirement savings arrangements** through hard or soft compulsion, financial incentives to join, and financial education initiatives tailored specifically to women.
- **Improve the level and frequency of women's contributions to retirement savings arrangements** with contributions from employers or spouses, financial incentives that target groups with large female representation (e.g. low-income groups), subsidies for maternity and caretaking, contribution limits that can be carried forward, and targeted communication to educate women on the importance of regular contributions.
- **Adapt the design of retirement savings arrangements to the career patterns of women** by allowing more flexibility with respect to contributions, improving the portability of plans, and adapting the fee structures to small account balances.
- **Improve investment returns on women's retirement savings** by implementing non-conservative default investment options and offering objective assessments of their risk tolerance to inform their investment decisions.
- **Increase women's own retirement benefit entitlements** by allowing spouses to share their pension rights with each other, facilitating the split of retirement benefit entitlements upon divorce, and increasing women's awareness of the option to share their former spouse's benefits, when it exists.
- **Increase the level of retirement income that women receive** by equalising retirement ages between genders, calculating lifetime retirement income based on unisex mortality tables where feasible, providing a subsidy directly to women, promoting pay-out options with survivor benefits, and encouraging the availability of pay-out solutions that increase payments over time.

1 Assessing the gender gap in retirement savings arrangements

This chapter assesses the difference in retirement income that men and women receive across OECD countries, and the extent to which retirement savings arrangements may contribute to this overall gender gap. It explores the main drivers of this gap in the labour markets, before looking into other factors that can create a gap in retirement income coming from retirement savings arrangements.

Women receive lower pensions than men worldwide. This is partly due to the fact that, overall, women tend to have earned less and had shorter careers than men during their working lives. The pensions received today by those who are already retired reflect past differences in their careers. However, the transmission mechanism varies across the different layers of the pension system.

This chapter estimates the gender gap in total retirement income in OECD countries and examines to what extent this may be attributed to retirement savings arrangements (i.e. funded pension plans).[1] This chapter aims to uncover any evidence of a difference in retirement income that men and women receive from retirement savings arrangements and touches upon some of the underlying drivers.

The analysis confirms the gap in retirement income that women receive from their retirement savings plans, occupational and personal plans, compared to men in certain countries. Differences in men and women's labour market outcomes have been narrowing, which should narrow the private pension gap between men and women over time, but other factors may continue to widen it. There is still a gap in the proportion of men and women covered by a retirement savings arrangement in many OECD countries. Women with retirement savings plans usually have a lower balance than men, and this gap compounds over their career. Additionally, the pay-out options that women may have at retirement could exacerbate the gap in retirement income further.

This chapter first defines what this publication considers as the gender pension gap. Secondly, it assesses this gap across OECD countries. Thirdly, it examines whether and to what extent retirement savings arrangements may play a role in this gender pension gap. The fourth section looks at factors in the labour markets that can explain the current gender pension gap, while the fifth section looks into other factors (beyond labour market inequalities) that can create a gap of retirement income coming from retirement savings arrangements. The last section concludes.

1.1. Measuring the gender gap in pensions

Individuals may receive income from several sources at retirement. Retirees may get a public (old-age) pension, they may also draw on their assets in retirement savings arrangements. Widow(er)s benefit from survivor's pensions in most OECD countries (OECD, 2018[1]). Some retirees may simply continue to work during retirement and earn some income from that work.

Men and women may not be on an equal footing in retirement. In particular, they may not receive the same benefit payments from the overall pension system (public and private) in a given year, creating a potential gap. [2]

A gap in retirement income, i.e. a gender pension gap, is the difference between the average retirement income of men and women in the latest year available. It is expressed as a percentage of men's average pension and is calculated over the population of pension beneficiaries aged 65+ for comparability purposes across countries.[3] Calculations exclude those with no pension at all. Work-related earnings for people aged 65+ are excluded from the calculations, as they do not represent a retirement income. One-off payments (i.e. lump sums) that can be received from retirement savings plans are not taken into account in the calculations of the gender pension gap, unless they are used to purchase an annuity product.

The analysis of the gender pension gap relies on multinational household survey data. Multinational household surveys contain information about streams of income from both the public and private pension systems for the elderly, and are harmonised across countries.[4] Some other sources (e.g. focus group analyses) can also provide insights and complement the analysis of the gender pension gap and its drivers (Box 1.1).

Box 1.1. Different sources for analysing the gender pension gap

The calculation of a gender pension gap requires knowledge of all the sources of income that men and women receive from the public and private pension arrangements.

Several sources provide information on the income of the elderly. These sources include supervisory data, tax data and survey data. Supervisory authorities compile information on benefit payments to retirees from private pension providers and the type of payment (e.g. lump sum payments, pensions). Tax and survey data can provide extensive information on the source of income for individuals by gender, taking into account all the income flows (from the public and the private pension systems) and the different providers (pension funds, insurance companies) of private pensions. Some other sources, such as focus group analyses, can also provide detailed information on the pension benefits retirees receive. Industry groups may also carry out studies on their clients for a better understanding of their preferences and behaviours.

The analysis of the gender pension gap in this publication is mainly based on household survey data as they include information on retirement income from public and private pension arrangements (unlike supervisory data), they are representative of the whole population through their sampling and weighting procedures (unlike focus group studies) and are easily available to the research community. This publication favours multinational household surveys as they cover multiple countries and compile information on retirement income in a standardised fashion (which may not be the case for tax data). Unfortunately, lump sum payments may not be considered as a (regular) retirement income in household surveys unless individuals purchase an annuity product with the lump sum payments. Household surveys are therefore useful for assessing a gender gap in regular retirement income but less appropriate for measuring a gender gap in pension wealth (that would take into account one-off payments as well as how long the regular payments are carried out).

However, household survey data contain useful demographic information about individuals (marital status, age, type of job). This information can be relevant to any analysis of the drivers of the gender pension gap during individuals' working lives.

1.2. Assessing the overall gender pension gap

This section examines the extent to which men and women receive a different retirement income from all (public and private) sources combined in retirement.

All reporting OECD countries have a gender pension gap when looking at the extent to which men and women receive different income at retirement (i.e. pensions) from all sources combined, public and private. The gap ranges from 3% in Estonia to 47% of men's average retirement income in Japan (Figure 1.1). On average, women aged 65+ receive 26% less income than men from the pension system in the OECD. In other words, women aged 65 or more receive around 74% of the retirement income of men from public and private pension arrangements on average in the OECD. These results are overall in line with previous work from the OECD on this subject using other sources (OECD, 2017[2]), although the size of the gap may vary to some extent for some countries depending on the underlying source (Box 1.2).

Figure 1.1. Gender gap in pensions in selected OECD countries, latest year available

Relative difference between men and women aged 65+ (among pension beneficiaries)

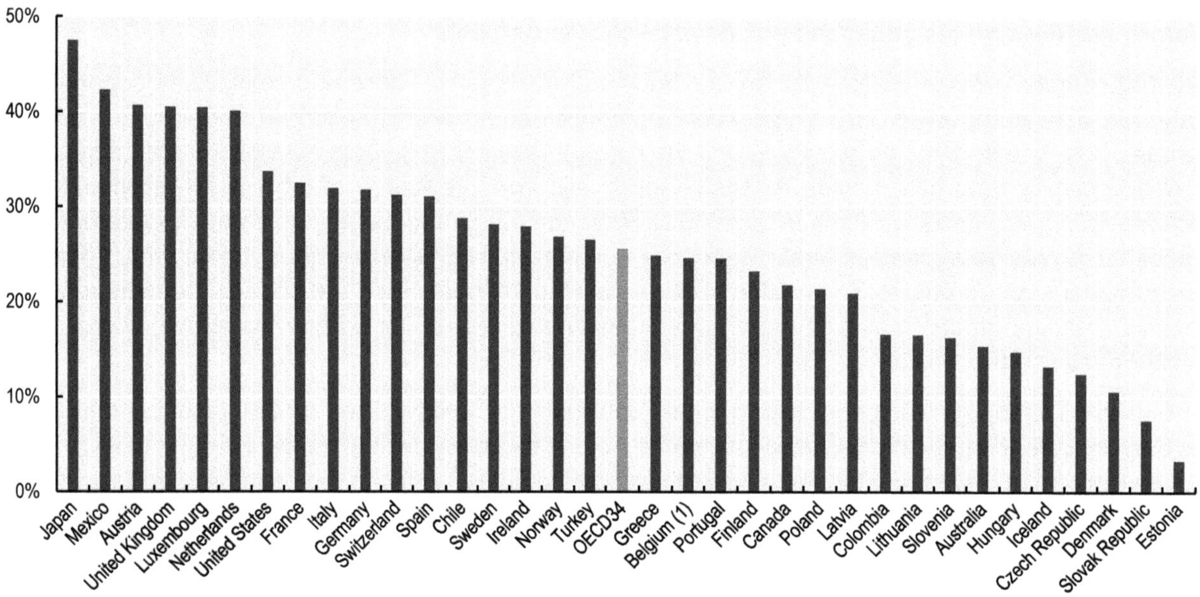

Note: The gender gap in pensions is calculated as the difference between the mean retirement income of men and women (aged 65+) over the mean retirement income of men (aged 65+), among pension beneficiaries. Calculations are based on the LIS, except for: France, Latvia and Portugal where the HFCS (Wave 3) was used; and Iceland, Sweden and Turkey where results come from the EU-SILC (published on Eurostat's website). Data come from the latest available survey, conducted in: 2013 for Japan, Luxembourg, the Netherlands, Norway and the Slovak Republic; 2014 for Australia; 2015 for Hungary and Slovenia; and after 2015 for all the other countries. Data refer to 2017 for Iceland and 2018 for Turkey. (1) In Belgium when partner A's pension rights are less than 25% of those of partner B, the pension of A is not paid out and B receives a family pension (calculated at 75% of wages instead of 60%).

Source: OECD calculations based on the LIS and the HFCS; Eurostat (for the EU-SILC).

StatLink https://doi.org/10.1787/888934230110

Box 1.2. Gender pension gaps according to several multinational household surveys

The size of the gender pension gap may vary across different household surveys. Several multinational household surveys gather standardised information on the retirement income of men and women in a number of countries. These surveys include the Household Finance and Consumption Survey (HFCS), the Luxembourg Income Study (LIS), the Luxembourg Wealth Study (LWS) and the European Union Statistics on Income and Living Conditions (EU-SILC). Altogether, these surveys cover all OECD countries but Israel, Korea and New Zealand. Annex 1.A briefly presents the variables on retirement income that these surveys cover.

These multinational surveys follow different approaches to standardise survey responses across countries. The HFCS and the EU-SILC define a common framework *ex ante* that participating national bodies can use to design a survey tailored to their own country. The underlying national surveys allow for the production of harmonised outputs across countries following the HFCS and the EU-SILC frameworks. By contrast, the LIS and the LWS harmonise the outputs of national surveys *ex post* to create international databases. The LIS and the LWS sometimes use the outputs of the HFCS and the EU-SILC surveys for European countries.

While all the previously mentioned surveys consistently show a gender pension gap in reporting OECD countries, the extent of this gap differs across surveys (Figure 1.2). Some of the largest discrepancies can be found for Austria with a gender pension gap varying between 31% and 41% depending on the survey, Germany with a gap between 32% and 40%, Luxembourg with a gap between 40% and 50%, the Slovak Republic with a gap between 5% and 15%, and the United Kingdom with a gap between 34% and 43%.

Figure 1.2. Gender pension gap in selected OECD countries according to different sources

Relative difference between men and women aged 65+ (among pension beneficiaries)

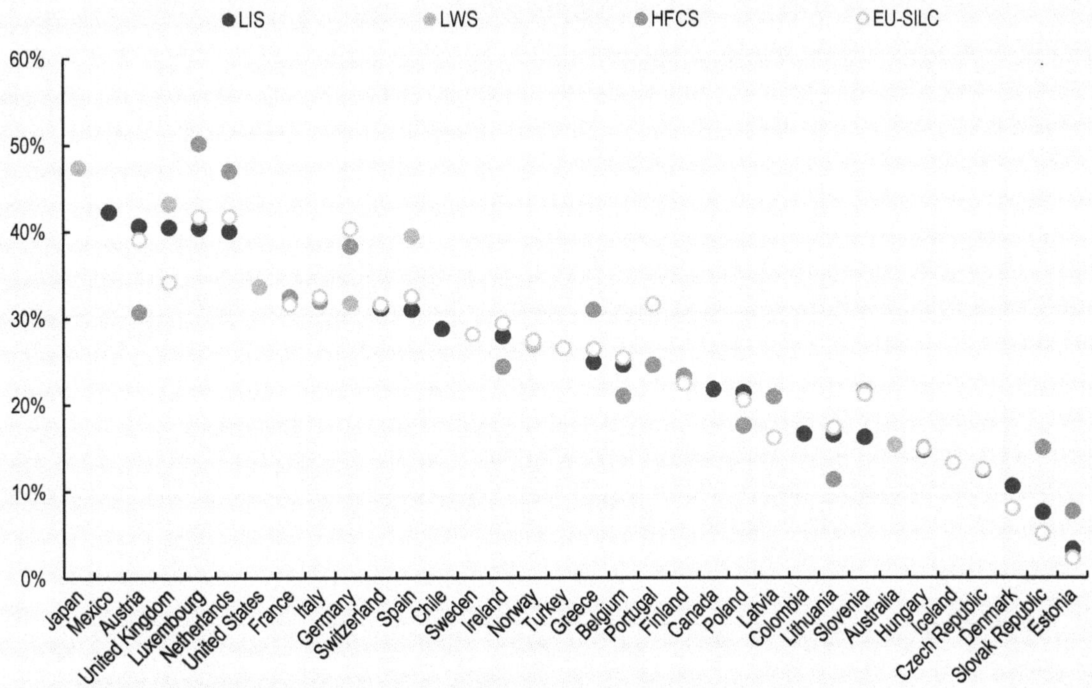

Note: This chart shows the gender pension gap across different surveys, conducted over the same (2-year) period in each country. Countries are ranked in the same order as in Figure 1.1.
Source: OECD calculations based on the HFCS, the LIS, the LWS; Eurostat (EU-SILC).

StatLink https://doi.org/10.1787/888934230129

Discrepancies across surveys may be the result of a combination of factors. These multinational surveys rely on different underlying national surveys. For instance, LIS and LWS data for Germany come from the German Socio-Economic Panel (GSOEP) while HFCS data are based on the Panel on Household Finances (PHF). The definition of retirement income may potentially be different across surveys. The HFCS questionnaire explicitly requests gross income from pensions (before tax and social contributions) among the core variables that all participating countries have to collect. The LIS and LWS databases do not specify whether retirement income is gross or net. The treatment of missing values also differs across surveys, as the HFCS and the LWS (for some countries) use a multiple imputation technique unlike the LIS. Finally, surveys have sometimes been conducted at different times, although surveys have been selected here in a way to ensure that this time difference is no more than two years.

The gender pension gap assessed in Figure 1.1 is based on the LIS and complemented by data from the HFCS and the EU-SILC. The LIS already covers a large number of OECD countries and compiles data over several decades through several waves of data collection, allowing for an analysis of the trends (over different samples though).

The gender pension gap has generally narrowed over the last decades. Figure 1.3 shows that the gender pension gap has declined in most reporting OECD countries since the early 2000s, especially in Canada (by 15 percentage points), Finland (by 8 percentage points) and the United States (by 8 percentage points). The gender gap has been closing relatively slowly in a third of the reporting countries, where the gap shrank by less than 5 percentage points in nearly two decades. However, some of these countries (e.g. Denmark and the Slovak Republic) already had a relatively low gender gap in the early 2000s (less than 15%) compared to other countries, leaving them less room for improvement than in other parts of the world. Yet, in a few countries, survey data suggest the gender gap would have remained the same or slightly increased since the early 2000s (e.g. in Austria and Italy).

Figure 1.3. Gender pension gap now and in the early 2000s in selected OECD countries

Relative difference between men and women aged 65+ (among pension beneficiaries)

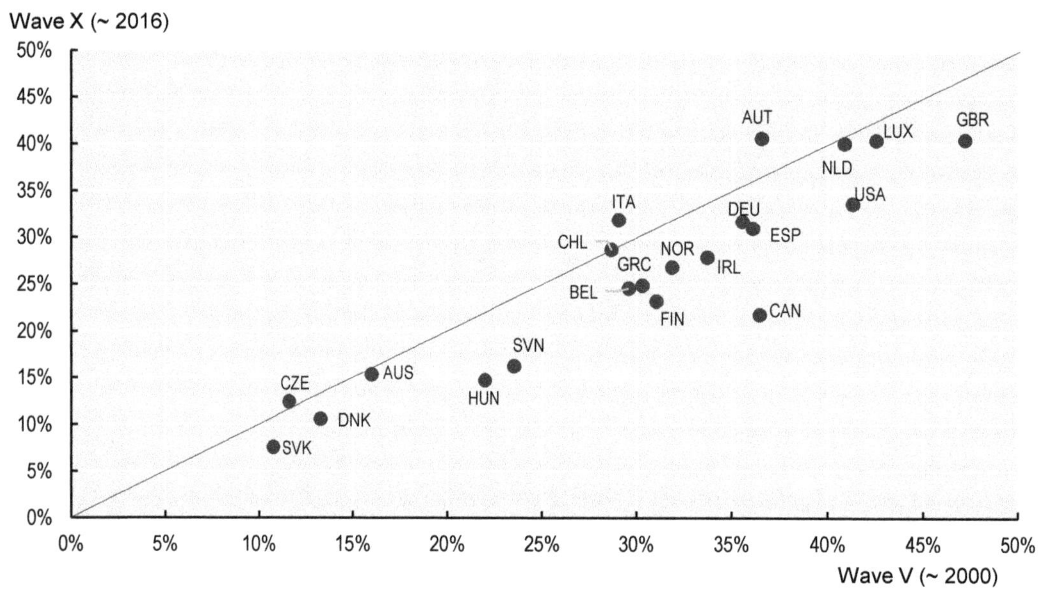

Note: This chart shows the gender pension gap in selected OECD countries (labelled with their ISO code) in Wave V (x-axis) and Wave X (y-axis) of the LIS, unless specified otherwise. Countries below the dotted line have experienced a decrease in the gender pension gap since Wave V (or VI) while those above have experienced an increase. ISO codes are available on the United Nation Statistics Division internet page at the following address: http://unstats.un.org/unsd/methods/m49/m49alpha.htm. Countries usually carried out the underlying survey of Wave V of the LIS between 1998 and 2002, and the underlying survey of Wave X of the LIS between 2015 and 2017. Data refer to Wave VI instead of Wave V for Luxembourg and Slovenia. Data refer to Wave IX instead of Wave X for Australia, Luxembourg, the Netherlands, Norway and the Slovak Republic. Data refer to Wave XI instead of Wave X for the United Kingdom and the United States.
Source: OECD calculations based on the LIS.

StatLink https://doi.org/10.1787/888934230148

1.3. Evidence of a gender gap in retirement income from funded sources

Women tend to receive lower retirement income than men when considering the total of all sources of retirement income. The extent to which retirement savings arrangements (i.e. occupational and personal pension plans) contribute to the overall gender pension gap depends on the prominence of retirement savings arrangements in the overall pension system, and on the difference in the retirement income that men and women receive from these arrangements.

Currently, retirement savings plans provide a regular stream of income only to a small proportion of old-age people in many European countries (Figure 1.4). In some countries, benefits can be paid, sometimes fully, as a lump sum, which may account for the small proportion of people receiving a regular private pension at retirement (e.g. in Belgium).[5] In some others, retirement savings plans were phased in only relatively recently, such as Estonia, Lithuania and the Slovak Republic that introduced second pillar pension plans after 2000 (in 2002, 2004 and 2005 respectively). Few people are already entitled to benefit payments from these arrangements. Retirement savings plans are therefore likely to have little impact on the overall gender pension gap in countries where they generate a regular income for a minority of old-age people only (whether men or women).

Figure 1.4. Proportion of individuals aged 65+ receiving a regular private pension, selected OECD countries, latest year available

In per cent

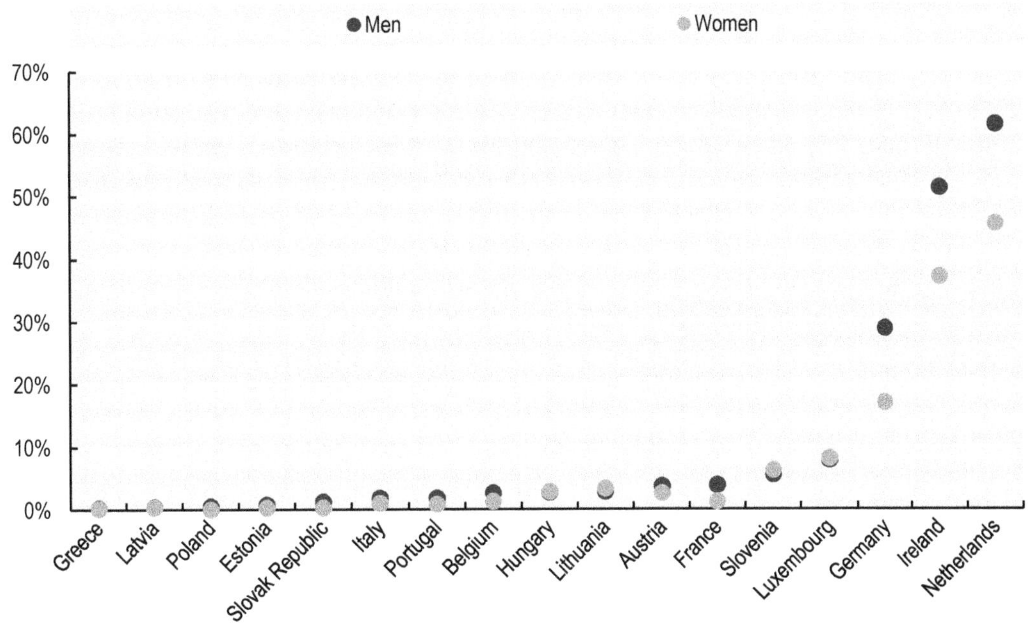

Note: This chart shows the proportion of men (respectively women) aged 65+ receiving a regular pension from occupational or personal plans over all men (resp. women) aged 65+. Pensioners who received a lump sum payment were not counted as receiving regular pension payments, unless they purchased an annuity. Data come from the third wave of the HFCS, primarily carried out between 2016 and 2018.
Source: OECD calculations based on the HFCS.

StatLink https://doi.org/10.1787/888934230186

In some countries, the proportion of people receiving private pensions is large but differs widely between men and women, thereby contributing to the overall gender pension gap. The proportion of women aged 65+ receiving private pensions is the largest in the Netherlands (46%), but still much smaller than the proportion of men receiving private pensions (61%). The difference is also particularly large in Ireland (37% for women compared to 51% for men) and Germany (17% for women, 29% for men). More men receive private pensions than women. They therefore benefit from an additional stream of income to complement public pensions compared with women in these countries, which may contribute to the overall gender pension gap there.

Additionally, when women get a pension from retirement savings plans, this income may be lower than men's, such as in Germany, Ireland and the Netherlands. These three countries have the highest proportion of women aged 65+ receiving a regular private pensions in Europe. Women receive on average 24% less income from their retirement savings plans (occupational and personal) than men in Ireland, 36% less in the Netherlands and 44% less in Germany. This average is calculated only over individuals receiving a private pension (zeros and lump sum payments are therefore excluded).

While currently few people in some countries are receiving private pensions, this may change in the future as retirement savings arrangements are gaining prominence in many countries (OECD, 2020[3]). It is therefore essential to understand what drives the gender pension gap, in particular among retirement savings schemes.

1.4. Labour-market factors driving the gender pension gap

The gender pension gap today is partly the result of different work histories between men and women and the way these differences are transferred through the different components of the pension system.

The gender pension gap is partly due to the lower proportion of women having a job compared to men. In the early 2000s, 48% of women aged between 15 and 64 were working on average in the OECD, compared to 69% of men (Figure 1.5, Panel A.1). This employment gap between men and women has been narrowing over the last decades, as more women had a job in 2018 compared to the early 2000s while the proportion of men with a job has declined over the same period. This has probably helped women to build up pension entitlements to levels that are more comparable to those of men, reducing the gender pension gap. The share of employed women is, however, still below the share of employed men on average in the OECD (50% of women compared to 66% of men).

The gender pension gap may also be the result of a historically larger proportion of women in part-time work compared to men. On average, 24% of women in the working-age population had a part-time job in 2000, compared to 7% of men in the OECD. The largest difference between men and women in part-time jobs was recorded in the Netherlands in 2000 (57% of women working part-time compared to 13% of men). The Netherlands also has one of the largest gender pension gaps (40% compared to 26% in the OECD on average), which may come from the difference in the shares of men and women in part-time jobs. Working part-time may exclude the worker from participating in pension systems in some countries. When it does not, working part-time still implies lower wages than working full-time and therefore lower pension entitlements in earnings-related pension schemes. Differences between the proportion of women and men in part-time jobs are still evident in 2018 (Figure 1.5, Panel A.2) and could contribute to the persistence of the gender pension gap in the future.

The current gender pension gap is also related to the gender wage gap. Among full-time workers, women were earning less than men on average in 2000 (Figure 1.5, Panel A.3). This gender wage gap is declining on average in the OECD, from 18% in 2000 to 13% in 2018. This decline could reduce the gender pension gap in the future. Lower differences in wages translate into lower differences in retirement income (with a time lag) if women are able to build up similar rights and save similar amounts as men during their working lives.

Other factors may contribute to the gender pension gap, such as women having shorter careers. Women's careers are one third shorter than those of men on average (OECD, 2017[4]). These shorter careers may be the consequence of career breaks following childbirth and caring responsibilities which tend to fall more heavily on women (children, elderly).

Figure 1.5. Factors potentially affecting the gender pension gap

A.1. Employment rates of men and women in the OECD, in 2000 and 2018

As a percentage of the working age population of men and women

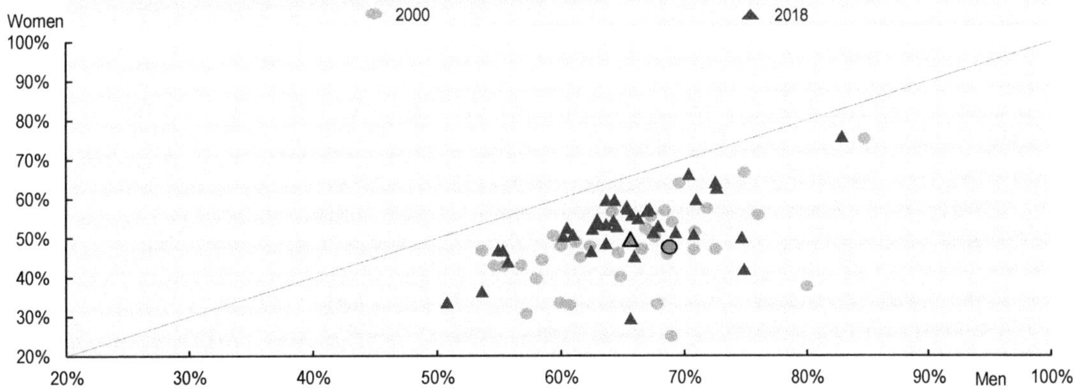

A.2. Share of men and women in part-time employment, 2000 and 2018

In per cent

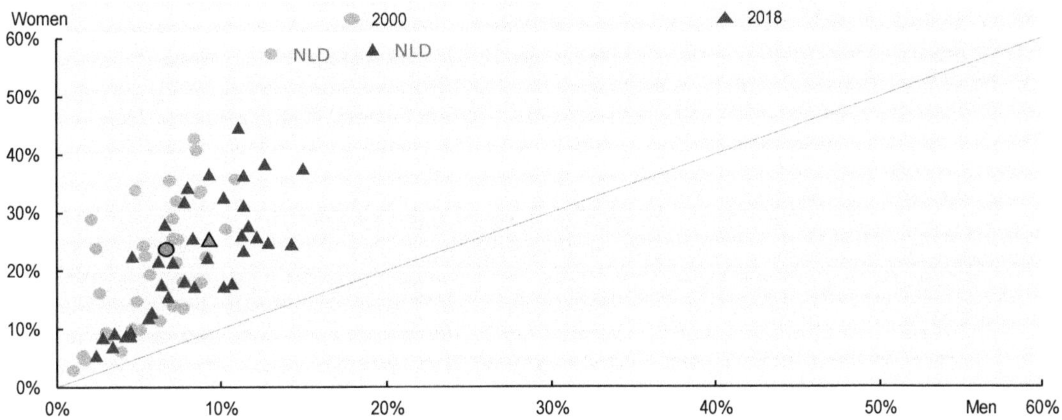

A.3. Gender wage gap in OECD countries, in 2000 and 2018

Relative difference between men and women

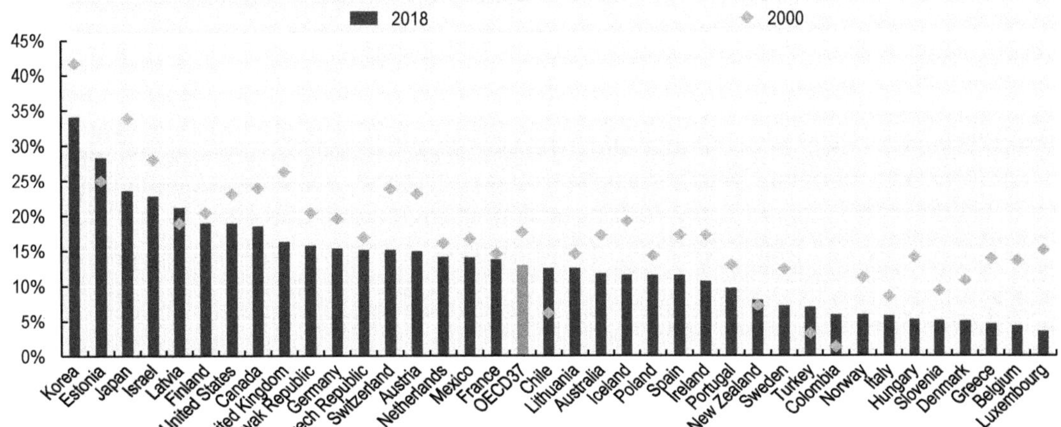

Note: **Panel A1**: Circles show the employment rates of men and women in 2000 while triangles show these rates in 2018 for all OECD countries. The red circle and the red triangle show the OECD average in 2000 and 2018 respectively. **Panel A2**: Circles show the share of men and women in part-time employment in 2000 while triangles show these rates in 2018 for all OECD countries. The red circle and red triangle show the OECD average in 2000 and 2018 respectively. **Panel A3**: The gender wage gap is defined as the difference between male and female median wages divided by the male median wages. OECD37 is the simple average of the gender wage gap among OECD countries.

Source: OECD Employment database.

StatLink https://doi.org/10.1787/888934230167

The way all these differences during working lives lead to different retirement income streams for men and women depends on the design of the pension system. The pension system is usually a combination of public and private programmes (OECD, 2019[5]), each reacting differently to differences during working lives (Table 1.1). The overall effect of the different factors on the gender pension gap depends on the importance of each component of the pension system.

Table 1.1. Impact of different labour market situations on rights and savings in different pension arrangements

	Public non-contributory	Public contributory	Funded / Private Occupational DB	Funded / Private Occupational DC	Personal (employment-related)	Other personal
Unemployment	Higher odds of relying on it if eligibility criteria met	Reduced or no entitlement	No access. Rights retained or transferred to another plan if already member	No access. Assets retained or transferred to another plan if already member	No access. Assets retained or transferred to another plan if already member	No automatic impact although it may limit ability to save for retirement
Part-time compared to full time	Higher odds of relying on it if eligibility criteria met	Depends on access criteria. Impact through lower wages	Depends on access criteria. Impact through lower wages	Depends on access criteria. Impact through lower wages	Depends on access criteria. Impact through lower wages	No automatic impact although it may limit ability to save for retirement
Lower wages	Higher odds of relying on it if eligibility criteria met	Lower entitlements (mitigated in the DB case depending on parameters in the formula)	Lower entitlements (mitigated depending on parameters in the formula)	Lower amount of assets accumulated for similar contribution rates	Lower amount of assets accumulated for similar contribution rates	No automatic impact although it may limit ability to save for retirement
Shorter careers	Higher odds of relying on it if eligibility criteria met	Lower entitlements (mitigated if the formula only takes into account the best years in the career instead of the full career)	Lower entitlements (mitigated if the formula only takes into account the best years in the career instead of the full career)	Lower amount of assets accumulated if not compensated	Lower amount of assets accumulated if not compensated	No automatic impact although it may limit ability to save for retirement

Note: See (OECD, 2019[5]) for more information on the access to retirement savings arrangements of individuals in non-standard forms of work (including part-time workers).

Work status and wage conditions can directly affect the access and the entitlements in employment-related contributory pension arrangements, whether pay-as-you-go or funded. For instance, unemployment affects individuals' entitlements from contributory public pension arrangements and savings in occupational and employment-related personal plans. Working grants pension rights to workers through contributions. Unemployment years may be counted in the formula for public pension payments (such as in France) up to a certain extent, but benefit entitlements may be lower than for people who have worked. In the funded and private pension system, access to occupational pension plans (and some personal plans) is restricted to those working. If individuals lose or quit their job (after the vesting period of pension rights), they will retain rights in defined benefit (DB) plans or assets in defined contribution (DC) plans unless they transfer these assets to another vehicle. The accrual of rights or assets in these plans may not keep up with the rights of members who are still working and paying contributions. Part-time work, lower wages, and shorter careers also reduce the entitlements from employment-related pension arrangements, although these effects could be mitigated depending on the formula of DB plans or partly offset if career breaks are compensated. For example, a DB career-average formula reduces differences in pensions related to career dynamism, but penalises more those with irregular or interrupted career patterns than a DB formula based on salaries in the best years (Lodovici et al., 2016[6]).

The effect of work status and wage conditions on the access and the possibility to save in a plan is in theory less automatic in a voluntary personal plan than in an employment-related one. Men and women can usually open a voluntary personal plan whether they are employed or not, working part-time or full-time, unconditional of their level of earnings or their time in employment.

By contrast, differences in careers between men and women increase the odds of women falling into poverty in retirement and relying on the protection of non-contributory programmes relative to men. Eligibility to these programmes may be subject to certain criteria in some countries (such as a certain number of years of residency, a certain number of contribution years to the public system). Some of these programmes may assess all income sources (such as social assistance that may be reduced depending on other retirement incomes) and may sometimes depend on other assets too.

1.5. Other factors driving the gender pension gap coming from retirement savings schemes

This section looks into other factors, beyond labour market inequalities, that can create a gap in retirement income, focusing on retirement savings arrangements, and therefore abstracting from public pensions. It first shows that women participate less than men in retirement savings plans, even after controlling for the gender employment gap. It then presents how the gap in rights and assets widens progressively during the accumulation phase among those participating in retirement savings plans. It finally explains how the gender gap during the accumulation phase can worsen at retirement.

1.5.1. Women participate less in retirement savings plans than men

The first step for building up savings for retirement is to be a member of a retirement savings plan. Individuals can voluntarily participate in a pension plan in most OECD countries if they wish. When they work, men and women may also be automatically enrolled in occupational plans or may have the possibility of joining the plan set up by their employers under certain conditions. The establishment of occupational plans is voluntary for employers in some countries (e.g. the United States), mandatory in others (e.g. Switzerland) or mandatory only in some sectors (e.g. the Netherlands). Individuals may also be members of several pension plans, occupational and personal.

While people may have several ways of accessing retirement savings plans (i.e. through work or independently), men tend to more commonly have a plan than women among European countries (Table 1.2).

The proportion of women with savings in a personal plan is usually close to but below the proportion of men with personal plans in Europe. More men have a personal plan than women in 14 out of 18 European countries. In 10 of these 14 countries, the difference in coverage is, however, below 2 percentage points. The largest difference was recorded in the Netherlands where 19% of women have a personal plan compared to 28% of men. By contrast, more women own a voluntary personal plan than men in four countries: Estonia, Finland, France and Latvia.

The proportion of women covered by an occupational plan is lower than men in most European countries, with Finland being one of the exceptions.[6] The coverage of women in occupational plans is comparable to men in Finland (around 85%), as participation in earnings-related pension plans (TyEL and other plans) is mandatory for public and private sector workers, farmers and self-employed individuals. Additionally, the employment gap between men and women is smaller in Finland (5 percentage points) than in the OECD on average (16 percentage points).

Table 1.2. Coverage of retirement savings plans in selected OECD countries, by gender, 2017

As a percentage of the working-age population

	Occupational / employment-related plan		Voluntary personal plan and life insurance		Total	
	Men	Women	Men	Women	Men	Women
Austria	12%	8%	16%	14%	24%	20%
Belgium	27%	18%	43%	41%	52%	48%
Estonia	..	..	14%	18%	..	..
Finland	85%	86%	18%	22%	86%	87%
France	5%	3%	26%	26%	28%	28%
Germany (1)	25%	18%	44%	43%	55%	49%
Greece	0%	0%	1%	0%	1%	0%
Hungary	..	..	13%	13%	..	..
Ireland	23%	16%	13%	9%	33%	23%
Italy	8%	4%	7%	5%	15%	9%
Latvia	..	..	11%	19%	..	..
Lithuania	..	..	9%	9%	..	..
Luxembourg	10%	7%	15%	12%	20%	15%
Netherlands	61%	59%	28%	19%	73%	68%
Poland	4%	4%	43%	42%	44%	43%
Portugal	2%	1%	10%	9%	11%	10%
Slovak Republic	26%	27%	13%	10%	33%	32%
Slovenia	9%	11%	10%	10%	18%	20%

Note: This table is based on data available in Wave 3 of the HFCS for all countries except Finland (Wave 2). ".." means not available. (1) The HFCS survey may underestimate the coverage of occupational pension plans, potentially due to an underreporting of enrolment in occupational plans and the classification of occupational plans for the public sector as statutory pensions.
Source: OECD calculations based on the HFCS.

StatLink https://doi.org/10.1787/888934230205

The gender employment gap accounts by itself for the difference in the proportion of men and women covered by an occupational plan in some countries, but not all. Calculating the proportion of men (respectively women) having an occupational pension plan over the employed population (instead of the working-age population) shows whether the gender employment gap has a differentiated impact. The difference between the proportion of men and women covered by occupational plans remains almost the same in Austria, France, Ireland and Italy for instance, even after controlling for the gender employment gap in these countries (Figure 1.6). By contrast, the difference in coverage declines in Germany (from 7 to 6 percentage points), Luxembourg (from 4 to 2 percentage points) and especially in the Netherlands where the gender gap in occupational plan coverage nearly disappears after controlling for the gender employment gap. While women were already more often covered by an occupational or employment-related pension plan than men among the working-age population in the Slovak Republic and Slovenia, this difference in favour of women further increases after adjusting for the gender employment gap. In Slovenia, this could be due to the fact that participation in an employment-related pension plan is voluntary for all employees except those in arduous and hazardous jobs and civil servants who tend to be more often women (OECD, 2017[7]).

Figure 1.6. Differences in the proportion of men and women having an occupational or employment-related pension arrangement, in selected OECD countries, 2017

In percentage points

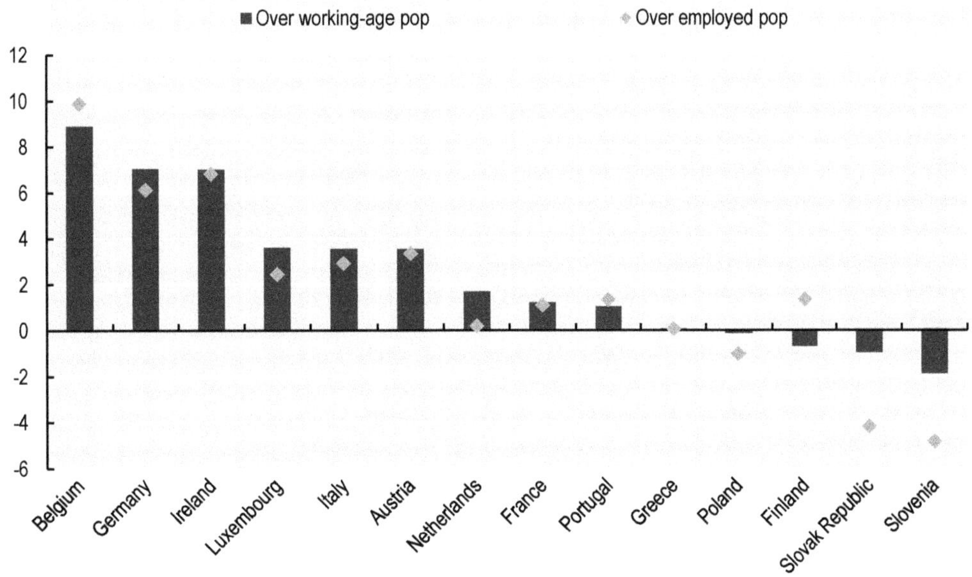

Note: This chart shows the difference (in percentage points) in the proportions of men and women covered by an occupational or employment-related pension plan. These proportions are calculated over the working-age population and over the employed population (to account for the gender employment gap). Calculations are based on data available in Wave 3 of the HFCS for all countries except Finland (Wave 2).
Source: OECD calculations based on the HFCS.

StatLink https://doi.org/10.1787/888934230224

The participation in an occupational plan may vary across sectors when the legislation does not require all employers to establish a plan on behalf of their employees. Access to an occupational plan then depends on the willingness of employers to set up a plan for their employees. A study from the Pew Charitable Trusts (2017[8]) found that full-time workers in some sectors (e.g. material moving) in the United States were more likely to have access to occupational plans than full-time workers in other sectors (e.g. wholesale and retail trade). Some employers may voluntarily set up occupational plans as part of a remuneration package to attract and retain skilled people.

In some countries, the difference in coverage of occupational plans between men and women probably results from the underrepresentation of women in sectors more likely to provide access to occupational plans. The proportion of women working in a given sector is inversely correlated with the coverage rate of occupational plans in this sector in a number of countries (Figure 1.7).[7] Women tend to work in sectors where fewer individuals are covered by an occupational plan such as education (code "P" in the NACE Rev. 2 Classification) or human health and social work activities (code "Q"). Women are underrepresented in manufacturing activities (code "C") where employers may provide wider access to occupational plans (such as in Belgium and Ireland).

Figure 1.7. Proportion of women working by sector and overall coverage of occupational or employment-related pension arrangements by sector, 2017

In per cent

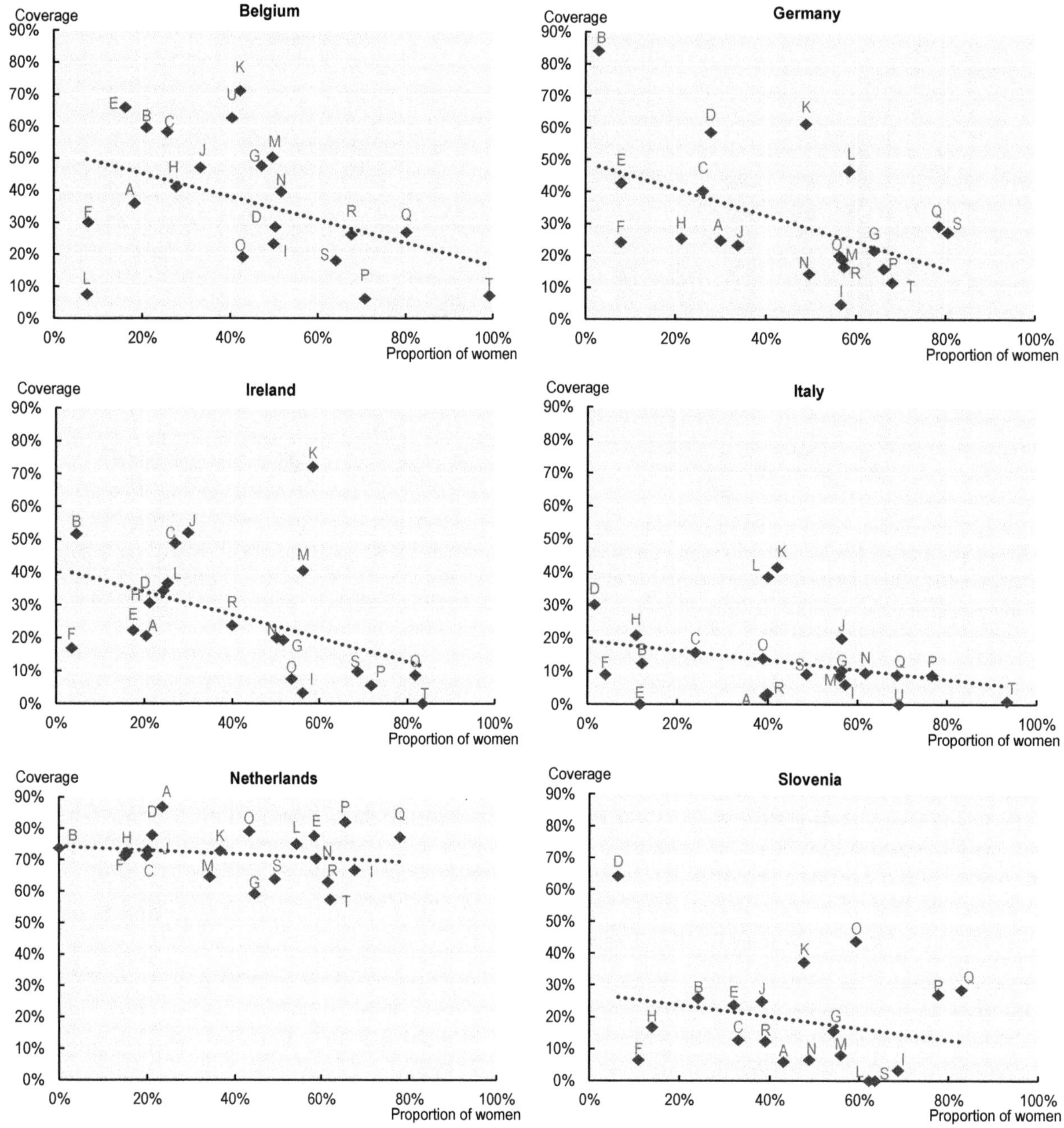

Note: The sectors follow the NACE Rev. 2 Classification. "A" stands for "Agriculture, Forestry and Fishing"; "B" for "Mining and Quarrying"; "C" for "Manufacturing"; "D" for "Electricity, Gas, Steam and Air Conditioning supply"; "E" for "Water supply; Sewerage, Waste Management and Remediation Activities"; "F" for "Construction"; "G" for "Wholesale and retail trade; repair of motor vehicles and motorcycles"; "H" for "Transportation and Storage"; "I" for "Accommodation and Food Service Activities"; "J" for "Information and Communication"; "K" for "Financial and Insurance Activities"; "L" for "Real Estate Activities"; "M" for "Professional, Scientific and Technical Activities"; "N" for "Administrative and Support Service Activities"; "O" for "Public Administration And Defence; Compulsory Social Security"; "P" for "Education"; "Q" for "Human Health and Social Work Activities"; "R" for "Arts, Entertainment and Recreation"; "S" for "Other Service Activities"; "T" for "Activities of Households as Employers; Undifferentiated Goods- and Services-producing Activities of Households for own use"; "U" for "Activities of Extraterritorial Organisations and Bodies".

Source: OECD calculations based on the HFCS.

StatLink https://doi.org/10.1787/888934230243

Women may face more barriers to joining occupational or employment-related plans when the access is subject to employment or earning conditions. In the United States, if employers decide to set up an occupational plan for their employees, they must provide access to this plan at least to all employees aged 21 and over and having 1 year or more of service (1 000 hours of work during the year). It may be more difficult for part-time workers – more often women - to qualify unless employers set wider access conditions. In other countries where participation in a plan is mandatory, access to the plan may be limited to those working in a formal job. Women who are more likely to be in informal work than men in Latin America (ILO, 2018[9]) could be left out from these mandatory plans (e.g. in Chile). Minimum earning requirements for joining a plan might also exclude women more than men from occupational plans. In Australia for instance, employers have to contribute to a plan on behalf of employees earning at least AUD 450 per month before tax. There is also an earnings floor in the United Kingdom to qualify for automatic enrolment in a plan. Women might be more penalised than men as they earn less than men on average. In the United Kingdom, 23% of employed women do not meet the qualifying criteria for automatic enrolment, compared to 12% of male workers (Pensions Policy Institute, 2020[10]).

The current difference in the proportion of men and women having a pension plan is likely to lead to differences in the proportion of retired men and women benefitting from retirement income in the future.

1.5.2. A gender gap in pension assets widens progressively during the accumulation phase

Women with retirement savings plans have historically accrued less in their plans than men in almost all European countries. Figure 1.8 shows that men hold more than twice the pension assets of women in Austria and Latvia (in voluntary personal plans). Women would have approximately the same amount of retirement savings only in the Slovak Republic and Slovenia among the reporting countries.

Figure 1.8. Gender gap in assets in all retirement savings arrangements, latest year available

Relative difference between men and women (among asset owners)

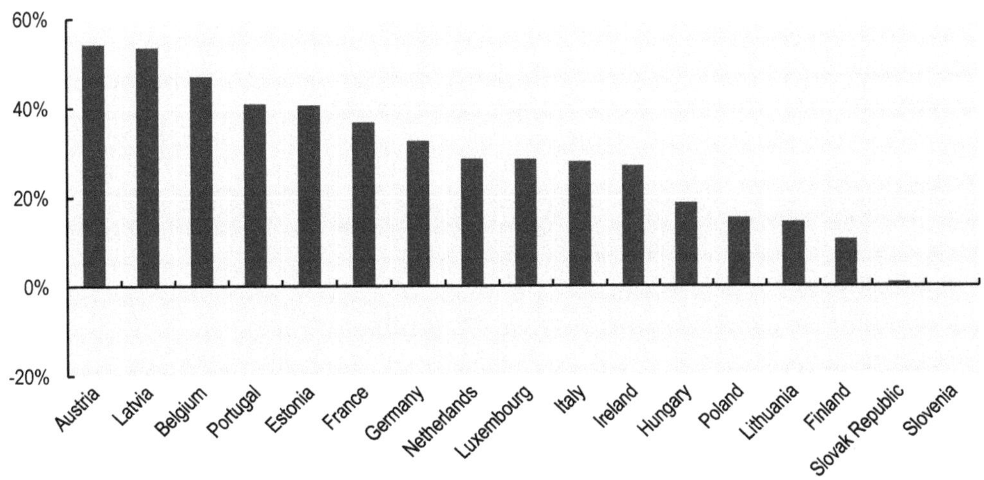

Note: The gender gap is defined as the difference between men and women's assets in all DC and personal retirement savings plans and the present value of all expected future benefit payments from DB plans as a percentage of men's, among asset owners. This indicator is calculated over the working-age population, based on data available in Wave 3 of the HFCS for all countries except Belgium and Finland (Wave 2). Data for Estonia, Hungary, Latvia and Lithuania refer to assets in voluntary personal plans only.
Source: OECD calculations based on the HFCS.

StatLink https://doi.org/10.1787/888934230262

This gap between the pension assets that men and women accumulate first emerges in the 25-34 year group and tends to widen from that point onwards. At the early stages of their careers, women and men have almost the same amount of assets (with a 2% difference in favour of men's pension assets) on average in a selection of European countries (Figure 1.9). The value of women's pension plans starts falling behind when they are between 25 and 34 years old. Women aged between 25 and 34 have 8% less than men in their pension plans. This gap widens between 35 and 44 years old when women have 30% less in their pension accounts than men. This analysis is based on the pension assets of different cohorts in 2017. An analysis of the gap in pension assets over time for the same cohort would help to confirm the findings based on different cohorts.[8]

Figure 1.9. Average amount of assets in retirement savings plans by gender and age group in selected OECD countries, latest year available

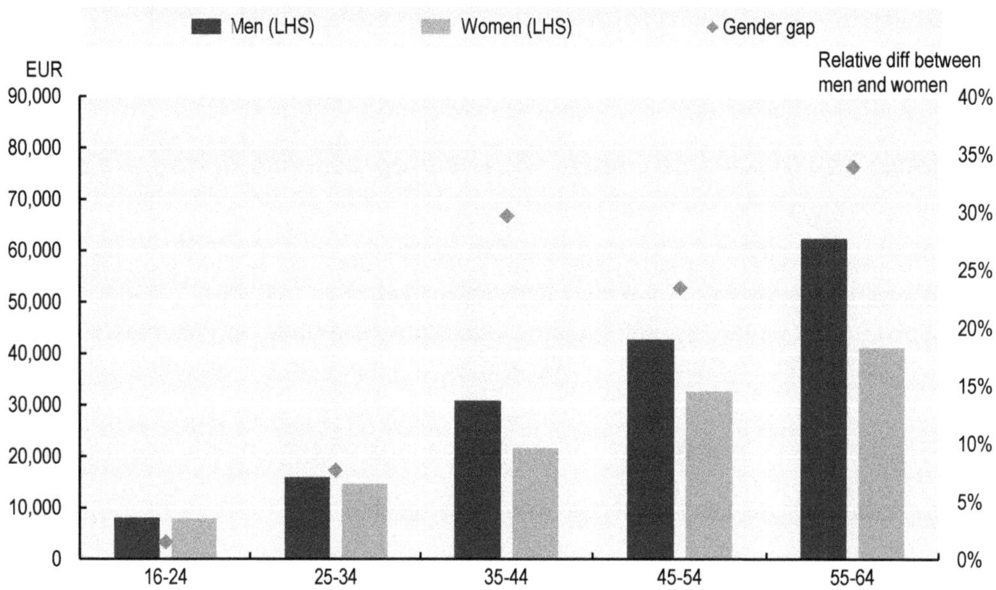

Note: This chart shows the average amount of assets in DC and personal retirement savings plans and the present value of all expected future benefit payments from DB plans for men and women among asset owners in a group of OECD countries on average (on the left-hand side). The chart also shows the difference between this average (of average pension assets) for men and for women relatively to men (on the right-hand side). The group of countries included in the calculations includes: Austria, Belgium, Estonia, Finland, France, Germany, Hungary, Ireland, Italy (except for the age group 16-24), Latvia, Lithuania (except for the age group 16-24), Luxembourg, the Netherlands, Poland, Portugal (except for the age group 16-24), the Slovak Republic and Slovenia. This indicator is calculated over the working-age population, based on data available in Wave 3 of the HFCS for all countries except Belgium and Finland (Wave 2).
Source: OECD calculations based on the HFCS.

StatLink https://doi.org/10.1787/888934230281

This gap in pension assets may be partly due to career breaks for parenting purposes between 25 and 44 years old (Mcguinness and Pyper, 2018[11]).[9] Additionally and because of the gender wage gap, a similar contribution rate for men and women would lead to lower savings overall for women compared to men.[10]

The gap in pension assets reaches its peak at the eldest ages (34% between 55 and 64 years old). This gap is the result of past differences in assets accumulated. The difference in asset values – in absolute monetary terms - widens over time as the interest earned compounds the value of the assets. Contributions are invested and generate investment income. Larger pension pots would earn more than smaller pots.

Different investment strategies between men and women could also explain differences in investment rates of return and thus in assets accumulated, *ceteris paribus*. Women could be more risk averse than men and may invest their assets more conservatively. When looking at investment allocations of both men and women outside retirement assets, women tend to hold more cash and money market funds – relatively lower risk investment – than men who hold rather stocks and shares in mutual funds that are riskier (Garnick, 2016[12]). Chapter 2 looks further into the risk aversion of men and women and the implications in terms of investment strategies that men and women select. A potential difference in the choice of investment strategy could contribute to differences in retirement savings outcomes, especially in a context of a growing prominence of DC plans where plan members make investment choices.

1.5.3. How the gender gap in retirement savings during the accumulation phase can materialise further at retirement

The amount of retirement income of men and women could also depend on their choices for the pay-out phase. Individuals can choose among different types of payments from retirement savings plans, such as lump sums, life annuities, programmed withdrawals, deferred life annuities or a combination of several options. If men and women select different pay-out options, this could have an impact on the income they receive from retirement savings plans.

Women may be less likely to receive a regular income from retirement savings arrangements – thus increasing the risk of a gap in retirement income between men and women - when annuity payments are conditional on eligibility criteria (such as a minimum contribution period). Men may be more likely to meet a criterion based on the length of the contribution period than women for example, as women have lower employment rates and shorter careers than men.[11]

Even if men and women both can and do choose to receive a regular retirement income through a life annuity, women may still receive lower pension payments than men for the same level of retirement savings if the price of the annuity takes into account the higher life expectancies of women compared to men.[12,13] As the previous section of this Chapter showed that women tend to have lower retirement savings than men when they reach retirement, the use of gendered mortality tables to price annuities could be expected to widen even further the difference in retirement income for men and women.

Differences in the pay-out phase between men and women could be expected to shrink in the future as some gaps between men and women in the labour market (e.g. gender employment gap, gender wage gap) slowly fade. Women may be more likely to reach retirement age with similar retirement assets as men in the long run.

1.6. Conclusions

This analysis confirms the well-documented existence of a gap in retirement income that men and women receive, the gender pension gap. The overall pension gap may partly reflect that women receive income from a retirement savings plan complementing their public pensions less often than men in some countries. And when they do, this income is generally lower than men's income.

This gap in retirement income is partly the result of past differences in labour market outcomes between men and women, such as the lower share of women employed, their shorter careers and their lower wages during their careers. These differences automatically affect savings in occupational plans set up by employers and potentially savings in personal plans too.

On top of these, women are less likely to participate in a funded pension plan during their career. This difference is partly due to the fact that women work in areas where workers are less likely to be covered by a funded pension plan in a number of countries. Women are also likely to accumulate a lower balance than men during their working lives. The gap in retirement assets appears when women are aged 25 to 34 and widens thereafter. This is when they are most likely to take a career break for parenting. Differences in retirement assets are likely to compound over time as these assets are invested in financial markets and yield investment returns. This gap may grow further when retiring depending on the pay-out options available to women and their features. Annuities in some countries take into account the fact that women will live longer than men and lead to lower retirement income payments for women compared to men, even for the same amount of accumulated assets.

References

Garnick, D. (2016), *Income Insights: Gender Retirement Gap.* [12]

Herrerías, R. and G. Zamarripa (2017), *Determinants of Density of Contribution for the Mexican Pension System.* [13]

ILO (2018), *Women and men in the informal economy: a statistical picture.* [9]

Lodovici, M. et al. (2016), *The gender pension gap: differences between mothers and women without children.* [6]

Mcguinness, F. and D. Pyper (2018), *The Gender Pay Gap*, http://www.parliament.uk/commons-library|intranet.parliament.uk/commons-library|papers@parliament.uk|@commonslibrary. [11]

OECD (2020), *Pension Markets in Focus.* [3]

OECD (2019), *Pensions at a Glance 2019: OECD and G20 Indicators*, OECD Publishing, Paris, https://doi.org/10.1787/b6d3dcfc-en. [5]

OECD (2018), *OECD Pensions Outlook 2018*, OECD Publishing, Paris, https://dx.doi.org/10.1787/pens_outlook-2018-en. [1]

OECD (2017), *Government at a Glance*, OECD Publishing, http://dx.doi.org/10.1787/gov_glance-2017-en. [7]

OECD (2017), *Preventing Ageing Unequally*, OECD Publishing, http://dx.doi.org/10.1787/9789264279087-en. [2]

OECD (2017), *The Pursuit of Gender Equality: An Uphill Battle*, OECD Publishing, http://dx.doi.org/10.1787/9789264281318-en. [4]

Pensions Policy Institute (2020), *The Underpensioned Index.* [10]

The Pew Charitable Trusts (2017), *Survey Highlights Worker Perspectives on Barriers to Retirement Saving.* [8]

Annex 1.A. Retirement income in different household surveys

Several multinational household surveys request information on retirement income that individuals receive. The way this information is collected varies across surveys, however. Some surveys already include a variable capturing the total retirement income while this variable can be created in other surveys by adding up the different retirement income streams. Annex Table 1.A.1 summarises the definitions of total retirement income and what this flow includes in four surveys: the Household Finance and Consumption Survey (HFCS), the Luxembourg Income Study (LIS), the Luxembourg Wealth Study (LWS) and the European Union Statistics on Income and Living Conditions (EU-SILC).

Annex Table 1.A.1. Definition of total retirement income in selected multinational household surveys

Survey	Definitions of total retirement income
HFCS	Gross income from public pensions and gross income from occupational and private pension plans. Income from public pension schemes includes old-age pensions, anticipated old-age pensions, partial retirement pensions, survivor's pensions, and disability pensions. Income from occupational and private pension plans refers to income from occupational pension schemes and to pensions and annuities received in the form of interest or dividend income from individual private insurance plans.
LIS	Pensions: public non-contributory pensions (universal and assistance pensions), public contributory pensions and private pensions (occupational and individual pensions).
LWS	Pensions: public non-contributory pensions (universal and assistance pensions), public contributory pensions and private pensions (occupational and individual pensions).
EU-SILC	Public pensions, private pensions, survivor's benefits and disability pensions.

The HFCS does not include a variable combining all the retirement income streams. The HFCS includes two main variables instead: "gross income from public pensions" and "gross income from occupational and private pension plans". Gross income from public pensions includes old age pensions, anticipated old-age pensions (i.e. regular payments to those who retire before the standard retirement age), partial retirement pensions (i.e. regular payments to those who only receive a portion of their full pension because they continue to work), survivor's pensions and disability pensions (i.e. regular payments to those below the standard retirement age who suffers from a disability impairing their ability to work or earn the minimum in the legislation). Gross income from public pensions also includes income from public pension systems abroad. Gross income from occupational and private pension plans covers income received from occupational pension schemes and pensions and annuities received in the form of interest or dividend income from individual private insurance plans.

The LIS database includes a variable on pensions called "pensions". This variable measures retirement income from all pillars (public, occupational and personal), all types (universal, assistance and insurance) and all functions (old-age, disability and survivors).

The LWS database also has a similar variable on pensions, also called "pensions" like in the LIS database. This variable is also supposed to cover public non-contributory, public contributory and private pensions.

The EU-SILC survey defines several variables relating to retirement income such as: old-age benefits, survivor's benefits, disability benefits and pensions from individual private plans. All these variables are collected on gross and net bases.

Lump sum payments are not included in retirement income in these surveys except in the EU-SILC where they are reported under "old-age benefits".

Notes

[1] This analysis focuses on the differences of retirement income between men and women and does not touch upon the overall level and adequacy of the retirement income of men and women.

[2] Differences between men and women could also relate to the cumulative amounts received by men and women over the whole retirement period (gap in pension wealth).

[3] There are differences in life expectancy between men and women across countries. If older cohorts tend to have less retirement income and women live longer than men, this cohort effect will be captured within the measure. In that case, differences across countries in the gender gap in life expectancy could explain some of the differences in the gender pension gap across countries (on top of other factors).

[4] The elderly population is defined as people aged 65 and over. Some household surveys – especially those on the whole population - may exclude people living in collective households and in institutions, such as the elderly in nursing homes or old people's homes. Institutions providing long-term care (excluding hospitals) host more women than men aged 65+ in all OECD countries. Excluding residents of these institutions may marginally distort the gender pension gap as they represent between 0% and 11% of all individuals aged 65+ across OECD countries according to the OECD Long-Term Care Resources and Utilisation database. Lithuania had the largest proportion of individuals aged 65+ receiving formal long-term care in institutions (other than hospitals) among OECD countries in 2018.

[5] In Belgium, people can receive benefits from their occupational plans as a single lump sum, as an annuity (fixed or lifetime) or as a combination of both. If the annuity that people could get is lower than EUR 659.79 annually, benefits have to be paid as a single lump sum.

[6] The Slovak Republic and Slovenia are other examples where the proportion of women covered by an occupational plan is higher than the proportion of men.

[7] The regression line in Figure 1.7 does not take into account the differences in the overall number of people (men and women) working in each sector.

[8] Figure 1.9 probably includes both an age effect (i.e. the gap in pension assets grows as people age) and a generational effect (i.e. men and women in the last age group were born at a different time than those in the first age group). Further analysis would be needed to disentangle the age and generational effects.

[9] McGuinness and Pyper (2018[11]) show that the gender pay gap between men and women grows after the birth of a first child in the United Kingdom.

[10] Different effective contribution rates by men and women could affect the gender gap in pension assets or entitlements. This dimension is left aside from this analysis due to lack of available data.

[11] This is the case for instance in Mexico (Herrerías and Zamarripa, 2017[13]).

[12] Women would however have the same pension wealth as men during retirement as they would receive lower pension payments from life annuity products, but for a longer period than men.

[13] Since 2012, the European Court of Justice has forbidden insurance companies from taking into account gender when pricing their annuity products. This rule implies that differences in life expectancy will not lead to lower benefit payments for women than for men for the same amount of accumulated assets in European countries.

2 Understanding the gender pension gap beyond labour market drivers through a literature review

This chapter explores the literature to shed light on some drivers of the gap in retirement income between men and women, beyond those directly linked to the labour market. It discusses some of the cultural and behavioural factors which may play a role in the gender pension gap by affecting individual decisions linked to retirement, and looks at the influence of societal interactions on retirement outcomes by gender.

This chapter reviews the existing literature to identify possible findings beyond those directly linked to labour market differences, to explain the gap in retirement income that men and women receive in retirement.[1]

Chapter 1 shows that labour market conditions, such as lower employment rates and the gender gap in income, coming from lower wages and career breaks are probably the main driver for the gap in retirement income between men and women. However, there might also be behavioural and cultural elements, which could explain part of the gender pension gap without being directly connected to labour market differences. In defined contribution funded pension schemes, participants often need to make several decisions about their pension savings, contrary to most defined benefit pay-as-you-go pension arrangements where no active decisions are required from individuals. For instance, participants may need to choose their contribution rate, their contribution period, and the investment strategy for their portfolio of assets. Hence, differences between men and women in attitudes and personal preferences may play a role in the gender gap in retirement savings in funded pensions.

Behavioural and cultural elements may influence the actions of men and women on an individual basis. For instance, women can be found to often be more risk averse than men. There is abundant literature on the gender difference in risk aversion, and this element may play a role in the gap in retirement income received by men and women. Part of the gender gap might also be explained by a difference in financial literacy, either actual or perceived. Men and women may furthermore demonstrate a difference in their attitude towards saving, i.e. their time preference, with women more likely than men to spend their income, either for themselves or for others, rather than to save it.

Attitudes and societal features may also play a role in the interactions and relationships between individuals, which might have an impact on the gender gap in retirement income beyond the direct effect cultural differences may have on labour market differences. Marital choices may be a factor in the gender pension gap, either through a possible shift in the decision-making process among couples, or through the different consequences of divorce or widowhood over retirement savings for men and women. Gender stereotyping may be at play, which could encourage women to opt for solutions that can be more conservative than what their actual risk preferences should imply. Communication campaigns may also influence the gender pension gap by omitting to take into account certain needs such as how to compensate for the decrease in salary and contributions during parental leave.

However, the situation is evolving, with women increasingly saving for retirement, and the concern about the gender pension gap getting higher up on the agenda of policy makers and pension arrangements stakeholders.

This chapter explores the potential behavioural and cultural drivers for the gap in retirement income between men and women. The first section discusses gender differences in risk tolerance described in the literature. The second section examines differences in the financial literacy of men and women. The third section looks at the impact of the marital status on funded pensions, while the fourth section explores the potential role of gender stereotyping on the gender pension gap. The fifth section calls attention to the influence of communication and framing on retirement outcomes. The last section concludes by highlighting some of the more recent trends in the gender gap in retirement income.

2.1. Gender differences in risk aversion

Labour market differences explain a large part of the gender gap in retirement income, however behavioural and cultural elements might also be at play. This section examines how differences in risk aversion may potentially affect the gender gap in retirement income. It first presents studies demonstrating a lower financial risk tolerance among women than men. It then looks at differences in attitudes towards gambling and competition. Finally, it discusses how factors such as marital status and financial literacy may affect risk aversion.

2.1.1. Women's lower tolerance for financial risk

Women tend to be more risk averse than men in the allocation of their financial assets. Garnick (2016[1]) shows that women in the United States tend to hold more low risk assets and less high risk assets than men, as part of their overall asset allocation. In 2014, women held, as a proportion of their overall assets, more low risk assets such as cash - 20.6% versus 15.6% for men, annuities - 11.4% versus 7.5% for men, and certificates of deposits - 7.1% versus 5.8% for men and had a lower allocation to higher risk assets such as stocks - 16.6% versus 21.1% for men, and mutual funds - 27.5% versus 33% for men.[2] The study also claims that default schemes in private pension arrangements, such as qualified default investment alternatives in private plans in the United States, have decreased the investment return differences between men and women.[3]

The gender difference in financial risk aversion may be linked to factors such as overall wealth and income stability. Fisher and Yao (2017[2]) estimate the level of financial risk tolerance of single men and women in the United States using a decomposition technique.[4,5] They find that while women do tend to exhibit lower levels of financial risk tolerance, with 39.6% of women (respectively 56.3% of men) reporting some risk tolerance, 11.4% (respectively 20.3%) high risk tolerance, and 2.6% (respectively 4.2%) substantial risk tolerance, this is determined not solely by their gender, but significantly by variables affecting their risk tolerance, in particular their level of income uncertainty and net worth. Indeed, income uncertainty exhibits a positive effect on financial risk tolerance for men, with men with uncertain incomes 66.4% more likely than men with certain income to declare having some risk tolerance, and 95.6% more likely to declare a high risk tolerance. For women, income uncertainty has a negative effect, decreasing the likelihood of having some risk tolerance by 14.1% compared to women with no income uncertainty, and by 6.8% for the high risk tolerance. For both men and women, an increase in net worth increases the odds of reporting high risk tolerance. Similarly, using a constant absolute risk aversion model to explain households' investment behaviour, Makarov and Schornick (2010[3]) demonstrate that poorer households are less likely to participate in the stock market, and that among those participating, the portion of wealth invested in risky assets increases with wealth.

The lower risk tolerance of women cannot be explained only by lower financial knowledge, lower confidence, or by lower wealth levels. Baeckstrom, Marsh and Silvester (2019[4]) use data from British individuals holding between GBP 50 000 and GBP 2.5 million to invest, in order to verify whether wealthier investors would exhibit dissimilar attitudes towards investment risk and confidence, compared to average investors.[6] Participants were asked to compare their own financial knowledge, risk appetite and confidence in their investment decisions to that of the general population. The study results show that women considered wealthy have similar confidence and financial knowledge levels compared to their male counterparts, and that risk tolerance is negatively correlated with investor age and positively with wealth. Regression analysis shows that investor risk tolerance, measured on a scale of 1 to 5, decreases by 0.2 for each additional 10 years of age, and is higher by 0.5 for investors with more than GBP 500 000 in wealth compared to investors with less than GBP 500 000. However, on average women in the panel still hold five percentage points more cash as a proportion of their investments than men, and consider themselves more risk averse in their investment decisions relative to men.

When provided with different investment strategy choices for their retirement savings, women are less likely to choose the high risk and high return option. Watson and McNaughton (2007[5]) examine the impact of gender on the superannuation fund risk preferences, and ultimately on the retirement benefits of staff in the Australian university sector, using data from members of the UniSuper defined contribution superannuation fund from 1997 to 2003.[7] Plan members were offered seven different investment strategies to choose from, corresponding to six risk categories – two of the strategies offering 100% allocation to shares differ in their investment focus rather than risk profile. For members unwilling or unable to make an investment choice, a default option in the balanced plan had been set up. In order to obtain meaningful data on individuals' risk preferences, the research eliminated those members who were allocated to the default plan, as the records did not allow differentiating those members who would have actively chosen the balanced strategy from those who would have stayed with the default plan in any case. The analysis shows that women in the panel are more risk averse than men, with 25% of men choosing the riskiest investment strategy versus 18% of women. Control variables were included in the regression in order to eliminate the potential interference of income and age profiles in the gender statistics, and women still generally chose less risky investment strategies than men for a similar age and level of income.

However, other studies argue that gender is only a minimal factor when studying retirement savings, and that structural labour market conditions only, rather than behavioural elements, drive the gender gap in retirement savings. Allport et al. (2019[6]) look at the impact of gender on retirement savings behaviour, in order to untangle the behavioural element from any structural factor, based on data from the United Kingdom's National Employment Savings Trust (NEST) covering over seven million occupational defined contribution plan members at the end of 2018, and broken down in several earning bands. The data show that women appear to have higher median contributions and pension account balances across all considered earning bands, except for the highest income group. However, the data allow distinguishing regular contributors to the pension plan from those only making occasional contributions, in order to control for any difference attributable to occasional contributors, which might distort the overall picture.[8] When focusing only on regular contributors, who made 12 contributions during the year 2018, the gender difference in median contributions and account balances disappears, except for individuals in the highest earnings band. The study also looks at attitudes towards saving, and shows that when controlling for earnings, there is no gender difference in voluntary contributions and active enrolment to the scheme. While more women actively opt in for pension contributions, this is attributable to the fact that three times more women in the sample earn less than the threshold for automatic enrolment. Additional contributions come equally from men and women - 50% each - with contribution levels higher for men, due to higher earnings. Hence, the authors conclude that gender is a minimal factor when studying retirement savings and that labour market conditions such as those linked to pay, positions, employment sectors, and career breaks drive the gender pension gap, rather than behavioural elements.[9]

Additionally, the increasing use of default parameters such as default investment strategies may reduce the impact of personal risk preferences on retirement outcomes between men and women. Default investment strategies are generally similar for all members or based on objective and gender-neutral parameters such as member age or time to retirement. Behavioural biases such as procrastination and inertia significantly limit the tendency of members to change their investment strategy once they are assigned one by default (OECD, 2018[7]). For example, Cronqvist et al. (2018[8]) show that in the absence of communication campaigns encouraging individuals to actively choose their own investment portfolio, only about 1% of those joining the Swedish Premium Pension system in 2016 declined the default fund and made an active choice. Hence, the implementation of defaults may alleviate the natural tendency of women to choose more conservative investment strategies.

Finally, differences in risk aversion levels between men and women may have different impacts on retirement outcomes at different times or for different cohorts depending on the performance of investment markets. On average over the longer-term, saving in a conservative investment strategy is expected to yield lower investment returns for retirement savings than a balanced or dynamic strategy. At times when financial markets fall however, risk averse savers with a defensive or conservative investment portfolio may end up with larger pension pots than savers with a dynamic or higher risk portfolio.

2.1.2. Different attitudes towards gambling and competition

Women tend to perceive risky situations more as a threat than a challenge. Arch (1993[9]) looks at explanations for the fact that while there are attempts to equalize opportunities for women to attain positions of power and status in society, change is not happening as rapidly as expected. The author uses experiments from different studies to demonstrate that women tend to see situations that present either a physical or a social risk, more like a threat and to choose avoiding options whereas men perceive them more as a challenge, which may explain a potential discrepancy in participation in opportunities. Larkin and Pines (2003[10]) also show that the perception of potential public humiliation rather than the likelihood of failure drives women more than men when considering participating in a public performance. In their experiment, they find that women are more concerned about doing poorly in public, and are less likely to risk entering a public competition by fear of disappointment.

Similarly, the attitude of men and women towards competition may be driven by societal factors. In their literature and research review of gender differences in preferences, Croson and Gneezy (2009[11]) look at how women and men react to competition in different studies. Overall, women tend to choose not to compete more often than men do. Yet research also demonstrates that women placed in a competitive environment perform just as well as men. Looking at experiments with children of different ages demonstrates that the gender difference seems to have appeared from a certain age rather than for all age groups, suggesting an environmental cause, which they characterise as backlash. Comparing a patriarchal society (the Maasai in Tanzania) and a matrilineal society (the Khasi in India), Gneezy, Leonard and List (2009[12]) also show that men choose to compete significantly more than women in the patriarchal societies, and that women choose to compete significantly more in matrilineal societies, reinforcing the assumption that the societal structure influences the willingness to compete.

Men may be driven more by speculation than women in their investment decision-process and portfolio choices. Based on a questionnaire addressed to clients of an Italian bank in 2013, and after controlling for sociological, demographic and economic variables, Marinelli, Mazzoli and Palmucci (2017[13]) find that gender still explains many differences in investment behaviours, namely in the investment decision process, in risk preferences and in portfolio characteristics.[10] The authors find no evidence of a difference in the quality of portfolios as illustrated by an assessment of liquidity and diversification. The data also show that women are more likely to declare relying on professional advice - 53.6% versus 44.3% of men, whereas men count more on autonomous decisions - 33.9% versus 26.3% of women. Men declare a greater risk tolerance, and to be driven more by speculation - 5% versus 2% of women, whereas women invest more with the aim of increasing their income. Consistent with this analysis, the survey by Ho (2018[14]) over Taiwanese finance students taking part in a virtual trading competition over 6 months shows that men are more likely to trade derivatives for speculation purposes than women in the sample, with a 20-percentage point difference in allocation between men and women.[11]

Women are less likely to gamble on events with objective probabilities, however, there is no effect of gender for subjective probabilities. Since most experiments demonstrating women's lower risk tolerance are based on gambling situations with an objective probability of winning and losing, Sarin and Wieland (2016[15]) look at risk aversion levels for situations such as cultural or sports events in the United States, where no objective probability of success can be derived. Based on several experiments using different types of elicitation methods, the authors find that there is no gender difference in risk aversion for events with a subjective probability of success.[12] The study compares these results to those obtained for gambles with objective probabilities, and finds that for gambles with objective probabilities, male respondents are twice as willing as women to pay to play the gambling game.[13] For subjective probability events however, gender does not seem to influence the bet valuation, which is only a function of the subjective probability of wining perceived by the participant.

The distribution of risk tolerance may be much more dispersed for men than for women. Based on individual portfolio choices in the mandatory Swedish Premium Pension plan (PPM), Säve-Söderbergh

(2012[16]) finds that there is little gender difference in portfolio risk for risk averse individuals, however men who choose risky portfolios take on significantly more risk than women who choose risky portfolios. The author examines the individual investment choices of participants by computing a measure of risk tolerance based on the standard deviation of the rate of return of funds in the pension portfolio for the past 36 months.[14] In this study, a similar proportion – around 62% - of both men and women choose to select funds to invest their contributions, as opposed to staying with the default investment strategy of the PPM, and women are more risk averse on average than men, with risk tolerance measures of 19.8 and 20.8 respectively.[15] However, when looking at the distribution of risk tolerance rather than at the mean, results indicate that the gender difference is explained in large part by risk tolerant men, i.e. men with a risk tolerance above the median male risk tolerance, who choose much riskier portfolios than risk tolerant women.

The gender difference in risk tolerance may be driven mostly by optimistic men who make significantly riskier choices than average men and women. Felton, Gibson and Sanbonmatsu (2003[17]) study the role of gender and optimism on the riskiness of investment choices of undergraduate business students from the Central Michigan University who participated in a portfolio simulation game on an individual basis.[16] The results of the game were both monetary, as participants could win up to USD 500, and academic since their results formed part of their grade. Optimism was evaluated through the Revised Life Orientation Test, and both men and women reported similar levels of optimism.[17] Risk indicators were built based on several parameters including the number of futures and options traded, the overall number of transactions, the number of companies invested in that traded on the Nasdaq stock market, on the New York Stock Exchange (NYSE) or on the American Stock Exchange (ASE).[18] The data show that male students are more likely than female students to invest in futures and options on average and that optimism is a significant predictor of investment in futures and options for men. The authors therefore argue that the difference between men and women's approach to futures and options is mostly driven by optimistic men, while optimism does not seem to affect the portfolio choices made by women. Looking at other risk indicators, men make significantly more transactions, and trade more on the Nasdaq market than women, and men have a standard deviation of their portfolio value approximately twice as large as that of women. The authors conclude that while male students take on significantly more risk than their female counterparts on average, the gender difference may be driven by optimistic men.

Over-confidence in their own capabilities and knowledge may hurt men's investment returns. Research on households from the United States finds that men are more likely to be over-confident in their investment decisions and experience than women, and that this leads them to negatively affect their investment returns by trading excessively (Barber and Odean, 2001[18]).[19] More (62.5%) men than women (47.8%) believe they have good or extensive experience, and more (2.8%) men than women (2.1%) believe they can outperform the market.[20] In addition, while both men and women tend to make poor portfolio decisions and to sell those stocks that have the best performances, women modify their portfolio less than men - 53% and 77% respectively, on an annual basis. Analysing the impact of over-confidence and excessive trading on net portfolio returns shows that men's returns are lowered by 2.65 percentage points a year, as opposed to 1.72 percentage points for women.

2.1.3. Impact of the marital status on risk aversion

Married individuals may be more risk averse, which can have long-lasting consequences on the gender pension gap (Hinz, McCarthy and Turner, 1997[19]). When controlling for income levels, using the share of stocks in pension investment portfolios as a risk tolerance measure shows that marriage reduces the risk tolerance of individuals in the United States.[21] Men invest more in stocks than women on average, 45% and 28% of their investment portfolio respectively. However, when breaking down risk tolerance by marital status, unmarried men demonstrate the riskiest investment profile, while married men and unmarried women show similar risk tolerance levels, and married women appear to be the most conservative in their investment risk profile.

However, the impact of marital status on financial risk tolerance may be more complex and vary by gender. Looking at participants in the Swedish PPM, Palme, Sundén and Söderlind (2004[20]) find that married men are less likely to accept financial risk than single men, but that married women are less risk averse than single women.[22] This analysis controls for the level of household income and expected pension benefits, and uses the standard deviation of the rate of return of the pension portfolio for the past 36 months as a measure of risk tolerance. The effect of the marital status on risk aversion for men and women can therefore not be considered as straightforward and might depend on additional parameters linked for instance to country specificities such as the overall pension system functioning.

2.1.4. Impact of financial education on risk aversion

Financial education may mitigate the gender gap in risk aversion. Comparing the general population in the United States to a sample of highly educated individuals, and to finance professors, Hibbert, Lawrence and Prakash (2013[21]) show that financial education lessens the gender difference in risk tolerance.[23] Comparing the general population with the highly educated shows that income and education are the most important variables in explaining risk aversion, however highly educated women are still significantly more risk averse than their male counterparts. Nevertheless the survey of finance professors shows no gender difference in risk aversion, with both male and female finance professors significantly less risk averse than the panel of highly educated participants.

The impact of financial education on risk aversion is also confirmed by comparing a sample of the general population's holding of investment in stocks to that of highly educated individuals and to economists in Denmark (Christiansen, Joensen and Rangvid, 2008[22]).[24] Economists in the panel are more likely to participate in the stock market – between 37% and 47% depending on years – than the overall panel, which has a participation rate of 23%, and than highly educated investors. The stock market participation rate of investors who are economists also increases significantly (by 6 percentage points) at the time when they complete their education, as does that of individuals moving in with an economist (by 5 percentage points). The duration of economics education also influences the stock market participation, as medium or long durations both significantly increase the stock market participation probability compared to a short economics education. Compared to several other education fields, having an economics education has by far the largest marginal effect on individuals' holding of stocks.

Perceived, rather than actual financial education, might also play a role in explaining risk aversion differences between genders.[25] The gender gap in stock market participation is usually explained by women's lower financial knowledge, their lower numeracy, their lack of familiarity with financial products or their lower risk tolerance. The study of German households by Bannier and Neubert (2016[23]) extends the analysis by looking at a larger universe of investment products and comparing standard risky products such as stocks and mutual funds to more sophisticated products such as hedge funds.[26] It also looks at different dimensions of financial knowledge, i.e. the actual versus the perceived financial literacy in order to examine the combined role of financial literacy and risk tolerance for investment decisions. While for men, a decrease in either the actual or the perceived financial literacy decreases the investment in standard risky products, for women only actual financial literacy appears meaningful. For both men (-11%) and women (-8%), standard risky investments decrease with risk tolerance. When controlling for actual financial literacy and risk tolerance together, gender does not play a significant role in investing in either standard or sophisticated assets.

Financial education may help increase the risk-return combination of investments, for a given level of risk tolerance. Comparing the levels of risk aversion of Chinese and American students, Pyles et al. (2016[24]) find that Chinese individuals tend to perceive themselves as more risk tolerant, although this does not necessarily translate into significant differences in portfolio composition. The authors also find that both American and Chinese female students exhibit lower risk tolerance levels than their male counterparts, and that financial education – assessed by having taking a finance class - increases the Sharpe ratio, which is a measure of the return of an investment compared to its risk. The results also show that the Sharpe ratio is unaffected by gender, meaning that women choose portfolios with a lower risk and return combination, which are as efficient as men's per value of risk.

2.2. Gender differences in financial literacy

Financial literacy is an important factor to ensure individuals have the knowledge and understanding to make choices that will affect when and in which material conditions they may retire. Men and women may exhibit differences in their understanding of financial concepts and in their attitudes towards saving (Atkinson and Messy, 2012[25]). This section first looks at the influence of gender on financial literacy and retirement readiness, and then examines the potential gender differences in priorities between spending and saving, before highlighting examples of retirement-related financial education campaigns targeted at women.

2.2.1. Differences in financial literacy

Women have lower levels of financial literacy overall. The OECD - International Network for Financial Education (INFE) pilot study on financial education examines the impact of several socio-economic factors such as age, gender and income on the level of financial knowledge in 14 countries (Atkinson and Messy, 2012[25]). Financial knowledge is evaluated by 8 questions covering key financial concepts, financial behaviours such as thinking before making a purchase, paying bills on time, budgeting, saving and borrowing, and attitudes towards long-term financial plans, as opposed to short-term. Results from the study show that women have much lower levels of financial knowledge than men in all of the countries studied except Hungary where results are similar for men and women. In several countries such as Norway, Poland and the United Kingdom for example, there is a 20-percentage point difference between men and women attaining a high knowledge score, in favour of men. Women are also less likely to gain high scores for financial behaviour, although this is not true for the Czech Republic, Estonia, Ireland and Norway where the opposite is found. In most of the countries surveyed, women are more likely to have a positive attitude towards long-term saving than men. Overall, none of the 14 countries surveyed has women score higher on the combined measure of financial literacy. The 2015 OECD/INFE survey of financial literacy, which expands the initial pilot study to include 30 countries, shows that the trend is still valid as women have less financial knowledge than men in 19 of the participating jurisdictions, with no significant gender differences in the remaining countries (OECD, 2017[26]).

Women's lower financial literacy may deter them from planning for retirement and may be linked to lower coverage by private pensions in several countries.

Men are more financially resilient than women in many countries. Taking into account financial knowledge reduces this gender difference (OECD, 2017[26]). Financial resilience denotes the ability of individuals to cope with a shock such as having to face major unexpected expenses, covering living expenses in case of an income loss, and supporting themselves in retirement independently of their spouse or family. In many countries participating in the 2015 OECD/INFE survey of financial literacy, men are more likely than women to report counting on their private pensions, accumulated financial and other assets to finance their retirement. Women are less likely than men to support themselves in retirement independently of their spouse in all 30 countries of the 2015 OECD/INFE survey of financial literacy, except Brazil, Korea and Lithuania. In several countries such as Belgium, Canada, New Zealand and Portugal, the financial resilience of women becomes closer to that of men when controlling for the level of financial knowledge.

Surveying women aged over 50 in the United States shows a strong positive correlation between financial literacy and planning (Lusardi and Mitchell, 2008[27]).[27] Overall, financial literacy results for the considered population are low, with 61.9% of respondents correctly answering a basic question on interest rates, as are the number of respondents (30.9%) who have ever attempted to plan for retirement. However, those respondents who can answer the financial literacy questions correctly, especially the question on risk diversification, plan significantly more than the overall sample.

Prior to the introduction of automatic enrolment to occupational pension schemes in 2012, many more women than men had a limited understanding of pensions and many more women than men also did not have appropriate private pension coverage in Great Britain (MacLeod et al., 2012[28]).[28] Overall 46% of women had never had a private pension at all, compared to 35% of men, and 23% of women actually had no resources at all for later life compared to 15% of men. This number increased to 42% for women with no educational qualifications, compared to 19% of all respondents. The study also showed that 71% of women, compared to 56% of men, felt that pensions seemed so complicated that they could not understand what was best to do. The study additionally found that 28% of women, compared to 13% of men, were "scared" by having to deal with their pension; and that 36% of women, compared to 25% of men, altogether avoided thinking of retirement.

In Ireland, crossing data from The Irish Longitudinal Study on Ageing (TILDA), and Growing Up in Ireland (GUI) surveys shows that women have lower levels of financial literacy than men, and that higher levels of female educational attainment reduce the gender gap for private and occupational pensions, throughout the income distribution (Nolan et al., 2019[29]). Almost 30% of boys aged 17 could correctly answer the three financial literacy questions of the GUI survey in 2014, compared to only 14% of girls of the same age. Similarly, for individuals aged over 54, the TILDA 2014 study shows that 17.2% of men could answer all financial literacy questions correctly, compared to 7.5% of women, and that women are more likely to answer 'don't know' to questions related to financial literacy than their male counterparts, by up to 9.9 percentage points. When decomposing the gender gap in occupational and private pensions according to educational levels attained, the authors find that higher education levels reduce the gender pension gap for all income groups, with higher effects for individuals in the lower deciles of the pension income distribution.

The gender gap in financial literacy is lower when women are involved in financial decision-making (Nolan et al., 2019[29]). While 54.5% of households in the Irish TILDA survey nominate the male partner as the key decision-maker for financial decisions, 74.4% nominate the female partner for family-related decisions. Financial literacy is higher for men on average, whatever the household decision-making combination, with a 0.54 point gap in favour of men in families where the man is in charge of financial decisions and the women in charge of family decisions, compared to 0.08 point when the woman is in charge of financial and the man in charge of family decisions, out of a maximum total score of 4.

2.2.2. Gender differences in priorities: spending versus saving

Women may prioritise more than men current spending for themselves or others over saving for retirement. Long-term planning can be linked to the level of financial knowledge, nevertheless it may also be influenced by a difference in priorities. Saving for retirement requires prioritising future over short-term well-being. It also implies saving for one-self rather than spending, potentially for others. Several pieces of research have shown a difference in preferences between men and women over these choices.

Women may be or feel more vulnerable to short-term financial hardship and hence avoid or delay saving for retirement. Just under half of men and women in the United Kingdom may not save adequately for retirement, and around 17% of both men and women do not save at all (Scottish Widows, 2018[30]).[29] Nevertheless a gender disparity exists among the younger cohorts, aged 22 to 29, in which 46% of men and 33% of women save adequately for retirement, while 17% of men and 25% of women do not save at all. The study argues that barriers to saving or to saving more for retirement are mainly linked to the absence of an access to emergency savings in case of financial hardship, with 42% of women aged 22 to 29 currently not saving for retirement confirming they would be likely to start, and an additional 19% currently contributing to a private pension likely to increase their savings, if they could have access to emergency funds in case of financial hardship. This is consistent with findings from Henry (2014[31]) in the United States, showing that the average share of consumption of American households devoted to personal insurance and pensions is highly dependent on their income level. Households in the lowest income quintile allocated 2.32% of their total consumption to pension and insurance on average over the period 1984-2012, compared to 13.92% for those in the highest income quintile.

Women may be more likely to spend their income on family members and gifts than men, thereby saving less, including for retirement. A study of couple households aged 55 and above in the United Kingdom shows that women are responsible for respectively 76% and 66% of household expenditures linked to the day-to-day needs of children under the age of 15 (including grand-children) and gifts (Age UK, 2018[32]). Conversely, men in the survey made 55% of expenditures related to savings.

Women take time off to care for a relative more often than men do, which is another way of prioritising current spending over future well-being.[30]

The gender employment gap has halved on average between the 1940s- and 1970s-born generations in OECD countries, nonetheless women are still more likely than men to work part-time and to take career breaks, which can create obstacles to adequate saving for retirement (OECD, 2017[33]). Women also bear most of the burden of unpaid household chores and are more likely to care for both children and older relatives.

Caregiving responsibilities can adversely affect the retirement savings and health of the individual providing this unpaid care, who is more often a woman than a man. American women are more likely to be caregivers for their family, with 56% of pre-retired women and 35% of pre-retired men, and 63% of retired women compared to 43% of retired men reporting having provided caregiving services (Rappaport et al., 2017[34]). Caregiving has emotional, physical and financial consequences for the caregiver. Among pre-retired respondents, 19% declare that caregiving has a major or catastrophic burden physically, 11% financially and 35% emotionally.[31] Women in the United States have a higher focus on others and are more likely to see their personal needs as secondary according to several surveys, focus groups and interviews (Rappaport, 2018[35]).[32]

Women, including the highly educated, often take career breaks to raise their children. In the United States, women work fewer years on average than men – 29 versus 38 respectively – mainly because of responsibilities linked to child-bearing and caring for the elderly (Garnick, 2016[1]).[33] Women increasingly take time off to raise their children, with almost 30% of stay-at-home mothers recorded in 2016, compared to 23% in 2000. Among the highly educated, this trend also holds with 25% of stay-at-home mothers having a university degree in 2016, compared to 7% in 1970.

Women taking career breaks to look after family may be the biggest factor in the gender pension gap. Looking at both public and private pension sources in the United Kingdom shows that the different working patterns between men and women are the largest factor explaining the difference in pension savings between men and women aged over 50, representing 47 percentage points of the 49% difference in pension wealth between men and women (Pensions Policy Institute, 2019[36]). This analysis interestingly does not note any behavioural or cultural effect in the gender pension gap linked to investment choices or risk aversion for instance. Policy options such as making sure employer contributions are based on the pre-maternity leave salary or are increased when taking time off or working part-time to take on caring responsibilities are proposed and quantitatively analysed to reduce the impact of caring duties on retirement savings.

Women also have a higher longevity, which implies a higher life expectancy in both health and disability, and a higher probability of living alone in retirement.[34] Women face healthcare costs 11% higher than men, because of their longer life expectancy, and these represent a growing portion of their retirement budget as they age (Garnick, 2016[1]). For instance at age 65, American women have a life expectancy of 19.5 years, made of 13.7 years in good health, and 5.8 years in mild or severe disability, compared to a total life expectancy of 15.3 years for men aged 65, of which 12.3 years in health and 3 years in disability. The associated long-term care costs incurred by women are therefore higher than for men, who are also more likely to have a family caregiver. The unpaid caregiving responsibilities of women can therefore imply less savings during working years, and also more spending in old age.

However, gender differences in attitudes towards long-term saving may not be universal (OECD, 2017[37]). In Norway for instance, over 80% of women, compared with 65% of men, achieve the minimum target score of three out of five for financial attitudes in the OECD/INFE survey, which assesses the preference for the long-term versus the tendency to live for today and spend rather than save.[35]

2.2.3. Examples of financial education campaigns aiming at improving the financial literacy of women

Several jurisdictions have put in place policy initiatives to address the gender gap in financial education (OECD, 2013[38]).

Financial education programmes may aim at informing women about the challenges and needs linked to retirement, with a focus on gender-related specificities and circumstances. For example, New Zealand's "Women in Super" network organises meetings and events since 2001, for women to learn more about the superannuation system and their specific needs linked to retirement. It was inspired by a similar initiative launched in Australia in 1994.

Other programmes are designed for particular groups of women that are considered as most vulnerable, such as young women, elderly women, low-income and marginalised women. Turkey's capital market board for instance launched a financial literacy programme in 2010 targeted at unemployed, unbanked and low-income women in order to increase their understanding of saving, debt and investment. In Singapore, the Tsao Foundation "Financial Education Programme for Mature Women" is designed for women between the ages of 40 and 60, and aims at helping them be financially independent in their older years.

2.3. Couples and the retirement income gap

Societal perceptions, attitudes and interactions may play a role in driving the gender gap in retirement income, in addition to individual behavioural biases that may affect women and have implications for their pension savings. This section examines dynamics of the pension gap for couples versus single individuals. It starts by focusing on financial decision-making at the household level, and then examines the impact of the marital status on the retirement outcomes of men and women.

2.3.1. Couples and financial decision-making

Financial decisions taken at the household level may not allow understanding the investment decision dynamics within couples. Bajtelsmit and Bernasek (1996[39]) propose several possible causes such as discrimination, choices, family responsibilities, as well as potential biological and social determinism for the wealth, income and employment differences explaining that American women on average have lower wealth levels than men, which is expected to increase their absolute risk aversion. However, the authors note that understanding the investment decision-making process within households is important to draw conclusions, especially related to gender differences.

There can be inconsistencies in the individual responses of household members related to financial decision-making, which can have implications for studying the gender pension gap. Members of Australian couples aged 21 to 80 years old asked to name the main household decision-maker for choices related to savings, investments and borrowings, report different answers (Johnston, Kassenboehmer and Shields,

2016[40]). Both men and women report similar frequencies of shared decision-making, around 70%. However, 22.6% of men report being the main decision-maker, which is confirmed by 15.7% of women, and 12.6% of women report being the main decision-maker, which is confirmed by 7.1% of men. These inconsistencies may have implications when analysing differences in financial education, risk aversion and ultimately the gender pension gap. Married couples are more likely to have a male decision-maker than cohabiting couples. Women with more education are more likely to be decision-makers. Couples with working females are more likely to have female decision-makers. The gender wage gap is significantly smaller when females are the decision-makers, from AUD 40 000 to AUD 8 000 in the studied sample. Finally, using detailed information on household wealth, the study finds that households in which the male is the main financial decision-maker are significantly more likely to hold financial assets and less likely to hold their wealth in real estate than households with either shared or female decision-making.

2.3.2. The marital status of retirees can influence their retirement income

Single women may experience an increased pension gap compared to married women. Couples may be able to mutualise their pension savings in order to manage their consumption smoothing, effectively reducing the gender pension gap. However, single retirees cannot and may suffer a higher gender pension gap.

The effect of having retirement savings on the income of single individuals aged over 65 in Canada is higher for women than for men (Richard Shillington et al., 2016[41]).[36] Although poverty in Canada has declined sharply between 1976 and 1995, it has been slowly increasing since 1996, especially for single individuals. Poverty rates for single individuals aged over 65 in Canada are higher for women than for men, at 28% and 24% respectively, compared with 11.1% for the overall population – including couples - of this age category in 2013. The authors focus on the difference of income for seniors depending on whether or not they have individual retirement savings, either occupational or personal, and excluding any payments from the public Canada or Quebec Pension Plan and show that the effect is greater for single individuals than for couples, and for women than for men. While the average family aged over 65 without a pension has an income of CAD 52 000, it reaches CAD 68 000 if there is a private pension plan. For single individuals, the difference is even greater since having a private pension increases income for single men from CAD 26 000 to CAD 46 000, as opposed to CAD 19 800 and CAD 39 000 for single women without and with a private pension respectively.

The proportion of women living in poverty increases with age, as more women are alone in old age. In the United States, women represent 57% of the 65 to 84 age group, and 71% of the 85 and above age group, and the proportion of women who are widowed increases with age, as does the proportion of women living in poverty (Bajtelsmit et al., 2005[42]).[37] The combination of women's higher life expectancy and of observed age differences within couples implies that women live increasingly longer alone. Women who outlive their male partner live on average 11.5 years alone, whereas only one third of males outlive their female partners, by an average of 8.8 years (Garnick, 2016[1]). Similarly, in the United Kingdom, 53% of men over the age of 80 live in a couple, compared to only 14% of women of the same age group (Portas, 2019[43]). And 75% of men with a defined contribution pension scheme believe it includes a financial benefit for their partner or dependents in event of their death whereas this is not an automatic feature of defined contribution schemes, implying that bereaved women may live on less income than they previously expected (Age UK, 2018[32]).[38]

Even within couples, a gender gap in retirement income may exist and increase with age and pension wealth. Focusing on individual-level occupational pension wealth for six European countries, Schneebaum et al. (2018[44]) demonstrate that there is an increase in the gender pension wealth gap as the absolute level of pension wealth and age - both strongly correlated - increase, at the disadvantage of women.[39] While most other parameters to quantify the wealth gap are observed for single households only because of the difficulty of correctly allocating assets within households, this result based on individual-level assets seems to show that the gap exists for the entire population, i.e. also for married couples or partners belonging to the same household.

The impact of a divorce on pension wealth can be significant, and increase the gender pension gap as pension savings may often be overlooked in divorce orders. In the United States, the poverty rate of divorced women is significantly higher than that of married women, at 20.4% and 4.3% respectively (Bajtelsmit et al., 2005[42]). The authors suggest this could be linked to a lack of awareness from the public that pension assets can be divided in a divorce, as other financial assets. In the United Kingdom, the median pension wealth of divorced women is reduced by 50% to GBP 26 100 compared to the overall female population, as opposed to approximately one third for men to GBP 103 500 (Now Pensions, 2019[45]). Out of the 118 142 divorce orders pronounced by British family courts in 2018, only 4 632 (i.e. less than 4%) included a pension attachment order, which divides pension entitlements accumulated during marriage between former spouses once they are in payment. However, other types of pension split orders also exist, such as pension offsetting and pension sharing orders (see Chapter 4 for further detail). Studying randomly selected divorce files in England and Wales courts between 2011 and 2012, Woodward and Sefton (2014[46]) found that 66% of files disclosed one or more relevant pension accounts but no pension split orders were pronounced, compared to 14% of cases which included an order to split pension assets between former spouses.[40]

The negative effect of divorce on women's retirement outcomes may be augmented as couples increasingly split at ages closer to retirement. New Zealand data from 1997 and 2019 shows that the median age for divorce has increased from 40.6 to 47 for men, and from 37.9 to 44.4 for women over the period. Dale and St John (2020[47]) argue that divorcing at later ages implies that there is less time to rebuild pension entitlements if there is an imbalance between the pension assets of former partners.

2.4. Gender stereotyping

Gender stereotyping refers to a generalised and preconceived view about some of the roles, capabilities and attributes performed or possessed by men and women. This section focuses on how gender stereotyping may play a role in several decisions and choices having an impact on the gender pension gap. It looks at the role gender may play on educational and career choices, before focusing on the gender imbalance in caregiving responsibilities and the impact of childcare costs on women's retirement savings. It then examines the influence of gender on the opening of a pension account and gifting by grandparents, and on recommendations provided by financial advisors.

2.4.1. From an early age in the choice of scientific topics, to career choices

Gender stereotyping and gendered expectations still drive educational and career choices (OECD, 2017[26]).

Gender stereotyping can have long-lasting effects for women's work and income prospects. Gender gaps persist in mathematics and numeracy across the OECD, and girls are more likely than boys to hold negative perceptions of their abilities in mathematics. This can deter women's work prospects and their ability to make important financial decisions. Several government-led initiatives targeted at women have recently been set up, such as in Poland to encourage women to participate in the stock market, or in Australia to prepare for important life events such as purchasing a home or having children. In most OECD countries, women still spend more time than men carrying out unpaid family work and there is a close link between the gender gap in paid and unpaid work hours, i.e. in countries where men and women share unpaid work hours more equally, they also spend a closer number of hours working in the labour market (OECD, 2017[26]).

The economic participation and progression of women may be affected by cultural and behavioural biases in the United Kingdom (Government Equalities Office, 2019[48]). Female students are under-represented in science subjects both at General Certificate of Secondary Education (GCSE) and A levels, and only 17% of small and medium-size enterprises (SMEs) are majority led by women, compared to 43% that are entirely led by men.[41] However, the over-representation of women in the public sector also implies that women with a pension are more likely to have a defined benefit plan than men, which may assist in reducing the gender pension gap (Now Pensions, 2019[45]).

2.4.2. Focusing on caregiving and the impact of childcare costs

In several countries, women still often are the primary family caregiver, and the moment in which the gender pension gap starts increasing coincides with the arrival of a child. In the United Kingdom, the average hourly gender pay gap between mothers and fathers, which is one of the main drivers of the gender pension gap, increases from around 10% to around 30% in favour of men from before the birth of a first child to the time the child is aged 13 (Mcguinness and Pyper, 2018[49]). The impact on hourly salary is compounded by the fact that when the first child reaches age 20, mothers have on average been working full-time for 10 years less than fathers. By that time, mothers have indeed on average worked part-time for seven years more than fathers, and have been out of paid work for three years more. Another study by Which? (2019[50]) notes that women working part time for ten years to take on caregiving responsibilities for children have pension pots between 15% and 20% lower than those working full time, and a likelihood 15% lower of receiving an adequate income in retirement.

Childcare costs may have a double effect on women's saving for retirement, both in absolute and relative terms. High childcare costs might imply leaving a full-time paid position, altogether or for a part-time one, hence decreasing pensionable salary and linked employer and employee contributions in absolute terms. They can also lead women to opt-out of non-mandatory schemes, or else reduce their voluntary contribution levels.

While automatic enrolment in the United Kingdom has enabled to increase the participation rate in the private occupational pension sector, childcare costs may play a role in women actively choosing to opt out (Prabhakar, 2017[51]). A focus group interview shows that the lack of affordability is the main reason for individuals to opt out after having been automatically enrolled by their employer, and that opt-out rates vary across different age groups.[42] Women in all age groups are more likely to opt out because of a lack of affordability. Women and not men, explicitly mention childcare costs as a reason for opting out.[43]

Childcare costs can make it financially more efficient in the short-term for women to reduce their working hours or leave employment (The People's Pension, 2019[52]; Imeson, 2019[53]). The labour market impact of childcare costs may be significant, with studies showing that up to half of the women in the United Kingdom have reduced their working hours after having children, and over a third have left employment after the birth of a child, primarily because it did not make financial sense, over the short term, to work compared to childcare costs. Long-term pension implications do not seem to form part of the parameters taken into account when deciding to reduce paid work because of childcare costs.

Women working part time following the birth of a child may have reduced opportunities and work prospects, in particular if childcare costs require them to reduce travelling to work time (Mcguinness and Pyper, 2018[49]). In the United Kingdom, gender differences in part-time working seem to explain more of the widening in the overall gender pay gap than the time women spend out of employment following the birth of a child. An increasing "gender commuting gap", i.e. the growing difference between the time men and women spend to travel to work in the 10 years following the birth a child, may imply that women have lower prospects of employment due to a constraint on their available time to commute to work, as travelling times for women decrease sharply from the birth of a child while they remain stable for men.

2.4.3. The effect of gender stereotyping on gifting by grandparents

Different gender perceptions and expectations from family members may influence the propensity of parents and grandparents to open a pension account and make contributions for their children and grandchildren. In countries where pension accounts may be opened for individuals before they start working, a gender difference in gifting patterns may have long lasting effects on the gap in pension assets between men and women. Tax data from the United Kingdom has shown that about 20 000 boys under the age of 16 had received money in a pension account for the fiscal year 2016-2017, compared to only about 13 000 girls of the same age. In addition, the tax relief of 20% attracted by contributions made on behalf of British children, which is added to the pension pot, and the compounding effect, may increase the impact of the difference in gifting patterns by family members towards young boys and girls.

2.4.4. Impact of gender stereotyping by advisors

Women may be more risk averse than men on average, nevertheless they are in addition, also often subject to gender stereotyping from financial advisors who assume an even greater risk aversion. Financial advisors may advise them on overly conservative investment options because of an unconscious bias.

Financial advisors may overestimate men's risk tolerance and underestimate women's because of gender stereotyping. Roszkowski and Grable (2005[54]) use four methods of regression and analysis to demonstrate that gender is a significant predictor of advisors' rating of risk tolerance, and that there is a tendency to overestimate men's risk tolerance and to underestimate women's.[44] Controlling for additional economical and educational factors that could explain the apparent gender stereotyping, the authors find that while there is a tendency to overestimate the risk tolerance of high income clients and to underestimate that of low income clients, gender remains the main predicting variable. Overall, they find a 0.41 correlation between advisors' estimates and actual risk tolerance indicators, and could not verify whether there is a difference in stereotyping between male and female advisors, due to the small sample of female advisors. This study shows that while women tend to exhibit lower risk tolerance levels, their investment choices may be further influenced or even limited by gender stereotypes demonstrated by investment advisors. Financial advisors should therefore rely on objective measures of risk tolerance in order to provide suitable advice to their clients and avoid being biased by stereotyping.

The gender difference in risk tolerance may be situational and amplified by the gender of financial advisors as wealthy women advised by male advisors report lower levels of risk tolerance, confidence and perceived financial literacy than wealthy women advised by female advisors (Baeckstrom, Marsh and Silvester, 2019[4]). The authors compare risk tolerance perception and the cash holdings of wealthy investors with and without an investment advisor, and find that having a financial advisor has an effect on risk tolerance and on cash holdings. Advised investors indeed report a higher risk tolerance perception and cash holdings 15% lower than self-advised investors. They also find that the gender of the financial advisor has a significant impact on the risk tolerance of advised women, as wealthy women advised by men feel less confident, less knowledgeable, more risk averse and hold 11% more cash than wealthy women advised by women. Wealthy women advised by women report the highest risk tolerance and make the lowest portfolio allocation to risk-free assets of the sample, including wealthy men. The authors therefore conclude that the gender difference in risk tolerance is situational rather than universally true for all women.

Financial advisors and fiduciaries should understand the specific financial needs of women and not assume women universally have a lower risk tolerance. In order to provide advice that is in their clients' best interest, it is important that financial advisors understand the ways in which income uncertainty and net worth may influence the risk tolerance levels of women, as the effects may be different for women and for men (Fisher and Yao, 2017[2]).

2.5. Communication and framing

This section looks at how communication and marketing may also be factors affecting the gap in retirement income between men and women. It starts by looking at how men and women may perceive information about retirement savings differently, then focuses on the need to target any communication campaign to its audience, including according to gender, before describing concrete examples of successful communication campaigns targeted at women.

2.5.1. Effect of information bias by gender

The way information is presented may play a different role in financial decision-making for men and women, alongside risk tolerance and financial literacy. For issues related to investment and pensions, women may be influenced more by information going against their preconceived notions. By using negative framing, i.e. by highlighting the potential financial losses associated with one or the other choice in an experiment, Agnew et al. (2008[55]) show that women are significantly more influenced by an information bias going against their preconceived notions.[45] When asked to choose between purchasing an annuity and investing their old age savings, women on average choose to annuitise more often than men, for a given level of risk aversion and financial literacy. Additionally, more risk averse individuals are more likely to choose an annuity rather than an investment option, regardless of gender. However, depending on whether the information is framed in favour of purchasing an annuity or in favour of investing, and controlling for the level of risk tolerance and financial literacy, men and women are influenced differently. While men are similarly influenced by information highlighting the disadvantages of investing or annuitising, women are significantly more influenced by an information bias towards investing that highlights the drawbacks of annuities. Taking into account the dissimilar impact of framing on men and women can be of particular importance when designing communication campaigns and when setting default investment strategies.

2.5.2. Need to target communication towards women

Although risk preferences may play a role, most of the gender difference in expected retirement benefits may be linked to contribution levels. Based on average returns expected for the different investment strategies available to Australian members of the UniSuper superannuation scheme, Watson and McNaughton (2007[5]) find that income, thus contributions, differences between men and women explain most of the difference in expected retirement benefits. Marketing and information campaigns targeted towards the specific needs of women can therefore be set up to better communicate towards women in order to increase their contributions and their financial education.

Women's behaviour may be more variable than men's and influenced by their environment. In addition to their work on risk preferences, Croson and Gneezy (2009[11]) look at social preferences and the impact of gender on altruism, envy, inequality aversion and reciprocity, comparing different studies using several methods such as ultimatum games, trust games or dictator games.[46] The authors find that while results across studies may vary, overall women tend to be more responsive to the conditions of the experiment. For example, in an ultimatum game, women respond more positively if the bargaining party is sitting opposite them rather than behind a curtain. Similarly, in the trust game, women trust less than men when they only have written information about the person they are asked to trust, and more than men when they are provided with a picture of this person. Women's behaviour can therefore be more variable than men's according to the context of the experiment, which could validate the need for targeted communication campaigns towards women, or specific training for financial advisors.

2.5.3. Examples of communication campaigns targeted at women

Targeted communication campaigns may be effective in increasing women's participation in private defined contribution plans. Anderson and Collins (2017[56]) examine the effect of a financial education campaign called EMPOWER (Embracing and Promoting Options for Women to Enhance Retirement) and designed to improve the participation of women to a supplementary occupational pension plan set up for non-school public agencies workers in Wisconsin. The campaign consisted of monthly emails to all workers in the agencies, posters in the workplace, invitations to webinars, and live events available to women workers only. The agencies which put EMPOWER in place were on average those with the highest initial gender gaps, and results were observed before and after the campaign, for men and women, for agencies participating and for those not participating in EMPOWER. The campaign is estimated to have had an overall effect of increasing participation by 2.6%, closing the gender gap by more than half. The effect was largest for younger workers, i.e. those who might not have been as aware of or preoccupied by their retirement options, and for lower-earning workers. However, the contribution rates of workers who were already participating did not significantly increase with the campaign.

Communication on the effects of specific life events, such as parental leave or divorce, on retirement income may be a way to increase women's awareness on retirement planning. Providing explanations on the potential effect of parental leave on retirement savings, and options to overcome these effects may help to address part of the gender gap in retirement income. Adapting communication to behavioural elements, such as risk aversion and confidence, and taking gender and life events into account when designing communication campaigns could be a solution to address the potential gender differences in behaviours related to pensions. This has only started to be considered by policy makers, pension schemes and trustees very recently (Imeson, 2019[57]).

2.6. Recent positive trends

The literature shows that differences in risk tolerance, financial literacy and in attitudes towards saving can have important effects on the gender gap in retirement savings. Societal factors such as the marital status, gender stereotyping and communication may also amplify this gap between men and women.

Although there is abundant literature on potential labour, behavioural, and cultural elements potentially explaining the gender gap in retirement income, research seems to indicate that the issue is now higher up on governments, policy makers, pension stakeholders, and investors' agenda. This indicates that solutions may be sought and that improvements may be expected in the future. Improvements in the imbalance between men and women's retirement income have already started to appear in several countries. For example, the European Commission's "Mind the gap in Pensions" project includes an analysis of some of the possible causes for the gender gap in pensions, including the impact of framing and career choices on the income received in retirement by men and women (Dekkers, Hoorens and Van Den Bosch, 2020[58]).

The Group of 20 (G20) endorsed a policy guidance on addressing women's and girls' needs for financial awareness and education in 2013 (OECD, 2013[59]). To overcome some of the challenges linked to the gender disparity in financial education and the gender differences in financial needs, policy guidance providing an international framework as well as delivery tools for policy makers was prepared by the OECD, and endorsed by leaders of the G20 in September 2013. It recommends considering national priorities and needs to identify and address the areas in which the development of financial education approaches targeted specifically at women and girls may be required.

The role of men and women in society has changed and gender stereotyping is decreasing in several jurisdictions. A change in mentalities with respect to the role of men and women in society has occurred in the United Kingdom since 1984, when 43% of respondents agreed that men should earn money while women should take care of the family, versus 8% in 2017. Additionally, there has been a shift in the representation of women in company boards and in prominent public roles (Government Equalities Office, 2019[48]).

There has been an increase in women's participation and savings rate in several OECD countries, which will eventually lead to a decrease in the gender gap in retirement savings. Working women aged 30 to 39 currently have a higher pension participation rate than men in the United Kingdom (Now Pensions, 2019[45]).

Active ownership by institutional investors might help reduce the occupational pension gap. Institutional investors such as for instance state pension funds in the United States have started showing more interest in the way companies treat gender neutrality, by asking them to disclose information on the gender pay and promotion gap for instance (Temple-West, 2019[60]). These pension funds see issues related to gender inequality as potential risks for the future and hence part of their fiduciary duty towards their members. The disclosure of information can affect the voting behaviour of investors in investee companies' annual general meetings. Active investors can decide to sanction management in their voting decisions if they think gender equality is not sufficiently targeted, or they can engage with management in order to initiate changes and improvements. Such active participation of investors in management decisions of companies can encourage companies to tackle the gender gap in their treatment of employees in several aspects, including in matters related to occupational pension and the gender pension gap.

Allowing defined contribution pension scheme members to choose their investment strategy may be positive, even for participants with a lower risk tolerance. Australia's UniSuper scheme moving from a single investment strategy to a choice between seven options with different risk and return profiles has had a positive impact on expected retirement incomes of both men and women, despite women choosing more conservative investment strategies than men on average (Watson and McNaughton, 2007[5]). Consistent with the recommendation to allow individual participants in defined contribution pension arrangements to choose their investment strategy stated from the OECD Roadmap for the Good Design of Defined Contribution Pension Plans (OECD, 2012[61]), imposing a single investment strategy may therefore not be a suitable solution to counterbalance the gender gap in retirement income.

References

Age UK (2018), *For love and money: Women's pensions, expenditure and decision-making in retirement.* [32]

Agnew, J. et al. (2008), *Who chooses annuities? An experimental investigation of the role of gender, framing, and defaults*, http://dx.doi.org/10.1257/aer.98.2.418. [55]

Allport, W. et al. (2019), *How the UK Saves: Effects of gender on retirement savings behaviour Member experience from the National Employment Savings Trust (NEST)*, Vanguard and NEST Insight. [6]

Anderson, D. and J. Collins (2017), *Can knowledge empower women to save more for retirement?*, https://crr.bc.edu/wp-content/uploads/2017/09/wp_2017-12.pdf (accessed on 25 February 2019). [56]

Arch, E. (1993), "Risk-Taking: A Motivational Basis for Sex Differences", *Psychological Reports*, Vol. 73/1, pp. 3-11, http://dx.doi.org/10.2466/pr0.1993.73.1.3. [9]

Atkinson, A. and F. Messy (2012), "Measuring Financial Literacy: Results of the OECD / International Network on Financial Education (INFE) Pilot Study", *OECD Working Papers on Finance, Insurance and Private Pensions*, No. 15, OECD Publishing, Paris, https://dx.doi.org/10.1787/5k9csfs90fr4-en. [25]

Baeckstrom, Y., I. Marsh and J. Silvester (2019), *Financial Advice, Wealth and Gender: Risk Tolerance, Knowledge and Confidence*, https://www.bloomberg.com/news/articles/2018-06-14/millionaires-now-control-. [4]

Bajtelsmit, V. and A. Bernasek (1996), *Why do women invest differently than men?*, Association for Financial Counseling and Planning Education, http://ssrn.com/abstract=2238. [39]

Bajtelsmit, V. et al. (2005), *Women and Pensions*, http://dx.doi.org/10.1111/j.1540-6296.2005.00047.x. [42]

Bannier, C. and M. Neubert (2016), "Gender differences in financial risk taking: The role of financial literacy and risk tolerance", *Economics Letters*, Vol. 145, pp. 130-135, http://dx.doi.org/10.1016/j.econlet.2016.05.033. [23]

Barber, B. and T. Odean (2001), *Boys will be boys:gender, overconfidence, and common stock investment.* [18]

Barker, A. (2018), "Increasing inclusiveness for women, youth and seniors in Canada", *OECD Economics Department Working Papers* No.1519, OECD Publishing, Paris, http://dx.doi.org/10.1787/83cb8b8d-en. [69]

Christiansen, C., J. Joensen and J. Rangvid (2008), "Are economists more likely to hold stocks?", *Review of Finance*, Vol. 12/3, pp. 465-496, http://dx.doi.org/10.1093/rof/rfm026. [22]

Cronqvist, H. et al. (2018), *When Nudges Are Forever: Inertia in the Swedish Premium Pension Plan*, https://ssrn.com/abstract=3099886. [8]

Croson, R. and U. Gneezy (2009), "Gender differences in preferences", *Journal of Economic Literature*, Vol. 47/2, pp. 448-474, http://dx.doi.org/10.1257/jel.47.2.448. [11]

Dale, M. and S. St John (2020), *Women and Retirement in a post COVID-19 world.* [47]

Dekkers, G., V. Hoorens and K. Van Den Bosch (2020), *Project text "Mind the Gap".* [58]

Even, W. and D. Macpherson (1990), "The Gender Gap in Pensions and Wages", *The Review of Economics and Statistics*, Vol. 72, pp. 259-265. [67]

Felton, J., B. Gibson and D. Sanbonmatsu (2003), "Preference for Risk in Investing as a Function of Trait Optimism and Gender", *Journal of Behavioral Finance*, Vol. 4/1, pp. 33-40, http://dx.doi.org/10.1207/S15327760JPFM0401_05. [17]

Fisher, P. and R. Yao (2017), "Gender differences in financial risk tolerance", *Journal of Economic Psychology*, Vol. 61, pp. 191-202, http://dx.doi.org/10.1016/j.joep.2017.03.006. [2]

Garnick, D. (2016), *Income Insights: Gender Retirement Gap.* [1]

Gherzi, S. et al. (2014), "The meerkat effect: Personality and market returns affect investors' portfolio monitoring behaviour", *Journal of Economic Behavior and Organization*, Vol. 107/PB, pp. 512-526, http://dx.doi.org/10.1016/j.jebo.2014.07.013. [68]

Gneezy, U., K. Leonard and J. List (2009), "Gender differences in competition: Evidence from a matrilineal and a patriarchal society", *Econometrica*, Vol. 77/5, pp. 1637-1664, http://dx.doi.org/10.3982/ECTA6690. [12]

Goverment Equalities Office (2019), *Gender equality at every stage: a roadmap for change*, HM Government. [63]

Government Equalities Office (2019), *Gender Equality Monitor*, HM Government. [48]

Government Equalities Office (2019), *The case for change*, HM Government. [62]

Henry, L. (2014), "Income inequality and income class consumption patterns", *Economic Commentary - the Federal Reserve Bank of Cleveland.* [31]

Hibbert, A., E. Lawrence and A. Prakash (2013), "Does knowledge of finance mitigate the gender difference in financial risk-aversion?", *Global Finance Journal*, Vol. 24/2, pp. 140-152, http://dx.doi.org/10.1016/j.gfj.2013.07.002. [21]

Hinz, R., D. McCarthy and J. Turner (1997), "Are women conservative investors? Gender differences in participant-directed pension investments", in *Positioning pensions for the twenty-first century*, The Pension Research Council (the Wharton School of the University of Pennsylvania) and University of Pennsylvania Press (Philadelphia). [19]

Ho, C. (2018), "The Effects of Social Interaction and Psychological Bias on Trading Behavior: Evidence from a Laboratory Experiment", *Journal of Mathematical Finance*, Vol. 08/01, pp. 178-196, http://dx.doi.org/10.4236/jmf.2018.81014. [14]

Imeson, S. (2019), *Bridging the gender pensions gap - How the industry can help improve retirement adequacy for women*, Pensions-expert.com, https://www.pensions-expert.com/Law-Regulation/How-schemes-can-play-their-part-in-bridging-the-gender-pensions-gap?ct=true (accessed on 23 August 2019). [53]

Imeson, S. (2019), *How schemes can play their part in bridging the gender pensions gap*, Pensions-Expert.com, https://www.pensions-expert.com/DC-Auto-enrolment/How-schemes-can-play-their-part-in-bridging-the-gender-pensions-gap?ct=true (accessed on 3 October 2019). [57]

Johnston, D., S. Kassenboehmer and M. Shields (2016), "Financial decision-making in the household: Exploring the importance of survey respondent, health, cognitive ability and personality", *Journal of Economic Behavior and Organization*, Vol. 132, pp. 42-61, http://dx.doi.org/10.1016/j.jebo.2016.09.014. [40]

Kesavayuth, D., R. Rosenman and V. Zikos (2016), "Retirement, personality, and well-being", *Economic Inquiry*, Vol. 54/2, pp. 733-750, http://dx.doi.org/10.1111/ecin.12307. [66]

Larkin, J. and H. Pines (2003), *Gender and Risk in Public Performance.* [10]

Lusardi, A. and O. Mitchell (2008), "Planning and financial literacy : how do women fare?", *American Economic Review: Papers & Proceedings*, Vol. 98/2, pp. 413-417, https://www.dartmouth.edu/~alusardi/Papers/AER-FinalPublishedVersion.pdf. [27]

MacLeod, P. et al. (2012), *Attitudes to pensions : the 2012 survey*, Department for Work and Pensions. [28]

Makarov, D. and A. Schornick (2010), *Explaining Households' Investment Behavior*, http://ssrn.com/abstract=1623785. [3]

Marinelli, N., C. Mazzoli and F. Palmucci (2017), "How does gender really affect investment behavior?", *Economics Letters*, Vol. 151, pp. 58-61, http://dx.doi.org/10.1016/j.econlet.2016.12.006. [13]

Mcguinness, F. and D. Pyper (2018), *The Gender Pay Gap*, http://www.parliament.uk/commons-library|intranet.parliament.uk/commons-library|papers@parliament.uk|@commonslibrary. [49]

Nolan, A. et al. (2019), *Gender, pensions and income in retirement*, Economic and Social Research Institute, Dublin, Ireland, http://dx.doi.org/10.26504/rs87. [29]

Now Pensions (2019), *Facing an unequal future Closing the gender pensions gap*, https://www.nowpensions.com/wp-content/uploads/2019/07/NP-gender-pensions-gap-report.pdf. [45]

OECD (2018), "Improving retirement incomes considering behavioural biases and limited financial knowledge", in *OECD Pensions Outlook 2018*, OECD Publishing, Paris, https://dx.doi.org/10.1787/pens_outlook-2018-8-en. [7]

OECD (2017), *G20/OECD INFE report on adult financial literacy in G20 countries*, http://www.oecd.org/daf/fin/financial-education/G20-OECD-INFE-report-adult-financial-literacy-in-G20-countries.pdf. [37]

OECD (2017), *Preventing Ageing Unequally*, OECD Publishing, Paris, https://doi.org/10.1787/9789264279087-en. [33]

OECD (2017), *The Pursuit of Gender Equality: An Uphill Battle*, OECD Publishing, Paris, http://dx.doi.org/10.1787/9789264281318-en. [26]

OECD (2013), *G20 OECD/INFE policy guidance on addressing women's and girls' needs for financial awareness and education*, http://www.oecd.org/daf/fin/financial-education/G20-Women-Girls-Fin-Ed-Policy-Guidance-2013.pdf. [59]

OECD (2013), *Women and Financial Education: Evidence, Policy Responses and Guidance*, OECD Publishing, Paris, https://dx.doi.org/10.1787/9789264202733-en. [38]

OECD (2012), *The OECD roadmap for the good design of defined contribution pension plans*, http://www.oecd.org/pensions/designingfundedpensionplans.htm. [61]

Palme, M., A. Sundén and P. Söderlind (2004), *INVESTMENT CHOICE IN THE SWEDISH PREMIUM PENSION PLAN*. [20]

Pensions Policy Institute (2019), *Understanding the Gender Pensions Gap*, http://www.pensionspolicyinstitute.org.uk. [36]

Portas, J. (2019), *Securing the financial future of the next generation*, Insuring Women's Futures. [43]

Prabhakar, R. (2017), "Why do people opt-out or not opt-out of automatic enrolment? A focus group study of automatic enrolment into a workplace pension in the United Kingdom", *Journal of European Social Policy*, Vol. 27/5, pp. 447-457, http://dx.doi.org/10.1177/0958928717717656. [51]

Pyles, M. et al. (2016), "Cultural influences on risk tolerance and portfolio creation", *Journal of Behavioral and Experimental Finance*, Vol. 9, pp. 43-55, http://dx.doi.org/10.1016/j.jbef.2016.01.001. [24]

Rappaport, A. (2018), *Women and Post Retirement Risks*, Society of Actuaries. [35]

Rappaport, A. et al. (2017), *Aging and Retirement Caregiving for Older Individuals: Perspectives of the Caregiver and the Care Recipient 2017 Risks and Process of Retirement Survey Report Retirement Survey Report Key Findings and Issues*, http://www.soa.org. [34]

Richard Shillington, B. et al. (2016), *An Analysis of the Economic Circumstances of Canadian Seniors*, Broadbent Institute. [41]

Roszkowski, M. and J. Grable (2005), "Gender Stereotypes in Advisors' Clinical Judgments of Financial Risk Tolerance: Objects in the Mirror Are Closer than They Appear", *Journal of Behavioral Finance*, Vol. 6/4, pp. 181-191, http://dx.doi.org/10.1207/s15427579jpfm0604_2. [54]

Sarin, R. and A. Wieland (2016), "Risk aversion for decisions under uncertainty: Are there gender differences?", *Journal of Behavioral and Experimental Economics*, Vol. 60, pp. 1-8, http://dx.doi.org/10.1016/j.socec.2015.10.007. [15]

Säve-Söderbergh, J. (2012), "Self-Directed Pensions: Gender, Risk, and Portfolio Choices", *Scandinavian Journal of Economics*, Vol. 114/3, pp. 705-728, http://dx.doi.org/10.1111/j.1467-9442.2012.01710.x. [16]

Schneebaum, A. et al. (2018), "The Gender Wealth Gap Across European Countries", *Review of Income and Wealth*, http://dx.doi.org/10.1111/roiw.12281. [44]

Scottish Widows (2018), *The 2018 annual women and retirement report.* [30]

Sierminska, E., J. Frick and M. Grabka (2009), "Examining the Gender Wealth Gap in Germany", *SSRN*, http://dx.doi.org/10.2139/ssrn.1424899. [64]

Temple-West, P. (2019), *Pension funds step up campaign to reduce gender pay gap*, Financial Times, https://www.ft.com/content/10f9caca-c1e0-11e9-a8e9-296ca66511c9 (accessed on 20 August 2019). [60]

The People's Pension (2019), *The Gender Pensions Gap: Tackling the motherhood penalty.* [52]

Thurley, D. et al. (2018), *Women and Pensions*, House of Commons Library, http://dx.doi.org/10.1111/j.1540-6296.2005.00047.x. [65]

Watson, J. and M. McNaughton (2007), "Gender differences in risk aversion and expected retirement benefits", *Financial Analysts Journal*, Vol. 63/4, pp. 52-62, http://dx.doi.org/10.2469/faj.v63.n4.4749. [5]

Which? (2019), *Top up the Pots - Achieving adequate retirement incomes with automatic enrolment.* [50]

Woodward, H. and M. Sefton (2014), *Pensions on divorce: an empirical study*, Cardiff University. [46]

Notes

[1] This literature review attempts to cover research from as many countries as possible, although some countries such as the United Kingdom and the United States may appear more often than others, reflecting the abundant literature currently available in these two OECD jurisdictions.

[2] 2014 data from the Cogent Reports and Investor Brandscape Custom Data Tables.

[3] The study refers to 401(k) and 403(b) private pension plans.

[4] 2013 United States Survey of Consumer Finances data.

[5] Married and partnered respondents were sampled out as the survey data would not allow to differentiate financial decisions made or influenced by spouses or partners. Final sample size: 2 246 individuals.

[6] Sample size: 500 individuals.

[7] UniSuper is the sole provider of retirement funds for Australian universities staff, both academic and general. Sample size: 32 061.

[8] This control was suggested by the observation that men in the lowest earnings brackets and who contribute occasionally have lower contributions and account balances than their gender counterparts, mostly attributable to more transient employment patterns and higher job turnover.

[9] Given that NEST does not cover the higher earnings categories of the population however, a caveat on data representativeness should be mentioned as results might therefore not hold for higher socio-economic groups.

[10] Sample size: 2 374 individuals.

[11] Sample size: 88 individuals.

[12] Elicitation methods used for the valuation of the bet included the price at which participants would be willing to sell a lottery ticket paying if their choice was correct, an ordinal comparison of outcomes, and a certainty equivalent, i.e. the amount that participants would accept for being indifferent between participating or not in the betting game.

[13] The objective probability game was a lottery game with 10 white balls and 20 yellow balls, asking participants to state how much they would be willing to pay to play a game where they would win USD 100 if a white ball was drawn.

[14] Data from the 1999 Swedish Household Survey on Income (HINK) and information on individuals' investment choices in the PPM individual accounts. Sample size: 17 987 individuals.

[15] This result may seem surprising given the low rate of people choosing their own investment funds previously presented in the study by Cronqvist et al. (2018[8]) for 2016. However, Cronqvist et al. (2018[8]) show that this rate is heavily dependent on communication campaigns, and went from 66.6% in 2000, to 18.4% in 2001 and down to 0.9% in 2019. Large communication campaigns were carried out in 2000 when the new Premium Pension system was introduced for all workers in Sweden, by both the Swedish government and individual funds, to encourage individuals to select their own investment funds instead of

choosing the default option. Communication and advertising efforts were significantly reduced in subsequent years, when only new entrants in the labour market were joining the PPM.

[16] Sample size: 66 individuals.

[17] The Revised Life Orientation Test (LOT-R) is a 10-item scale that measures how optimistic or pessimistic people feel about the future. It was developed in 1994 by psychologists Scheier, Carver and Bridges.

[18] In this analysis, the number of futures and options traded is considered as showing a greater risk tolerance through speculation, stocks traded on the Nasdaq are considered more volatile hence positively associated with risk tolerance, while stocks traded on the NYSE or the ASE are considered to represent more traditional blue-chip companies and hence negatively associated with risk tolerance.

[19] Sample size: 37 664 households.

[20] The gender difference being statistically significant for both indicators.

[21] Data from the 1990 survey of participants in the Federal government's Thrift Savings Plan (TSP).

[22] Data from the 2010 Longitudinal INdividual DAta panel (LINDA) and information on individuals' investment choices in the PPM individual accounts in 2010. Sample size 244 750 individuals.

[23] The general population data is drawn from the 2004 Federal Reserve Board's Survey of Consumer Finance – SCF, of which 4 216 adults with a college degree were considered highly educated. The finance faculty sample size was 1 147.

[24] The general population sample was built from the Danish Institute of Governmental Research data, covering 10% of the Danish population from 1997 to 2001, i.e. more than 400 000 individual investors with annual data. Highly educated individuals were the 19 233 individuals in the panel with at least 18 years of schooling, corresponding to holding a master's degree or above. Economists were the 5 148 individuals in the sample with economics education of 2, 4 or 6 years beyond high school.

[25] Perceived financial education refers to an individual's own assessment of their financial literacy compared to the average person, while actual financial education can be assessed by objective means such as through questionnaires or surveys.

[26] Based on 2 047 responses from the German household survey SAVE for 2009.

[27] Sample size: 758 individuals.

[28] Sample size: 1 949 randomly selected adults.

[29] Data based on 5 148 adults in the United Kingdom for the year 2018. Adequate saving for retirement defined for individuals as either saving at least 12% of income or expecting that their main retirement income will come from a defined benefit plan.

[30] This may be due to personal preferences and/or to societal expectations.

[31] 2017 Society of Actuaries' Risks Survey.

[32] Combining data from the 2014 American Community Survey, the 2017 Society of Actuaries' Risks and the Process of Retirement Survey, focus groups and interviews.

[33] 2014 data from Social Security Administration.

[34] According to the 2017 Society of Actuaries Risk Survey, 87% of women aged 85 and over are single – either unmarried or widowed, compared to 49% of men aged 85 and over.

[35] Sample size: 1 031 individuals.

[36] Statistics Canada and OECD data.

[37] United States Census Bureau 2000 data.

[38] Survey of people aged between 55 and 70, and living with a partner. Sample size: 1 010.

[39] Based on data from the Household Finance and Consumption Survey (HFCS) for Austria, Belgium, France, Germany, the Slovak Republic and Spain.

[40] Sample size: 369. In 20% of cases, no relevant pensions were disclosed by members of the couple.

[41] Majority-led meaning controlled by a single woman or having a management team of which a majority were women.

[42] Sample size: 44 individuals. Opt-out rates were 7% for participants under 30, 9% for participants aged 30 to 49, and 23% for those aged 50 and above.

[43] Reasons to opt out mentioned were lack of affordability, the presence of more financially attractive alternatives to a pension, and limited time for returns to be generated by a private pension for some participants aged 50 and above.

[44] Sample size: 183 financial advisors in the insurance industry and 290 clients.

[45] Using a sample of 845 United States participants aged 19 to 89.

[46] In an ultimatum game, one player - the allocator - is endowed with a sum of money and asked to split it between herself and an anonymous player - the recipient. The recipient may either accept the allocator's proposal or reject it, in which case neither of the players will receive anything. In a trust game, one player can send all, some, or none of her endowment to a second player. The amount sent is multiplied by 3, and received by the second player, who can then decide to return as much or as little of the money in her possession to the first player. A dictator game is similar to the second stage of a trust game, as only one player chooses whether and how much of her endowment to send to another anonymous player.

3 What drives the gender pension gap? Case studies from the United States, Germany and Finland

There is a well-documented gap in retirement income between men and women. Women generally receive less than men from retirement savings arrangements in part because they tend to have earned less and have had shorter careers than men. But a key question is whether these are the only factors that explain the gender pension gap. This chapter uses case studies of three OECD countries to explore which factors drive the gender gap in pension coverage, assets and entitlements in retirement savings arrangements for working-age people, to determine what aspects of pension policy design might explain the gender gap in pensions.

Women generally receive a lower pension income than men in part because they tend to have earned less and have had shorter careers than men. This is a common explanation for the gender pension gap. However, it is less clear to what extent factors other than labour market factors may also contribute to the gender pension gap. Chapters 1 and 2 explore what some of these factors may be. This chapter complements their content by using case studies from three OECD countries to delve deeper into the question of what drives gender differences in some pension indicators.

The analysis in this chapter shows that while labour market factors remain a significant reason why women may end up with lower retirement income than men, that is only part of the story. Rather, delving deeper into case studies of different countries reveals that other factors are often at play, and that there is room for policy intervention to address the sources of the gender pension gap.

It explores how different features of policy design, demographic characteristics, incomes, workplace choices, and career trajectories contribute to gaps in pension coverage, assets, and entitlements in retirement savings arrangements. Understanding drivers of these gaps is important because individuals' future retirement income is, at least in part, a function of whether someone has a pension plan and how much they save in defined contribution (DC) plans or accumulate in entitlements in defined benefit (DB) plans. Unpacking the contribution of different drivers of the pension gap makes it possible for policy makers to understand how much differences between men and women's careers can affect their pensions. Conversely, if career disparities cannot explain differences in retirement income outcomes, a different explanation, such as pension policy or behavioural biases might better explain the gender pension gap.

This chapter considers these questions through case studies of three OECD countries: the United States, Germany, and Finland. It examines what drives gender disparities when it comes to coverage, assets, and entitlements accrued for both occupational pension arrangements and personal pension arrangements separately.

The analysis starts by using econometric analyses to explore why, in some countries, women may be less likely to have a pension plan through their workplace. For people who do have a pension plan linked to their employment, it also explores why assets or entitlements from those plans might differ between men and women. The analysis shows that the industry people work in and the number of hours they work can be related to whether or not a person has a pension plan from their workplace (for example, in the United States and Germany). Workplaces in some industries are significantly more likely to offer plans to their workers than other industries, and those industries happen to be male-dominated. A similar effect is seen in the type of work that people do. In the United States, some plans may only be offered to full time workers, which can disadvantage women. While in Germany such distinctions are not made within workplaces, it remains that workplaces that tend to hire workers with more standard and stable careers are also those that offer workplace pension plans to their employees. Again, this can disadvantage women. When coverage of occupational pension plans is universal, there is no meaningful difference in pension plan coverage between the genders (for example, Finland). However, in all the countries studied, when it comes to the assets or entitlements individuals may have from their occupational pension plans, labour market factors such as income and years of work appear to be the main drivers of a potential gender gap in accumulated assets or entitlements.

With respect to personal pension plans, the analysis shows that there is no clear sign that women are less likely to have taken out a personal pension plan than men. Instead, in Finland, the opposite appears true, that women in some age groups are more likely to have personal pension plans. While this is a positive sign, the same is not true of the amount of assets people accumulate in those plans. In Finland and Germany, the amounts women contribute to those plans are significantly less than men, as are the assets they manage to accumulate in those plans. Even after accounting for labour market factors, those differences are still evident, pointing to a potential behavioural bias between men and women.

This chapter proceeds as follows. Section 3.1 summarises the plans analysed in this chapter. Section 3.2 outlines the approach taken in the analysis. Sections 3.3 and 3.4 explore the drivers of the pension gaps in occupational pension plans and personal pension plans respectively in the three countries analysed. Section 3.5 discusses the results and concludes.

3.1. Summary of pension plans analysed in this chapter

The analysis focusses on funded and private occupational or personal pension arrangements available in three countries, the United States, Germany, and Finland.[1] Annex 3.A contains details of the data used in this analysis for the three countries.

The case study of the United States considers the voluntary occupational schemes, which can be DB or DC. In the United States, individual employers or groups of employers may voluntarily establish a complementary occupational pension plan for their employees. The plan sponsor decides what type of plan to establish. If a private employer offers a DB plan, participation is automatic and thus compulsory for covered employees. In the case of DC plans (such as 401(k) plans), participation may be automatic or voluntary depending on the plan type and its rules. In some cases, employees can choose whether to participate in a pension plan that is offered by their employers. Most occupational DC plans are 401(k) plans, where an employer can also make a matching contribution to the employee's account. In the survey the data is based on, the question refers to these as a pension or retirement plan that an individual has through their job or their union. The question specifically excludes Social Security Railroad Retirement and individual retirement accounts (IRAs). This chapter does not consider drivers of gaps in personal pension plans in the United States.

For the case study on Germany, the analysis in this chapter focusses on private funded occupational and personal pension plans. Like in the United States, private occupational pension plans, or workplace pension plans, are voluntary in Germany. Access to the schemes is usually determined by collective agreements negotiated at the sector or company level, and are seen as a means of attracting and retaining staff.[2] To collect this information, the German survey underlying the data used in this analysis asks respondents whether they have at least one contract for an occupational pension plan. The survey clarifies that occupational pension plans mean pension funds, pension schemes, retirement funds and direct pension commitments by the employer.[3] This analysis also considers personal pension plans in Germany, which people take out for their own private saving purposes. In gathering this information, the survey questionnaire refers to all types of personal pension plans, providing examples such as the "Riester pension" or the private “Basic Pension” ("Rürup pension"), as well as non-government-subsidized private retirement pensions.

For the case study on Finland, this chapter explores occupational and personal pension plans. The Finnish occupational pension plan that is considered in this analysis is the statutory pension provided under the Employees Pensions Act (TyEL). It is a partially funded DB arrangement that is compulsory for all private sector employees in the country. It stands in contrast to the other case study countries, where the study considers voluntary occupational pension arrangements. Finally, the case study also considers personal pension plans in Finland, which do not form a large part of the pension system in the country, but are informative nonetheless in discerning people's behavioural patterns.

3.2. Approach

The analysis considers two key factors that can lead to a gender gap in pensions: whether a person is covered by a pension plan, and the assets or entitlements they accumulate in that pension plan. This analysis considers the drivers of each of those factors separately.

The analysis relies on econometric modelling to examine the magnitude and statistical significance of different drivers of coverage and assets and entitlements. The approach used makes it possible to assess whether these drivers explain all the difference in pension outcomes between genders, or whether there is something else driving the gaps. Details of the methodology are available at Annex 3.B and full results of the econometric analysis at Annex 3.C. For brevity, only high-level summaries of the results are included in the main text of this chapter.

The analysis relies on two main models (which are explained in more detail in Annex 3.B). The first model uses logistic regressions to investigate drivers of pension plan coverage. In those regressions, the response variable is a relevant indicator (dummy) variable of whether an individual is covered by a pension plan. The approach is used to analyse coverage of occupational pension plans and personal pension plans. The second model relies on regressions using a two-part model to determine the drivers of the value of assets, entitlements, and contributions of people who were covered by a pension plan.

Readers should note that the analysis in this chapter relies on survey data. A key shortcoming of doing so is that people can under-report retirement plan coverage because people are often simply unaware that they have workplace pension arrangements. When they do have pension plans, whether occupational or personal, many also do not know the value of those plans. Therefore, the analysis in this chapter makes a key assumption that men and women do not differ in the way they under-report coverage or mis-report the value of their pension plans.

Many features of individuals' working lives can cumulatively lead to gender gaps in pension income. The main ones are differences in wages, career lengths, type of work, and contribution levels. Chapter 1 contains a fuller discussion of these factors. This chapter explores which factors contribute to a gender gap in pension income and the effect their inclusion has on a gender indicator.

3.3. Drivers of the pension gaps in occupational pension plans

This section first considers drivers of a difference in coverage of occupational pension plans between men and women for the three countries. Then, for the people who are covered by an occupational pension plan, it explores why the assets, entitlements, and contributions in those plans may differ between men and women.

3.3.1. Coverage gap

United States

Women perform worse than men in almost all indicators of occupational plan coverage in the United States. Table 3.1 shows aggregate outcomes for coverage indicators. First, it shows that women are less likely than men to be covered by an occupational pension plan. The data shows that women are also generally less likely to be eligible for a plan through their work. This is related to the question of coverage in the United States since individuals may not be eligible for occupational plans through their employers, and if they are eligible, they may not participate in that plan. Table 3.1 shows that even among people who are eligible for an occupational plan through their workplace, women less commonly participate in that plan (by making contributions, for example). These results are evident across all age groups, although the differences are starker for the older groups. To delve further into whether these differences are significant enough to be statistically meaningful, what follows explains the results of a econometric model that analyses these factors.

Table 3.1. Comparison of men and women's coverage and participation in occupational plans

		All	Individuals aged:			
			15-29	30-44	45-59	60-64
Covered by an occupational plan	Male	48%	35%	52%	52%	42%
	Female	42%	30%	46%	46%	35%
Eligible for an occupational plan	Male	64%	51%	65%	68%	65%
	Female	60%	48%	63%	64%	56%
Participating in an occupational plan if they are eligible for one	Male	55%	36%	55%	62%	57%
	Female	49%	33%	51%	55%	51%

Note: Individuals are treated as being covered by an occupational plan if they have an occupational pension plan from their current or a previous employer. Individuals are treated as being eligible for an occupational plan if they are employed and either reported that they are eligible for an occupational plan or reported that they were participating in an occupational plan.
Source: Calculations based on a sample of working-age individuals (aged 15-64) from the 2017 PSID survey. Sample is weighted by individual weights.

The results of econometric modelling show that the differences in coverage, eligibility, and participation in occupational plans are statistically significant in most age groups (Table 3.2). The analysis shows that the odds of women having a pension plan through their workplace was 77.8% of the odds of males having a workplace pension plan (22.2% less) in 2017. This lower likelihood of women having an occupational pension plan (whether from a current or previous employer) persists across the age cohorts analysed, and to a similar magnitude, although the statistical significance of the result for the youngest cohort is weaker. Table 3.2 shows that there is also a statistically significant difference in eligibility and participation between the genders. However, the aggregate differences are mostly driven by older cohorts. While women have lower odds of being eligible for an occupational plan through their workplace, this overall result appears to be driven by workers aged 45 and older. The gap between men and women is greatest with respect to participation in plans, when workers are eligible. The modelling shows that overall, the odds of women participating in a plan when eligible are 77.2% of the odds of males doing so. This result is mostly driven by people aged between 30 and 59.

Table 3.2. Relative probability (females to males) of being covered, eligible, and participating in an occupational pension plan in the United States

Cohort	All (age 15-64)	15-29	30-44	45-59	60-64
Pension plan coverage	0.778	0.789	0.777	0.788	0.734
Pension plan eligibility	0.852	0.888	0.928	0.817	0.677
Participation if eligible	0.772	0.889	0.725	0.680	1.636

Note: The table presents odds ratios. Green cells indicate odds ratios that are statistically significant at the 95% confidence level or higher. Orange cells indicate odds ratios that are statistically significant at the 90% confidence level. Uncoloured cells indicate no statistical significance at the 90% confidence level or higher. The dependent variables are pension plan coverage (whether an individual has an occupational plan from their current or previous employer); pension plan eligibility (whether an individual is eligible for a pension plan through their employer); participation if eligible (whether an individual is participating in a retirement pension plan from their employer if they are eligible for one). Detailed logistic regression results are at Tables 3.C.1-3.C.2 of Annex 3.C.
Source: Calculations based on a sample of working age individuals (aged 15-64) from the 2017 PSID survey.

To unpack these aggregate results, the analysis then accounted for other characteristics that may be driving the gaps, but are somehow associated with gender. The econometric analysis added those characteristics gradually, to see whether gender continues to have a statistically significant relationship with eligibility and participation, even after accounting for other characteristics that may lead to gender gaps (Annex 3.C). This approach aims to account for the fact that it is often not gender alone that explains a gender pension gap, but rather, factors associated with gender. When the modelling accounts for more of these characteristics, the explanatory power of gender diminishes, which shows that the model successfully accounted for and measured drivers that relate to gender. When the model includes enough drivers such that gender loses all predictive power, it is possible to conclude that the model is accounting for most drivers associated with gender that have a bearing on eligibility and participation. Detailed results are available at Annex 3.C, but the tables that follow summarise the results when all explanatory variables are included alongside the gender indicator, for brevity.

The predictive power of gender diminishes entirely after accounting for other factors likely to be associated with gender but which have a bearing on occupational plan eligibility and participation, suggesting that gender alone is not what drives occupational plan eligibility and participation. Table 3.3 shows gender to be uncoloured (not statistically significant at the 90% confidence interval or higher) when other relevant drivers are included in the analysis. The same analysis could not be conducted for drivers of coverage of occupational pension plans from any employer, since most possible drivers available in the data refer to features of an individual's current employment.

Table 3.3. Drivers affecting occupational pension plan eligibility and participation in the United States

Cohort	All (age 15-64)	15-29	30-44	45-59	60-64
Dependent variable: Whether eligible for a plan					
Female indicator	1.004	0.975	1.089	1.044	0.611
Attended college	1.741	2.408	1.926	1.524	1.581
In job for less than 1 year	0.317	0.438	0.279	0.372	0.261
Government employee	2.325	1.219	2.376	2.749	4.012
Part-time worker	0.168	0.199	0.151	0.185	0.096
Employed in a small or micro business	0.320	0.342	0.323	0.318	0.238
Industry with high pension coverage	2.094	2.504	2.301	1.754	1.494
Covered by union contract	2.235	1.940	2.268	1.911	6.234
Dependent variable: Whether participating in a plan, if eligible					
Female indicator	0.809	0.890	0.819	0.755	1.071
Attended college	1.390	1.608	1.767	1.466	1.296
In job for less than 1 year	0.395	0.663	0.500	0.336	0.335
Government employee	1.975	1.762	2.138	1.392	5.352
Part time worker	0.479	0.348	0.281	0.914	0.260
Employed in a small or micro business	0.716	0.609	0.786	0.808	0.551
Industry with high pension coverage	2.195	2.655	1.812	2.555	1.768
Covered by union contract	2.075	1.684	1.555	3.375	1.896

Note: The table presents odds ratios. Green cells indicate odds ratios that are statistically significant at the 95% confidence level or higher. Orange cells indicate odds ratios that are statistically significant at the 90% confidence level. Uncoloured cells indicate no statistical significance at the 90% confidence level or higher. The dependent variables are: pension plan eligibility (whether an individual is eligible for a pension plan through their employer); participation if eligible (whether an individual is participating in a retirement pension plan from their employer if they are eligible for one). Independent variables are: female indicator; whether the individual attended college; whether the individual was in their current job for less than one year; whether the individual works for the federal, state or local government; whether the individual was employed on a part-time basis (less than 30 hours per week); whether the individual was employed in a business that is classified as either micro or small (fewer than 10 employees or between 10 and 50 employees respectively); whether the individual works in an industry that overall has high occupational plan coverage (more than 60% of employees in that industry are covered by an occupational plan); and whether the individual's current job is covered by a union contract. Detailed logistic regression results are at Table 3.C.4 and Table 3.C.5 of Annex 3.C.
Source: Calculations based on a sample of working age individuals (aged 15-64) from the 2017 PSID survey.

The results show that, broadly speaking, the following variables tend to drive eligibility for occupational plans in the United States:

- Whether an individual is employed on a full-time or part-time basis. In the United States, it is not unusual for retirement plans to be restricted to workers with full-time or near full-time schedules (Kobe, 2010[1]). Furthermore, females are much more likely to be working part time than men (Table 3.4).[4] This is therefore is a key driver of the eligibility gap.
- Industry of work. The industries men and women work in are likely to explain much of the difference in occupational plan coverage between the genders. Men are more likely to work in industries that tend to have higher occupation plan coverage rates compared with women (such as manufacturing, mining, and technical services) (Table 3.4 and Figure 3.1). As such, they are more likely to be eligible for a workplace pension plan.
- The length of time an individual has been at a workplace. In the United States, employers are more likely to offer pension plans to people who have worked there longer. Some plans also have minimum service requirements. The modelling results show that being in a job for less than a year significantly reduces the odds of an individual being eligible for a workplace plan. However, the data also show that the genders are about equally likely to have been in a job for under a year (Table 3.4). The fact that women and men do not have large differences in the likelihood of being in a job for less than a year suggests it is unlikely to explain much of the gender gap in coverage or eligibility for a pension plan.
- Public / private sector mix. The data show that government workers are significantly more likely to have an occupational pension plan than private-sector workers. Women are over-represented in government work. As such, this can act to narrow the gender pension gap to a small degree.
- Firm size. In the United States, workers in smaller firms are much less likely to have a plan available to them. This is borne out in the modelling, which shows that individuals employed in small or micro businesses are significantly less likely to be covered by or eligible for an occupational plan. However, the data show that employment in these smaller businesses is about evenly split between the genders, with a slight tilt towards males. As such, this factor is unlikely to drive the gender pension gap in the United States.

Table 3.4. Gender split of key eligibility and participation predictors for the US

	Females	Males
Attended college	74%	66%
In job for less than 1 year	12%	12%
Government employee	24%	16%
Part time worker	16%	7%
Employed in a small or micro business	50%	52%
Industry with high pension coverage	43%	48%
Covered by union contract	15%	15%

Note: See descriptions in note to Table 3.3. Percentages refer to proportions of men and women falling within each category.
Source: Calculations based on a sample of working age individuals (aged 15-64) from the 2017 PSID survey.

Figure 3.1. Percentage of women employed by industry compared to the percentage of people with occupational plans by industry

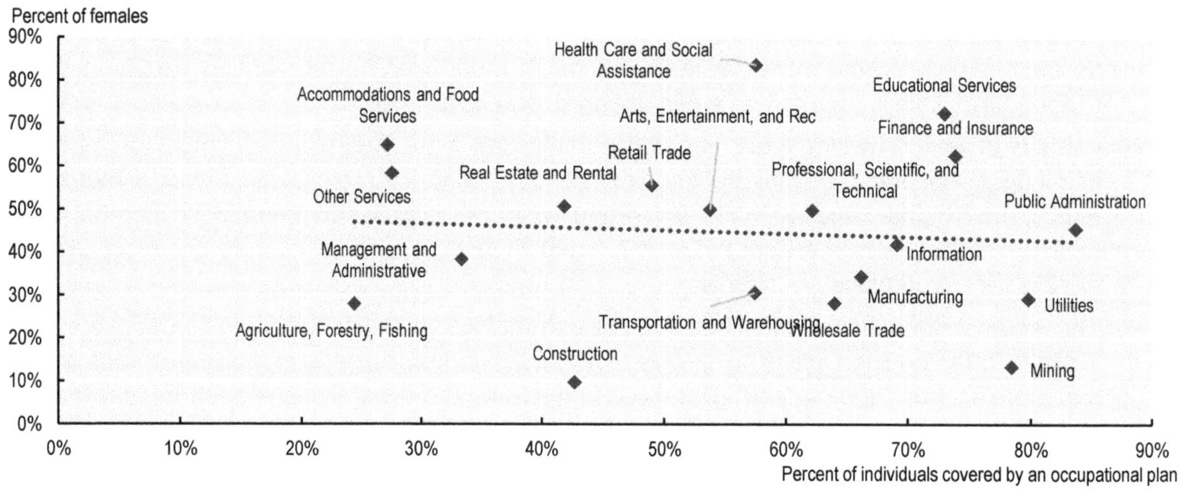

Source: Calculations based on a sample of working age individuals (aged 15-64) from the 2017 PSID survey.

Women are less likely to be participating in a pension plan, even when they are eligible for one, and this may be related to behavioural factors. When it comes to participation in a pension plan, when an individual is eligible for that plan, Table 3.2 shows that overall, the odds of a woman participating in a workplace plan are about 77% of the odds of men doing so.[5] However, this difference is only statistically significant for the two cohorts of people aged 30-59. In the youngest cohort (aged 15-29), no such difference in participation exists between the genders, suggesting that younger generations may be exhibiting different behavioural trends than their predecessors. Those differences persist even after the model accounts for whether a person attended college, was in job for a short time period, and is a government employee. Controlling for part-time work has a small impact on the odds that women participate in a pension plan if eligible, but a statistically significant difference persists even after controlling for this variable. Whether or not an individual works for a small business similarly appears to have little bearing on the statistical significance and odds of a woman, participating in a pension plan compared to a man. What ultimately appears to affect the statistical significance of gender as a predictor is controlling for the variables discussed as well as whether a person works in an industry with high pension coverage and is covered by a union contract (Table 3.3). Intuitively, these factors should not alone affect a person's decision to participate in a pension plan if they are eligible, suggesting that there may be some related behavioural factors at play.

Germany

The aggregate results from the Household Finance and Consumption Survey (HFCS) data show that Germany has a gender gap in occupational plan coverage – 24% of men and 19% of women reported being covered by funded occupational pension plans through their workplace.[6]

The econometric modelling shows that these differences are statistically meaningful across most age groups. The odds of women having a pension plan through their workplace was 73.6% of the odds of men being covered by a workplace pension plan (26.4% less) in 2015 (Table 3.5). However, analysing age cohorts separately shows that individuals in the age cohorts over 45 and below 30 mostly drive this result. The gap in occupational plan coverage in Germany was particularly large in the cohort of individuals aged 45-59 and 60-64. For those individuals, the odds of women having occupational pension plans were 65% and 45.5% of the odds of men, respectively. For younger workers, on the other hand, there was no statistically significant difference between men and women's occupational plan coverage for workers in the

30-45 age cohort, and statistically significant difference at a lower level of confidence for the 15-29 age cohort. This suggests that for the younger generation of workers, the coverage gap might be closing.

Table 3.5. Relative probability (females to males) of being covered by an occupational pension plan in Germany

Cohort	All (age 15-64)	15-29	30-44	45-59	60-64
Germany	0.736	0.601	0.999	0.650	0.455

Note: The table presents odds ratios. Green cells indicate odds ratios that are statistically significant at the 95% confidence level or higher. Orange cells indicate odds ratios that are statistically significant at the 90% confidence level. Uncoloured cells indicate no statistical significance at the 90% confidence level or higher. Detailed logistic regression results are at Table 3.C.6 of Annex 3.C.
Source: Calculations based on a sample of working age individuals (aged 15-64) from the HFCS Wave 2 data. Data relate to survey responses collected between 2013 and 2015.

Of the cohorts of individuals with statistically significant gaps in occupational plan coverage in Germany, the employment gap appears to explain the difference. When the model is adjusted to control for whether or not an individual was an employee, it shows that a positive and statistically significant relationship exists between an individual having an occupational pension plan in Germany and being employed (as opposed to self-employed). Importantly, when that variable is included in the model, the statistical significance of gender disappears for most age groups (Table 3.6). This suggests that the coverage gap is linked to differences in likelihoods of men and women being in the labour market. The data on men and women's employment accords with this finding. It shows that in the year the HFCS survey was conducted, 75% of men compared to 68% of women aged between 14 and 65 received employee income in the last 12 months. Similarly, data on participation rates by gender show a gap of about ten percentage points in favour of men in Germany.[7] This gap is evident across all age cohorts. While men are slightly more likely to be self-employed in Germany, and therefore not covered by an occupation pension plan, this does not fully offset the effect the gender employment gap has on occupational plan coverage.

Table 3.6. Drivers affecting occupational pension plan coverage in Germany

Cohort	All (age 15-64)	15-29	30-44	45-59	60-64
Female indicator	1.044	0.946	1.416	0.869	0.499
Hours worked	1.022	1. 042	1.013	1.023	1.006
Employed as a worker	2.979	2.953	3.150	2.823	3.102

Note: The table presents odds ratios. Green cells indicate odds ratios that are statistically significant at the 95% confidence level or higher. Orange cells indicate odds ratios that are statistically significant at the 90% confidence level. Uncoloured cells indicate no statistical significance at the 90% confidence level or higher. Detailed logistic regression results are at Table 3.C.6 of Annex 3.C.
Source: Calculations based on a sample of working age individuals (aged 15-64) from the HFCS Wave 2 data. Data relate to survey responses collected between 2013 and 2015.

The number of hours an individual worked, which on average differs by gender, was also a statistically significant predictor of occupational plan coverage in Germany. Table 3.6 shows that the more hours an individual tended to work, the greater their odds of having an occupational pension plan. However, German law prohibits a fund's rules from discriminating between full-time and part-time employment for the purpose of company pension plan coverage. As such, hours worked alone is unlikely to be the cause of lower coverage, but rather, it suggests that firms whose workers have more standard and stable hours are also those who are more likely to offer pension plans to their workers. This matters for the gender pension gap because the data show that women are more likely to be in jobs that generally involve fewer hours, suggesting they are in the latter category.

Another potential factor at play in explaining the coverage gap is the company size. Men are more likely to be employed in larger companies than women are, and analysis by the Germany Ministry of Labour and Social Affairs has shown that larger companies are much more likely to offer occupational plans to their employees (Bundesministeriums für Arbeit und Soziales, 2020[2]). However, due to a lack of relevant information in the data source used, the econometric analysis did not include firm size in the analysis of drivers of company pension plan coverage in Germany. Notwithstanding, but it is likely to be an important factor explaining the coverage gap.

Another important difference not included in the analysis of pension plan coverage in Germany is the industry of employment. In Germany, access to workplace pension plans is usually determined by collective agreements negotiated at sector or company level or by company agreements. There are relatively large disparities between coverage across different industries. Coverage of company pension plans is highest in industries such as credit and insurance, mining and quarrying, electricity and gas supply, and water supply, which tend to be male-dominated.[8] Others, such as health, veterinary and social services, and education and teaching have slightly lower coverage rates and are female dominated. On the other end of the spectrum are industries such as accommodation and food services, and administrative and support services, which are female dominated. As such, the sector or company can have a bearing on gender differences in coverage. While the sample data was not large enough to permit this variable to be included in the modelling, a high-level analysis of gender distribution by industry confirmed that it was likely an important driver.

Finland

Gender is not a key factor explaining any differences in coverage of occupational plans in Finland. Occupational plans are mandatory in Finland, so there is no strong reason for there to exist a gender difference in occupational plan coverage. The overall figures in Chapter 1 show that the difference in occupational plan coverage is small – 85% of men and 86% of women are covered by occupational pension plans. The results in Table 3.7 confirm this expectation, as they show that the gender indicator is not a statistically significant predictor of occupational plan coverage for any age cohort. Table 3.8 shows that the main predictor of whether an individual has an occupational plan in Finland relates to whether they are working. In any event, there does not appear to be a strong enough gender difference between the likelihood of having an occupational pension plan by gender, as having one such plan only depends on an individual having had employment at some point in their lifetimes. As such, no more analysis was needed for this case study, and it could proceed to an analysis of the drivers of differences in asset values and entitlements in occupational pension plans.

Table 3.7. Relative probability (females to males) of being covered by an occupational pension plan in Finland

Cohort	All (age 15-64)	15-29	30-44	45-59	60-64
Finland	1.056	1.059	0.944	1.149	1.042

Note: The table presents odds ratios. Green cells indicate odds ratios that are statistically significant at the 95% confidence level or higher. Orange cells indicate odds ratios that are statistically significant at the 90% confidence level. Uncoloured cells indicate no statistical significance at the 90% confidence level or higher. Detailed logistic regression results are at Table 3.C.7 of Annex 3.C.
Source: Calculations based on a sample of working age individuals (aged 15-64) from the HFCS Wave 2 data. Data relate to survey responses collected between 2013 and 2015.

Table 3.8. Drivers affecting occupational pension plan coverage in Finland

Cohort	All (age 15-64)	15-29	30-44	45-59	60-64
Female indicator	0.931	0.893	0.957	0.945	0.933
Employed as a worker	9.012	9.910	14.60	9.068	3.869

Note: The table presents odds ratios. Green cells indicate odds ratios that are statistically significant at the 95% confidence level or higher. Orange cells indicate odds ratios that are statistically significant at the 90% confidence level. Uncoloured cells indicate no statistical significance at the 90% confidence level or higher. Detailed logistic regression results are at Table 3.C.7 of Annex 3.C.
Source: Calculations based on a sample of working age individuals (aged 15-64) from the HFCS Wave 2 data. Data relate to survey responses collected between 2013 and 2015.

3.3.2. Assets and entitlements

For people who do have occupational pension plans, it is possible to further investigate the drivers of overall gender pension gaps by exploring what might explain differences in the values of assets or entitlements accrued in those plans. This section proceeds by exploring the drivers of DC account values, expected DB income, employer contributions, mandatory employee contributions, and voluntary employee contributions in the United States. It will then explore drivers of differences in DC account values or DB entitlements for Germany and DB entitlements in Finland. It shows that, for the most part, unlike drivers of plan coverage, differences in assets and entitlements are more linked to labour market outcomes.

United States

Men generally have greater accumulated assets or entitlements in their occupational plans compared with women in the United States. The data from the United States contain information about asset balances, expected pay-outs from DB plans, and contributions behaviour for people who do have occupational plans. Table 3.9 shows that on average, across all age groups, men accumulated larger balances in occupational DC accounts than women. The same result is evident for expected income from DB plans. Furthermore, of people who do have occupational plans, men tend to contribute greater amounts of money both mandatorily and voluntarily, and their employers contributed more overall as well. The same pattern can be seen in results for median values, which can be a better indicator for when distributions are skewed.

Table 3.9. Comparison of men and women's average and median assets, entitlements, and contributions to occupational plans

In USD

Average		All	Individuals aged:			
			15-29	30-44	45-59	60-64
Accumulated amounts in defined contribution account	Male	211 504	33 969	137 884	308 884	367 125
	Female	138 015	29 747	93 427	231 761	195 064
Expected DB plan income	Male	44 435	N/A	49 557	43 247	40 447
	Female	29 441	N/A	32 425	29 705	26 372
Mandatory contributions by individuals	Male	4 469	2 689	4 095	5 149	4 017
	Female	3 561	2 705	2 868	4 032	4 646
Voluntary contributions by individuals	Male	7 313	4 449	6 459	8 388	9 688
	Female	5 149	3 052	4 759	5 815	6 866
Contributions by employers	Male	4 583	2 744	4 279	5 328	4 880
	Female	3 209	2 390	3 455	3 194	3 331

Median						
Accumulated amounts in defined contribution account	Male	86 000	16 000	60 000	150 000	170 000
	Female	60 000	12 000	40 000	100 000	134 000
Expected DB plan income	Male	36 000	N/A	40 600	36 000	35 000
	Female	26 000	N/A	26 000	26 400	25 200
Mandatory contributions by individuals	Male	2 750	1 830	2 200	3 975	3 000
	Female	2 610	1 830	2 304	3 094	3 900
Voluntary contributions by individuals	Male	4 800	3 000	4 260	5 359	6 140
	Female	2 940	2 000	2 750	3 220	3 480
Contributions by employers	Male	3 048	2 250	2 915	3 540	3 793
	Female	2 010	1 710	2 100	2 120	2 000

Note: The results for assets in DC accounts refer to amounts accumulated in DC plans with an individual's current employer. Expected DB plan income refers to the annual amounts individuals expect to receive from a DB plan with their current employer in retirement. The level of individual and employer contributions refers to annual contribution amounts as reported by individuals. Where individuals reported those amounts as a percentage of their pay, the contribution amount was calculated based on reported income.
Source: Calculations based on a sample of working age individuals (aged 15-64) from the 2017 PSID survey. Sample is weighted by individual weights.

The results of regression analyses confirm the overall findings in these descriptive statistics (Table 3.10). The first row shows that the gender differences for key indicators of plan assets, entitlements, and contributions are statistically significant for almost all cohorts of individuals. That is, the gap between men and women's DC asset values, expected DB income, and contributions are large enough to be statistically meaningful. An exception is the level of mandatory contributions by employees, for which gender was not a statistically significant predictor.

Table 3.10. Summary of analysis: Drivers of gaps in occupational plan assets, entitlements, and contributions

	Value of DC account	Expected DB income	Employer contributions	Mandatory employee contributions	Voluntary employee contributions
Statistically significant overall gender difference?	Yes, except for youngest cohort	Yes (note no data for youngest cohort)	Yes, except youngest cohort	No	Yes
Whether the effect persists after controlling for:					
Years of participation in plan	Yes	Yes	Yes	No change	Yes
Whether the person has children	Yes	Yes	Yes	No change	Yes
Income	No	No	No	No change	No

Note: The variables analysed are as follows. Value of DC account: the level of accumulated assets in an individual's occupational DC account. Expected DB income: the amount an individual expects to receive annually from their DB pension plan. Employer contributions: the level of employer contributions to individuals' occupational pension plans, of individuals whose employers make contributions. Mandatory employee contributions: the level of mandatory contributions by individuals to occupational pension plans, of individuals who are required to make mandatory contributions. Voluntary employee contributions: the level of voluntary contributions by individuals to occupational pension plans, of individuals who do make voluntary contributions. The analysis was conducted using a two-part model, which fits a binary choice model for the probability of observing a positive-versus-zero outcome. Conditional on a positive outcome, an OLS regression was fit for the log of the positive outcome. Detailed regression results are available at Tables 3.C.8 – 3.C.12 of Annex 3.C.
Source: Calculations based on a sample of working age individuals (aged 15-64) from the 2017 PSID survey.

The results show that years an individual participated in an occupational pension plan, as well as income, are key drivers of the level of assets, entitlements, and contributions to occupational pension plans in the United States. This is possible to discern once the analysis accounts for other factors that are related to gender but also have a bearing on the results for the indicators being analysed. Table 3.10 summarises the broad outcomes of analyses that account for such possible drivers of the gender gaps discussed. Indeed, these drivers have a relationship with gender. Women tend to work fewer years overall than men, since they are more likely to take time off for parenting or other caring responsibilities. This means they have fewer years during which they are building up their assets or entitlements to pensions. Similarly, women experience a well-documented gender pay gap that persists even in younger generations.[9] These results are unsurprising, but an important finding from the analysis is that after accounting for all these factors in the model, gender was no longer a statistically significant predictor of the gaps in occupational plan assets, entitlements, and contributions when it comes to workplace pension plans. This suggests that differences in labour market outcomes, mainly years of work and income gaps, are likely to account for most of the observed differences.

There are some exceptions to these trends. Analysing the youngest age cohort (individuals aged 15-29) did not show statistically significant differences in account balances in DC plans. The same analysis was not possible for expected income from DB plans since the sample size was too small. However, this gap was also not evident for employer contributions to occupational plans for individuals in that age group. This is not to say that the gender gap in pension assets is disappearing. Rather, the 15-29 age bracket might simply align with years before career breaks (such as for parenting) and may simply reflect a period prior to the emergence of gender-based differences in income and employment. To illustrate, Figure 1.9 of Chapter 1 shows that in OECD countries, at the early stages of individuals' careers, women and men have almost the same amount of assets, but this gap widens with time.

Germany

The analysis of the drivers of the level of occupational plan assets and entitlements for those individuals who do have occupational plans shows that the overall difference between genders is statistically significant (Table 3.11). However, most cohorts of individuals do not show a statistically significant difference in asset or entitlement values between men and women, with the exception of the cohort aged 45-59. The analysis therefore suggests that while there appears to be a gap in occupational plan assets and entitlements in Germany, it may not be wide enough to be statistically meaningful over most age cohorts or the data sample was not large enough to determine the drivers of a gender gap with certainty.

Table 3.11. Drivers of gaps in occupational plan assets and entitlements in Germany

Cohort	All (age 15-64)	15-29	30-44	45-59	60-64
Female indicator	-0.540	-1.305	-0.480	-0.447	-0.810

Note: Dependent variable is the log of occupational pension plan assets or entitlements. Green cells indicate predictors that are statistically significant at the 95% confidence level or higher. Orange cells indicate predictors that are statistically significant at the 90% confidence level. Uncoloured cells indicate no statistical significance at the 90% confidence level or higher. Detailed regression results are at Table 3.C.13 of Annex 3.C.

Source: Calculations based on a sample of working age individuals (aged 15-64) from the HFCS Wave 2 data. Data relate to survey responses collected between 2013 and 2015.

Considered together, the results of an analysis of coverage and assets/entitlements in German occupational pension schemes suggest that differences in the overall asset level or value of entitlements in occupational plans in Germany might be explained by a coverage gap due to men being more likely to be in paid employment or in workplaces that offer plans to their employees. Any differences in the value of assets/entitlements between people in occupational pension plans is less evident, but if it exists, would mostly be related to income and work experience and gender does not appear to be a strong driver.[10]

Finland

The results for Finland, on the other hand, show a significant gender gap in pension plan entitlements that persists across all the age cohorts analysed. The overall figures show that for individuals in the cohorts aged 30-45, 45-60 and over 60, women have systematically lower pension plan entitlements than men. Analysis of the cohort aged 15-29 reveals the opposite result: women have systematically higher pension entitlements than men.

Table 3.12. Drivers of gaps in occupational plan assets and entitlements in Finland

Cohort	All (age 15-64)	15-29	30-44	45-59	60-64
Results when only considering gender					
Female indicator	-0.002	0.302	-0.12	-0.16	-0.10
Results when controlling for other drivers					
Female	-0.102	0.221	-0.094	-0.263	-0.152
Tertiary educated	0.326	-0.123	0.219	0.331	0.468
Log age	4.868	7.956	3.969	4.603	5.613
Coupled	0.106	0.144	0.0883	0.124	0.356
Previously coupled	0.093	-0.078	0.180	0.143	0.306
Interaction: Working (employee or self-employed) × Total income	0.105	0.222	0.141	0.0651	0.029

Note: Dependent variable is the log of occupational pension plan assets or entitlements. Green cells indicate predictors that are statistically significant at the 95% confidence level or higher. Orange cells indicate predictors that are statistically significant at the 90% confidence level. Uncoloured cells indicate no statistical significance at the 90% confidence level or higher. Detailed regression results are at Table 3.C.14 of Annex 3.C.

Source: Calculations based on a sample of working age individuals (aged 15-64) from the HFCS Wave 2 data. Data relate to survey responses collected between 2013 and 2015.

Gender differences are still evident even after the analysis accounts for education, age, relationship status, and income. However, the data set used does not make it possible to control for years of work history, which can be a significant driver of differences in entitlements. A crude way to circumvent this issue is to assume that the primary reason for career breaks is parenting, and a crude way to isolate individuals who have not taken career breaks is to consider only single people. Interestingly, after restricting the population to single individuals, the statistical significance of the female coefficient disappears for the cohort aged older than 35. This adds some weight to the possibility that differences in career lengths explain the apparent gender gap in pension entitlements in Finland.

However, an analysis of the cohort aged 15-35 shows that women, including single women, have systematically higher pension entitlements than men even after controlling for age, education, and income. This result might signal a generational shift in the gender pension entitlements gap in Finland. However, it may also be due to this group being less likely to have experienced long career breaks than older age groups.[11] As such, the finding may support the view that taking career breaks for parenting may be a key driver of gender gaps in occupational pensions in Finland.

Table 3.13. Drivers of gaps in occupational plan assets and entitlements for single individuals in Finland

Cohort	All (age 15-64)	15-34	35-64
Results when only considering gender			
Female indicator	0.0386	0.186	0.091
Results when controlling for other drivers			
Female	0.084	0.196	-0.030
Tertiary educated	0.261	0.021	0.318
Log age	5.157	6.716	3.564
Interaction: Working (employee or self-employed) × Total income	0.167	0.220	0.093

Note: Larger age cohorts were needed for this analysis because single people represented a smaller sample size. Dependent variable is the log of occupational pension plan assets or entitlements. Green cells indicate predictors that are statistically significant at the 95% confidence level or higher. Orange cells indicate predictors that are statistically significant at the 90% confidence level. Uncoloured cells indicate no statistical significance at the 90% confidence level or higher. Detailed regression results are at Table 3.C.15 of Annex 3.C.
Source: Calculations based on a sample of working age individuals (aged 15-64) from the HFCS Wave 2 data. Data relate to survey responses collected between 2013 and 2015.

3.4. Drivers of the pension gaps in personal pension plans

This section considers the drivers of the pension gap in personal pension plans. Gaps in personal pension plan coverage have some similarities to occupational pension plans, because much of the gap can be related to labour market differences. But unlike occupational pension plans, differences in personal pension plan coverage and asset values can have a lot to do with personal qualities and individual behaviours, as discussed in Chapter 2. Those qualities and behaviours cannot be captured effectively using the data at hand. Notwithstanding, it is possible to draw some conclusions regarding other key drivers of why individuals might take out personal pension plans, and what drives the asset values in those plans. Readers should note that it was not possible to conduct the same analysis for personal pension plans for the United States, and this section will proceed with an analysis of Germany and Finland.

3.4.1. Coverage

Germany

The analysis on Germany only shows a statistically significant gender gap in coverage of personal plans for individuals in the 45-59 age cohort (Table 3.14).[12] In this age group, the odds of women having a personal pension plan were 77.4% of the odds of men having one. While there is no systematic gender coverage gap across all cohorts, it is important to bear in mind that the years leading to retirement are when people are more likely to voluntarily start saving for retirement. As such, the older age cohorts are particularly relevant when analysing personal pension plans.

Table 3.14. Relative probability (females to males) of being covered by a personal pension plan in Germany

Cohort	All (age 15-64)	15-29	30-44	45-59	60-64
Female indicator	0.926	0.863	1.214	0.774	0.727

Note: The table presents odds ratios. Green cells indicate odds ratios that are statistically significant at the 95% confidence level or higher. Orange cells indicate odds ratios that are statistically significant at the 90% confidence level. Uncoloured cells indicate no statistical significance at the 90% confidence level or higher. Detailed logistic regression results are at Table 3.C.16 of Annex 3.C.
Source: Calculations based on a sample of working age individuals (aged 15-64) from the HFCS Wave 2 data. Data relate to survey responses collected between 2013 and 2015.

Employment and education gaps are likely to explain the gender gap for personal pension plan coverage in Germany. After controlling for individuals' incomes and whether they received a tertiary education, the gender predictor loses its statistical significance for the 45-59 age cohort (Table 3.15). This suggests that the relationships between gender and income and gender and education are likely to explain much of the difference. As such, the gender wage gap, which disadvantages women financially can also have a bearing on the likelihood that they would take out personal pension plans. Intuitively, this would suggest that people with lower financial means are less likely to take voluntary steps to start saving in personal pension plans. A similar effect is evident when it comes to education. People who have completed tertiary education are significantly more likely to take out personal pension plans. This is likely true both because of better financial knowledge but also because people with tertiary education tend to have higher incomes. There is also an important relationship between tertiary educational attainment and gender for the age cohort that exhibits a difference in personal pension plan coverage. Of people in the 45-59 age group, German women are significantly less likely to have attained a tertiary education, unlike younger age cohorts, where tertiary education attainment tends to be closer to gender parity.[13]

Table 3.15. Drivers affecting personal pension plan coverage in Germany

Cohort	All (age 15-64)	15-29	30-44	45-59	60-64
Female indicator	1.182	1.084	1.672	0.912	0.881
Work income	1.175	1.234	1.178	1.118	1.101
Tertiary education	1.550	1.255	1.399	1.613	0.970

Note: The table presents odds ratios. Green cells indicate odds ratios that are statistically significant at the 95% confidence level or higher. Orange cells indicate odds ratios that are statistically significant at the 90% confidence level. Uncoloured cells indicate no statistical significance at the 90% confidence level or higher. Detailed logistic regression results are at Table 3.C.16 of Annex 3.C.

Source: Calculations based on a sample of working age individuals (aged 15-64) from the HFCS Wave 2 data. Data relate to survey responses collected between 2013 and 2015.

Another interesting outcome from the analysis is that for the cohort aged 30-44, after accounting for income and educational attainment, women were more likely to have a personal pension plan than men. This suggests that something else might be at play which may warrant further research.

Finland

In contrast to the case of Germany, the overall figures for Finland show that women are more likely to have personal pension plans than men. Table 3.16 shows that overall, the odds of women having a personal pension plan were about 22.8% higher than those of men. Women aged between 30 and 59 appear to be driving this result. While it should be noted that personal pension plans are a very small component of Finland's retirement income system overall, the results remain interesting.

Table 3.16. Relative probability (females to males) of being covered by a personal pension plan in Finland

Cohort	All (age 15-64)	15-29	30-44	45-59	60-64
Female indicator	1.228	1.325	1.140	1.337	1.094

Note: The table presents odds ratios. Green cells indicate odds ratios that are statistically significant at the 95% confidence level or higher. Orange cells indicate odds ratios that are statistically significant at the 90% confidence level. Uncoloured cells indicate no statistical significance at the 90% confidence level or higher. Detailed logistic regression results are at Table 3.C.17 of Annex 3.C.

Source: Calculations based on a sample of working age individuals (aged 15-64) from the HFCS Wave 2 data. Data relate to survey responses collected between 2013 and 2015.

While income and education are associated with higher personal plan coverage in Finland, factors associated with gender are also likely to be driving the positive gender coverage gap in favour of women. Table 3.17 shows that this gender coverage gap persists even after controlling for key factors that might affect coverage. It shows that, in line with intuition on the matter, higher income levels and attaining a tertiary education are all associated with higher odds of having a personal pension plan in Finland. Finland can be contrasted with Germany, since women are more likely to have attained a tertiary education in Finland. However, controlling for these factors in the econometric analysis (see also Annex 3.C) leaves the relevance of the gender indicator virtually unchanged, suggesting that other factors associated with gender are likely to be driving the positive gender coverage gap.

Table 3.17. Drivers affecting personal pension plan coverage in Finland

Cohort	All (age 15-64)	15-29	30-44	45-59	60-64
Female indicator	1.179	1.336	1.200	1.261	1.056
Work income	1.130	1.547	1.105	1.097	1.066
Tertiary education	1.594	0.950	1.082	1.496	1.814

Note: The table presents odds ratios. Green cells indicate odds ratios that are statistically significant at the 95% confidence level or higher. Orange cells indicate odds ratios that are statistically significant at the 90% confidence level. Uncoloured cells indicate no statistical significance at the 90% confidence level or higher. Detailed logistic regression results are at Table 3.C.17 of Annex 3.C.
Source: Calculations based on a sample of working age individuals (aged 15-64) from the HFCS Wave 2 data. Data relate to survey responses collected between 2013 and 2015.

3.4.2. Assets and contributions

This section considers divers of differences in personal plan assets and contributions for individuals that have personal pension plans.

Germany

Labour market factors appear to be the primary reason women accumulate less than men in personal pension plans in Germany. The figures from the modelling on Germany show that overall, of people who do have personal plans, women tend to accumulate less assets in those plans. But after controlling for total income, years spent in the workforce, and entitlements in occupational pension plans, the explanatory power of the gender coefficient disappears. This suggests that women's career lengths and incomes are the primary drivers of their lower personal pension savings. However, for the cohort of people aged 30-45 there is no statistically significant difference between men and women's personal plan assets. Notwithstanding, the sample size is small, making the result uncertain (and at odds with the results for contributions shown in Table 3.19). On the other hand, for the cohort of individuals aged 45-60, the reverse is evident: women have systematically lower personal plan assets than men, and this difference persists even after controlling for variables such as education, age, time in employment, marital status and income.

When considering contributions to personal pension plans, the analysis shows that women tend to contribute significantly less than men to their plans (Table 3.19). This result is evident across almost all cohorts, with the exception being the oldest age cohort. The result holds even after controlling for predictors such as income, age, education, years of work experience, and the level of entitlements in occupational plans. While including these predictors diminished the effect of the gender coefficient, it remained statistically significant and negative for the age groups 15-29 and 45-59. This suggests that after controlling for education, work history, income, and occupational plan balance, women still contribute to personal plans less than men. It points to something more than simply labour market outcomes, but possibly a behavioural effect leading women to save less than men.

Table 3.18. Drivers of gaps in personal plan assets in Germany

Cohort	All (age 15-64)	15-29	30-44	45-59	60-64
Results when only considering gender					
Female indicator	-0.385	-0.696	-0.068	-0.446	-0.159
Results when controlling for other drivers					
Female	-0.085	-0.402	0.164	-0.322	0.288
Tertiary educated	0.806	1.71	0.821	0.436	0.658
Log total time in employment	1.231	0.913	1.009	0.665	1.005
Coupled	-0.29	-0.628	-0.213	-0.381	-0.222
Previously coupled	-0.551	0.485	-0.900	-0.54	-0.383
Interaction: Working (employee or self-employed) × Total income	0.035	0.118	0.054	0.036	0.001
Interaction: Value of occupational plan × has occupational plan	0.017	0.016	0.012	0.015	0.007

Note: Dependent variable is the log of personal pension plan assets. Green cells indicate predictors that are statistically significant at the 95% confidence level or higher. Orange cells indicate predictors that are statistically significant at the 90% confidence level. Uncoloured cells indicate no statistical significance at the 90% confidence level or higher. Detailed regression results are at Table 3.C.18 of Annex 3.C.
Source: Calculations based on a sample of working age individuals (aged 15-64) from the HFCS Wave 2 data. Data relate to survey responses collected between 2013 and 2015.

Table 3.19. Drivers of gaps in personal plan contributions in Germany

Cohort	All (age 15-64)	15-29	30-44	45-59	60-64
Results when only considering gender					
Female indicator	-0.423	-0.643	-0.291	-0.503	-0.204
Results when controlling for other drivers					
Female	-0.262	-0.634	-0.119	-0.386	0.049
Tertiary educated	0.524	0.739	0.481	0.366	0.419
Log total time in employment	0.42	0.296	0.239	0.136	0.159
Coupled	-0.08	-0.097	-0.142	-0.151	0.511
Previously coupled	-0.163	-0.233	-0.301	-0.184	0.206
Interaction: Working (employee or self-employed) × Total income	0.067	0.07	0.079	0.075	0.079
Interaction: Value of occupational plan × has occupational plan	0.024	0.078	0.007	0.034	-0.017

Note: Dependent variable is the log of contributions to personal pension plans. Green cells indicate predictors that are statistically significant at the 95% confidence level or higher. Orange cells indicate predictors that are statistically significant at the 90% confidence level. Uncoloured cells indicate no statistical significance at the 90% confidence level or higher. Detailed regression results are at Table 3.C.19 of Annex 3.C.
Source: Calculations based on a sample of working age individuals (aged 15-64) from the HFCS Wave 2 data for Germany. Data relate to survey responses collected between 2013 and 2015.

One shortcoming of this analysis, which readers should bear in mind, is that Riester plans come with a government subsidy, which does not appear in the data on individual contributions. That government subsidy can have the effect of better equalising asset gaps between the genders and the data on contributions would not account for this. Notwithstanding, it would not change the key findings of what may drive gender gaps where they exist.

Finland

In Finland, an overall gender gap in assets accumulated in personal pension plans is mostly driven by the cohorts aged 30-59 (Table 3.20).

Table 3.20. Drivers of gaps in personal plan assets in Finland

Cohort	All (age 15-64)	15-29	30-44	45-59	60-64
Results when only considering gender					
Female indicator	-0.153	-0.029	-0.304	-0.183	0.259
Results when controlling for other drivers					
Female	-0.178	0.034	-0.338	-0.175	0.232
Tertiary educated	0.496	0.085	0.510	0.412	0.865
Log age	2.911	3.973	3.505	3.266	-8.452
Coupled	-0.205	-0.215	-0.139	-0.314	-0.226
Previously coupled	-0.210	-2.509	-0.080	-0.468	0.222
Interaction: Working (employee or self-employed) × Total income	0.065	-0.041	0.054	0.050	0.045

Note: Dependent variable is the log of personal pension plan assets. Green cells indicate predictors that are statistically significant at the 95% confidence level or higher. Orange cells indicate predictors that are statistically significant at the 90% confidence level. Uncoloured cells indicate no statistical significance at the 90% confidence level or higher. Detailed regression results are at Table 3.C.20 of Annex 3.C.
Source: Calculations based on a sample of working age individuals (aged 15-64) from the HFCS Wave 2 data. Data relate to survey responses collected between 2013 and 2015.

The results show that other factors, such as having a tertiary education, age, marital status, and income earned can also be related to the assets accumulated in a personal pension plan in Finland. Individuals with a tertiary education, higher incomes, and more time in employment tend to save more in their personal pension plans. Furthermore, people who are living in couple are more likely to have accumulated greater amounts in their plan than those who are no longer in couple. Notwithstanding, in the cohorts aged 30-44 and 45-59, a statistically significant difference in the assets accumulated between the genders persists even after controlling for these factors.

A similar pattern is evident when examining contributions to personal pension plans. Women overall contribute less than men, and this result is mainly driven by the 30-59 age group. The gender difference persists even after controlling for typical labour market and educational outcomes, which suggests, like in the case of Germany, a possible behavioural bias between men and women when it comes to saving in personal plans.

Table 3.21. Drivers of gaps in personal plan contributions in Finland

Cohort	All (age 15-64)	15-29	30-44	45-59	60-64
Results when only considering gender					
Female indicator	-0.144	-0.349	-0.151	-0.144	-0.181
Results when controlling for other drivers					
Female	-0.162	-0.356	-0.192	-0.116	-0.242
Tertiary educated	0.172	0.381	0.251	0.087	0.462
Log age	1.846	1.956	1.550	2.562	8.100
Coupled	-0.082	-0.169	-0.116	-0.003	-0.284
Previously coupled	-0.145	N/A	0.025	-0.119	-0.759
Interaction: Working (employee or self-employed) × Total income	0.026	-0.038	0.017	0.038	0.034
Interaction: Value of occupational plan × has occupational plan	0.006	0.108	0.014	0.003	-0.014

Note: Dependent variable is the log of contributions to personal pension plans. Green cells indicate predictors that are statistically significant at the 95% confidence level or higher. Orange cells indicate predictors that are statistically significant at the 90% confidence level. Uncoloured cells indicate no statistical significance at the 90% confidence level or higher. Detailed regression results are at Table 3.C.21 of Annex 3.C.
Source: Calculations based on a sample of working age individuals (aged 15-64) from the HFCS Wave 2 data for Finland. Data relate to survey responses collected between 2013 and 2015.

3.5. Discussion and conclusion

This chapter analysed drivers of the gender gap in potential pension income, for three OECD countries: the United States, Germany and Finland. The focus of the analysis was to unpack causes of differences in retirement savings outcomes by gender, other than the typical labour market explanations.

The chapter focussed on what might drive gaps between the genders when it comes to pension plan coverage, and for people who are covered by a pension plan, what drives differences in the assets or entitlements accumulated in those plans. There are, as always, some shortcomings when conducting this type of analysis. First, what this chapter explored was only some of the many potential pathways for working life factors to affect retirement incomes. Of course, many other factors, whose analysis was outside the scope of the analysis described in this chapter, could affect retirement incomes. These include different life expectancies between the genders, different behavioural biases, the fact that couples may pool income sources, the effect of relationship breakdowns, and so on.[14] Notwithstanding, the chapter shows that it is possible to discern how some key features of the accumulation phase in some countries can lead to gender pension gaps in the future.

The analysis showed that for occupational pension plans, gender differences in coverage could be explained by factors other than labour market outcomes, but not for differences in assets or entitlements accumulated. The case studies for the United States and Germany showed that the industries women tend to be employed in and the type of work they do, which is more likely to be part time, can lead to a difference in the likelihood that they have a pension plan with their workplace. The same is not true for Finland, which does not have a gender gap in occupational plan coverage because funded pension plans are mandatory for all workers.

The findings suggest that there is room for policy interventions in the United States and Germany to encourage more employers to offer plans to all workers, particularly in instances where coverage rules may disproportionately impact women. The analysis showed that this is potentially the main area policy makers can use pension policy design to improve outcomes for women, since gender gaps in occupational pension plan assets and entitlements appear to be mostly explained by labour market differences.

When it came to personal plans in Germany and Finland, there was no clear sign that women were less likely to have a personal plan, but a behavioural disparity may lead women to contribute less to plans when they have one. The analysis showed that men and women were about equally likely to have a personal pension plan in Germany, and women were more likely to have one in Finland. Notwithstanding, in both case studies, women contributed less to their plans than men, and accumulated lower assets in their plans than men. This result proved true even after the modelling accounted for potential labour market differences between men and women. The results suggest that something else, such as a behavioural disparity, might be at play. Of course, the question about what behavioural traits might drive people to contribute more to their plans is not something that is easy to pinpoint using survey data. Notwithstanding, it is valuable to discern that *something* other than typical labour market factors may be leading to differences in gender outcomes, suggesting that there may be room for policy makers to address such shortcomings. For instance, upon further examination policy makers might conclude that behavioural biases such as risk aversion might explain different attitudes to retirement saving among the genders. As such, they may choose to tailor financial education programmes to counter such outcomes.

References

Belotti, F. et al. (2015), "twopm: Two-part models", *The Stata Journal*, Vol. 15/1, pp. 3-20, https://journals.sagepub.com/doi/pdf/10.1177/1536867X1501500102 (accessed on 1 February 2021). [3]

Bundesministerium für Arbeit und Soziales (2020), *Ergänzender Bericht der Bundesregierung zum Rentenversicherungsbericht 2020 gemäß § 154 Abs. 2 SGB VI (Alterssicherungsbericht 2020)*, https://www.bmas.de/SharedDocs/Downloads/DE/Rente/alterssicherungsbericht-2020.pdf;jsessionid=50F4F18C7380CF9FD520DD4816F94A30.delivery2-replication?__blob=publicationFile&v=1 (accessed on 18 February 2021). [9]

Bundesministerium für Familie, Senioren, F. (2016), *Atlas zur Gleichstellung von Frauen und Männern in Deutschland*. [6]

Bundesministeriums für Arbeit und Soziales (2020), "Arbeitgeber- und Trägerbefragung", https://www.bmas.de/SharedDocs/Downloads/DE/PDF-Publikationen/fb567-endbericht.pdf?__blob=publicationFile&v=1 (accessed on 25 January 2021). [2]

Cooper, D., K. Dynan and H. Rhodenhiser (2019), "Measuring Household Wealth in the Panel Study of Income Dynamics: The Role of Retirement Assets", *6*, No. 19, Federal Reserve Bank of Boston, https://psidonline.isr.umich.edu/Guide/Quality/DataComparisons.aspx. [4]

Kobe, K. (2010), *Small Business Retirement Plan Availability and Worker Participation Research Paper*, https://www.sba.gov/sites/default/files/rs361tot.pdf (accessed on 14 January 2021). [1]

O'Rand, A. and K. Shuey (2007), "Gender and the Devolution of Pension Risks in the US", *Current Sociology*, Vol. 55/2, pp. 287–304, http://dx.doi.org/10.1177/0011392107073315. [5]

OECD (2021), *Gender wage gap* (indicator), https://dx.doi.org/10.1787/7cee77aa-en (accessed on 25 January 2021). [7]

OECD (2019), *Pension Markets in Focus 2019*, https://www.oecd.org/daf/fin/private-pensions/Pension-Markets-in-Focus-2019.pdf (accessed on 28 January 2021). [8]

Annex 3.A. Data

Panel Study of Income Dynamics (PSID)

The analysis of the United States in this chapter relies on data from the Panel Study of Income Dynamics (PSID), a longitudinal household survey conducted by the Survey Research Center at the Institute for Social Research at the University of Michigan. The dataset is a rich source of demographic and financial information dating back to 1968.

The PSID dataset is useful because it provides both household-level and individual-level information on a range of demographic and financial variables. The family household file contains information on gender, marital status, education, income, housing, children, employment history, pension plan coverage, pension plan values, and contributions to pension plans. The PSID pension module has detailed information about the head of household and any spouse's retirement accounts (DC and DB) at their current employers and at as many as two previous employers each. It collects information about the balance of retirement accounts (IRAs), although this information is only reported in total for the household.

The PSID has some shortcomings. For instance, it does not track the upper end of the wealth and income distribution. Another issue is that not all people who report having DC retirement accounts know the value of those accounts. In some years, the PSID survey asked these people whether the account value lay within a certain range. In this analysis, where individuals only reported that value as a range, the midpoint was used.[15] The same issue arises for people who were asked their expected future income from a DB plan. If people did not know their potential income from their DB plan, the questioners asked them for an estimate as a percentage of their salary. The analysis in this chapter calculates the expected DB income in such cases, based on the stated percentage and the individual's reported income. However, since this chapter focuses on gender-based differences, it is unlikely that the data shortcomings will affect the results (since it is unlikely that males and females systematically differ in their abilities to recall account information).

Household Finance and Consumptions Survey (HFCS)

The analysis for Germany and Finland relies on Wave 2 of the Household Finance and Consumption Survey data. The data was published by the European Central Bank in 2016 and provides household-level data in 20 Euro area countries for the second wave. Those data relate to survey responses collected between 2013 and 2015 for European countries.

The HFCS data is useful in that it contains many variables that could have a strong relationship with coverage and asset/entitlement levels in the working-age population. The HFCS data include information about individuals' age, income, education, marital status, employment history, work type, hours worked, and pension assets or entitlements for both personal and occupational plans.

The HFCS data on occupational plan assets or entitlements is different for Germany and Finland. The data for Germany refer to assets or entitlements in private occupational plans. The German survey which collects HFCS data (the German Panel on Household Finances (PHF)) refers to these plans as 'company pension plans'. The occupational plan data for Finland refer to the present value of future entitlements from employer-provided occupational pension schemes.[16] The personal pension plan data for both countries refer to the total value of all of an individual's voluntary pension plan assets.

Readers should note that the HFCS data for Germany are based on the Panel on Household Finance of the Deutsche Bundesbank. This sample contains only around 4 500 households and is not collected specifically for gathering data on occupational or private pensions.

Annex 3.B. Methodology

The analysis of the coverage and asset/entitlement gaps was done in two stages. The first uses logistic regressions to investigate drivers of pension plan coverage, with occupational and personal plan coverage analysed separately. In those regressions the response variable is an indicator (dummy) variable of whether an individual was covered by each type of pension plan (occupational and personal). In the case study of the United States, the indicator dummy referred separately to whether an individual was eligible for a pension plan through their workplace, and whether they participated in a pension plan if they were eligible. The second stage uses a two-part model to determine the drivers of the value of assets or entitlements in funded pensions for people with personal or occupational plans, which are analysed separately (following the approach outlined in Belotti et al. (2015[3])). Using a two-part model made it possible to cater to a situation where a regression is conditional on a positive outcome, that is, that an individual has a relevant pension plan. The second part of the two-part model estimated the log of the dependent variable using ordinary least squares regression. The log transformation helps overcome shortcomings that come with having right skewed dependent variables. For results that examine the level of assets, entitlements or contributions to pension plans where an individual has one such plan, the chapter only reports the results from the second part. Rather than report results for the first part, instead the analysis relies on logistic regression analysis, to account for there being more information on whether an individual has a particular plan, than the amounts in that plan. This is because individuals were more likely to answer questions about whether or not they had a plan than the amount of assets in a plan, since they are less likely to know the latter.

In both stages of the modelling, the econometric analysis explores the effect of different relevant drivers by including them in the regressions incrementally. This makes it possible to see how the explanatory power of the female indicator changed as the regressions featured more of the predictors.

These analyses consider the whole of the population as well as cohorts of individuals in the following age groups: 15-29; 30-44; 45-59; over 60. Splitting the population into cohorts makes it possible to judge whether and how results change as younger generations benefit from an equalising playing field across genders. Some factors typically associated with gender pension gaps, such as gender pay gaps, have trended downward in OECD countries in recent years. Splitting the sample into cohorts is one way to track how the drivers of the gender pension gap may be changing in statistical significance and magnitude over time.

Readers should note that the analysis presented in this chapter makes it possible to examine the factors that drive the gender gaps in pensions, but the approach of using logit and a two-part model does not make it possible to understand the relative contribution or importance of different factors to the gender gaps in pensions. In the academic literature, such an analysis is typically done using a Oaxaca-Blinder decomposition approach. The data did not permit such a decomposition technique for the analysis in this chapter.

Annex 3.C. Detailed modelling results

Annex Table 3.C.1. Results from logistic regressions: odds ratios predicting occupational pension plan coverage in the United States (gender predictor only)

Cohort	(1)	(2)	(3)	(4)	(5)
Female indicator	0.778***	0.789*	0.777***	0.788***	0.734**
	(0.706 - 0.856)	(0.623 - 1.001)	(0.672 - 0.900)	(0.664 - 0.934)	(0.550 - 0.979)
Constant	0.935*	0.542***	1.081	1.075	0.729***
	(0.872 - 1.003)	(0.454 - 0.646)	(0.971 - 1.203)	(0.949 - 1.219)	(0.595 - 0.893)
Observations	11 999	2 332	5 099	3 421	1 147
Pseudo R2	0.00283	0.00242	0.00285	0.00256	0.00423

Note: Table presents odds ratios. Confidence intervals are reported in parentheses; *** p<0.01, ** p<0.05, * p<0.1. Cohort numbers refer to the following age groups: Cohort 1: All working age individuals (aged 15-64); Cohort 2: individuals aged 15-29; Cohort 3: individuals aged 30-44; Cohort 4: individuals aged 45-59; Cohort 5: individuals aged 60-64. The dependent variable is an indicator variable of whether the individual is covered by an occupational pension plan from their current or a previous employer. The only independent variable is an indicator of being female.
Source: OECD Secretariat calculations. Calculations were based on a sample of working age individuals (aged 15-64) from the 2017 PSID survey.

Annex Table 3.C.2. Results from logistic regressions: odds ratios predicting occupational pension plan eligibility in the United States (gender predictor only)

Cohort	(1)	(2)	(3)	(4)	(5)
Female indicator	0.852***	0.888	0.928	0.817*	0.677**
	(0.762 - 0.953)	(0.698 - 1.130)	(0.784 - 1.098)	(0.662 - 1.009)	(0.462 - 0.992)
Constant	1.756***	1.039	1.817***	2.135***	1.850***
	(1.618 - 1.905)	(0.866 - 1.247)	(1.608 - 2.053)	(1.828 - 2.494)	(1.413 - 2.423)
Observations	9 194	1 979	4 126	2 456	633
Pseudo R2	0.00114	0.000635	0.000248	0.00178	0.00673

Note: Table presents odds ratios. Confidence intervals are reported in parentheses; *** p<0.01, ** p<0.05, * p<0.1. Cohort numbers refer to the following age groups: Cohort 1: All working age individuals (aged 15-64); Cohort 2: individuals aged 15-29; Cohort 3: individuals aged 30-44; Cohort 4: individuals aged 45-59; Cohort 5: individuals aged 60-64. The dependent variable is an indicator variable of whether the individual is eligible for an occupational pension plan from their current employer. The only independent variable is an indicator of being female.
Source: OECD Secretariat calculations. Calculations were based on a sample of working age individuals (aged 15-64) from the 2017 PSID survey.

Annex Table 3.C.3. Results from logistic regressions: odds ratios predicting occupational pension plan participation in the United States (gender predictor only)

Cohort	(1)	(2)	(3)	(4)	(5)
Female indicator	0.772***	0.889	0.725**	0.680**	1.636
	(0.645 - 0.925)	(0.612 - 1.291)	(0.557 - 0.944)	(0.472 - 0.979)	(0.752 - 3.556)
Constant	6.033***	2.370***	5.928***	9.433***	7.373***
	(5.274 - 6.901)	(1.784 - 3.147)	(4.871 - 7.213)	(7.144 - 12.45)	(4.598 - 11.82)
Observations	5 422	922	2 534	1 586	380
Pseudo R2	0.00254	0.000599	0.00396	0.00527	0.00784

Note: Table presents odds ratios. Confidence intervals are reported in parentheses; *** p<0.01, ** p<0.05, * p<0.1. Cohort numbers refer to the following age groups: Cohort 1: All working age individuals (aged 15-64); Cohort 2: individuals aged 15-29; Cohort 3: individuals aged 30-44; Cohort 4: individuals aged 45-59; Cohort 5: individuals aged 60-64. The dependent variable is an indicator variable of whether an individual participated in an occupational pension plan if they were eligible to do so. The only independent variable is an indicator of being female.
Source: OECD Secretariat calculations. Calculations were based on a sample of working age individuals (aged 15-64) from the 2017 PSID survey.

Annex Table 3.C.4. Results from logistic regressions: odds ratios predicting occupational pension plan eligibility in the United States

	Cohort 1					Cohort 2					Cohort 3				
Female indicator	0.697***	0.934	0.919	0.986	1.004	0.725**	0.864	0.884	0.977	0.975	0.775**	1.057	1.009	1.086	1.089
	(0.609-0.797)	(0.807-1.080)	(0.787-1.072)	(0.843-1.153)	(0.857-1.177)	(0.550-0.956)	(0.647-1.154)	(0.650-1.202)	(0.714-1.338)	(0.707-1.344)	(0.637-0.942)	(0.859-1.302)	(0.810-1.256)	(0.870-1.355)	(0.869-1.363)
Attended college	1.778***	1.861***	1.778***	1.672***	1.741***	2.662***	2.577***	2.377***	2.209***	2.408***	2.159***	2.192***	2.060***	1.861***	1.926***
	(1.533-2.061)	(1.590-2.178)	(1.501-2.106)	(1.408-1.984)	(1.463-2.072)	(1.967-3.601)	(1.874-3.544)	(1.671-3.381)	(1.541-3.165)	(1.650-3.515)	(1.717-2.714)	(1.730-2.777)	(1.597-2.657)	(1.432-2.419)	(1.472-2.519)
In job for less than one year	0.323***	0.301***	0.302***	0.315***	0.317***	0.456***	0.453***	0.438***	0.451***	0.438***	0.321***	0.298***	0.290***	0.289***	0.279***
	(0.269-0.387)	(0.249-0.365)	(0.244-0.373)	(0.254-0.391)	(0.254-0.395)	(0.334-0.622)	(0.330-0.624)	(0.312-0.615)	(0.318-0.638)	(0.307-0.626)	(0.244-0.422)	(0.224-0.396)	(0.214-0.392)	(0.212-0.393)	(0.203-0.382)
Government employee	3.515***	3.896***	3.586***	2.802***	2.325***	2.134***	2.403***	1.861***	1.401	1.219	3.599***	4.178***	3.811***	2.918***	2.376***
	(2.868-4.308)	(3.132-4.847)	(2.821-4.558)	(2.189-3.587)	(1.794-3.013)	(1.444-3.154)	(1.581-3.654)	(1.169-2.963)	(0.860-2.283)	(0.713-2.086)	(2.652-4.884)	(3.015-5.789)	(2.676-5.429)	(2.028-4.197)	(1.626-3.472)
Part time worker		0.131***	0.147***	0.162***	0.168***		0.159***	0.177***	0.179***	0.199***		0.124***	0.134***	0.145***	0.151***
		(0.091-0.173)	(0.111-0.195)	(0.122-0.217)	(0.126-0.224)		(0.092-0.274)	(0.096-0.327)	(0.096-0.335)	(0.104-0.378)		(0.084-0.183)	(0.088-0.202)	(0.094-0.222)	(0.099-0.232)
Employed in a small or micro business			0.284***	0.310***	0.320***			0.315***	0.348***	0.342***			0.278***	0.313***	0.323***
			(0.244-0.330)	(0.266-0.362)	(0.274-0.374)			(0.233-0.427)	(0.255-0.473)	(0.249-0.470)			(0.223-0.346)	(0.250-0.391)	(0.258-0.406)
Industry with high pension coverage				2.085***	2.094***				2.497***	2.504***				2.298***	2.301***
				(1.779-2.444)	(1.784-2.458)				(1.808-3.448)	(1.803-3.477)				(1.822-2.900)	(1.820-2.909)
Covered by union contract					2.235***					1.940**					2.268***
					(1.649-3.031)					(1.090-3.453)					(1.420-3.622)
Constant	1.551***	1.685***	3.386***	2.411***	2.158***	0.767*	0.879	1.760***	1.195	1.090	1.236*	1.339***	2.843***	2.006***	1.838***
	(1.353-1.779)	(1.460-1.944)	(2.842-4.035)	(1.996-2.913)	(1.776-2.622)	(0.570-1.031)	(0.648-1.193)	(1.217-2.546)	(0.798-1.789)	(0.712-1.669)	(1.000-1.527)	(1.076-1.666)	(2.169-3.727)	(1.499-2.683)	(1.356-2.491)
Observations	7,704	7,518	7,142	7,136	7,038	1,656	1,602	1,494	1,491	1,442	3,611	3,532	3,362	3,360	3,320
Pseudo R2	0.0802	0.134	0.186	0.202	0.207	0.0671	0.106	0.148	0.175	0.181	0.0886	0.141	0.198	0.218	0.223

	Cohort 4					Cohort 5				
Female indicator	0.669***	0.910	0.952	1.016	1.044	0.389***	0.665	0.519**	0.526*	0.611
	(0.513-0.872)	(0.679-1.221)	(0.700-1.295)	(0.744-1.387)	(0.763-1.428)	(0.228-0.665)	(0.360-1.228)	(0.273-0.986)	(0.276-1.005)	(0.316-1.181)
Attended college	1.388**	1.547***	1.532***	1.488**	1.524***	1.243	1.627	1.532	1.451	1.581
	(1.048-1.837)	(1.146-2.090)	(1.114-2.106)	(1.081-2.049)	(1.110-2.093)	(0.731-2.114)	(0.875-3.025)	(0.794-2.953)	(0.769-2.740)	(0.836-2.990)
In job for less than one year	0.326***	0.300***	0.324***	0.351***	0.372***	0.306**	0.281**	0.241*	0.241**	0.261*
	(0.213-0.498)	(0.189-0.476)	(0.191-0.550)	(0.204-0.605)	(0.216-0.640)	(0.096-0.975)	(0.089-0.885)	(0.057-1.014)	(0.058-0.998)	(0.064-1.063)
	3.797***	4.063***	3.929***	3.247***	2.749***	6.134***	5.780***	6.070***	4.971***	4.012***

Government employee	(2.503-5.760)	(2.604-6.341)	(2.412-6.399)	(1.986-5.309)	(1.664-4.542)	(2.778-13.54)	(2.457-13.60)	(2.416-15.25)	(1.984-12.46)	(1.607-10.02)
Part time worker		0.138***	0.160***	0.184***	0.185***		0.0833***	0.0990***	0.103***	0.0962***
		(0.079-0.241)	(0.093-0.273)	(0.106-0.317)	(0.107-0.319)		(0.038-0.184)	(0.044-0.220)	(0.046-0.232)	(0.040-0.229)
Employed in a small or micro business			0.289***	0.303***	0.318***			0.220***	0.235***	0.238***
			(0.215-0.389)	(0.225-0.410)	(0.235-0.430)			(0.116-0.417)	(0.123-0.451)	(0.123-0.458)
Industry with high pension coverage				1.733***	1.754***				1.616	1.494
				(1.278-2.351)	(1.293-2.380)				(0.864-3.021)	(0.796-2.803)
Covered by union contract					1.911**					6.234***
					(1.096-3.332)					(1.821-21.34)
Constant	2.280***	2.345***	4.262***	3.182***	2.838***	2.433***	2.768***	6.911***	5.767***	4.524***
	(1.769-2.939)	(1.801-3.054)	(3.106-5.849)	(2.242-4.517)	(1.994-4.039)	(1.498-3.951)	(1.647-4.652)	(3.396-14.06)	(2.670-12.46)	(2.047-10.00)
Observations	1 988	1 948	1 869	1 868	1 860	449	436	417	417	416
Pseudo R2	0.0695	0.122	0.170	0.179	0.182	0.101	0.209	0.273	0.278	0.306

Note: Confidence intervals are reported in parentheses; *** p<0.01, ** p<0.05, * p<0.1. Cohort numbers refer to the following age groups: Cohort 1: All working age individuals (aged 15-64); Cohort 2: individuals aged 15-29; Cohort 3: individuals aged 30-44; Cohort 4: individuals aged 45-59; Cohort 5: individuals aged 60-64. The dependent variable is an indicator variable of whether the individual is eligible for an occupational pension plan from their employer. Individuals are treated as being eligible for an occupational plan if they are employed and either reported that they are eligible for an occupational plan or reported that they were participating in an occupational plan. Independent variables are: female indicator; whether the individual attended college; whether the individual was in their current job for less than 1 year; whether the individual works for the federal, state or local government; whether the individual was employed on a part time basis (less than 30 hours per week); whether the individual was employed in a business that is classified as either micro or small (fewer than 10 employees or between 10 and 50 employees respectively); whether the individual works in an industry that overall has high occupational plan coverage (more than 60% of employees in that industry are covered by an occupational plan); and whether the individual's current job is covered by a union contract.
Source: OECD Secretariat calculations. Calculations were based on a sample of working age individuals (aged 15-64) from the 2017 PSID survey

Annex Table 3.C.5. Results from logistic regressions: odds ratios predicting occupational pension plan participation in the United States

	Cohort 1					Cohort 2					Cohort 3				
Female indicator	0.675***	0.701***	0.729***	0.785**	0.809**	0.721	0.739	0.781	0.886	0.890	0.662***	0.713**	0.775*	0.817	0.819
	(0.553-0.822)	(0.575-0.856)	(0.593-0.894)	(0.638-0.965)	(0.656-0.999)	(0.482-1.078)	(0.492-1.110)	(0.515-1.184)	(0.579-1.356)	(0.578-1.369)	(0.501-0.876)	(0.537-0.947)	(0.579-1.038)	(0.608-1.098)	(0.607-1.105)
Attended college	1.461***	1.463***	1.422***	1.367***	1.390***	2.099***	2.064***	1.801**	1.666**	1.608*	1.843***	1.866***	1.860***	1.749***	1.767***
	(1.165-1.833)	(1.164-1.838)	(1.124-1.799)	(1.079-1.732)	(1.090-1.772)	(1.311-3.363)	(1.278-3.333)	(1.111-2.921)	(1.019-2.723)	(0.963-2.684)	(1.288-2.638)	(1.296-2.687)	(1.278-2.705)	(1.205-2.540)	(1.202-2.598)
In job for less than one year	0.368***	0.370***	0.359***	0.371***	0.395***	0.682	0.693	0.614**	0.620**	0.663*	0.473***	0.468***	0.489***	0.485***	0.500***
	(0.276-0.490)	(0.278-0.492)	(0.266-0.484)	(0.273-0.504)	(0.289-0.541)	(0.428-1.085)	(0.436-1.102)	(0.384-0.983)	(0.389-0.989)	(0.409-1.076)	(0.308-0.726)	(0.304-0.722)	(0.309-0.774)	(0.303-0.777)	(0.311-0.806)
Government employee	3.170***	3.138***	3.049***	2.413***	1.975***	3.129***	3.268***	2.757***	2.073**	1.762*	3.059***	2.998***	2.952***	2.458***	2.138***
	(2.361-4.256)	(2.336-4.215)	(2.245-4.140)	(1.769-3.290)	(1.421-2.747)	(1.803-5.427)	(1.901-5.617)	(1.583-4.802)	(1.158-3.712)	(0.941-3.299)	(1.955-4.784)	(1.916-4.691)	(1.847-4.718)	(1.533-3.940)	(1.299-3.521)
Part time worker		0.427***	0.400***	0.484***	0.479***		0.313**	0.309**	0.334**	0.348**		0.275***	0.244***	0.280***	0.281***
		(0.277-0.659)	(0.257-0.623)	(0.305-0.769)	(0.302-0.760)		(0.114-0.858)	(0.113-0.847)	(0.122-0.919)	(0.129-0.938)		(0.146-0.519)	(0.126-0.474)	(0.143-0.547)	(0.146-0.543)
Employed in a small or micro business			0.629***	0.680***	0.716***			0.536***	0.573***	0.609**			0.700**	0.749*	0.786
			(0.513-0.770)	(0.554-0.836)	(0.581-0.881)			(0.356-0.807)	(0.379-0.867)	(0.400-0.928)			(0.521-0.940)	(0.555-1.010)	(0.582-1.060)
Industry with high pension coverage				2.152***	2.195***				2.620***	2.655***				1.777***	1.812***
				(1.747-2.651)	(1.777-2.710)				(1.729-3.971)	(1.741-4.048)				(1.320-2.393)	(1.343-2.446)
Covered by union contract					2.075***					1.684					1.555
					(1.412-3.047)					(0.807-3.515)					(0.875-2.763)
Constant	4.342***	4.424***	5.424***	3.659***	3.275***	1.352	1.401	1.983***	1.252	1.212	3.317***	3.359***	3.837***	2.914***	2.730***
	(3.521-5.354)	(3.578-5.471)	(4.289-6.859)	(2.828-4.734)	(2.489-4.310)	(0.854-2.141)	(0.879-2.235)	(1.197-3.283)	(0.723-2.168)	(0.680-2.159)	(2.344-4.692)	(2.362-4.776)	(2.607-5.646)	(1.914-4.434)	(1.745-4.271)
Observations	4 945	4 933	4 744	4 738	4 694	855	853	817	814	796	2 367	2 362	2 264	2 262	2 241
Pseudo R2	0.0548	0.0594	0.0663	0.0854	0.0891	0.0446	0.0515	0.0657	0.0992	0.0957	0.0530	0.0637	0.0676	0.0785	0.0793

	Cohort 4					Cohort 5				
Female indicator	0.628**	0.633**	0.648*	0.714	0.755	0.905	1.084	0.930	0.978	1.071
	(0.410-0.960)	(0.413-0.970)	(0.419-1.005)	(0.461-1.105)	(0.485-1.175)	(0.365-2.242)	(0.453-2.594)	(0.378-2.287)	(0.406-2.356)	(0.451-2.545)
Attended college	1.449*	1.461*	1.440	1.402	1.466	1.238	1.242	1.251	1.243	1.296
	(0.937-2.241)	(0.944-2.260)	(0.919-2.256)	(0.892-2.204)	(0.928-2.315)	(0.502-3.050)	(0.500-3.084)	(0.500-3.126)	(0.491-3.145)	(0.520-3.228)
In job for less than one year	0.271***	0.274***	0.266***	0.309***	0.336***	0.307	0.312	0.346	0.319	0.335
	(0.132-0.555)	(0.135-0.555)	(0.127-0.557)	(0.142-0.669)	(0.157-0.722)	(0.071-1.349)	(0.077-1.274)	(0.076-1.567)	(0.066-1.529)	(0.070-1.603)
Government employee	2.478***	2.448***	2.420***	1.859**	1.392	6.972**	7.460**	7.250**	6.031**	5.352*
	(1.405-4.368)	(1.389-4.315)	(1.349-4.344)	(1.016-3.400)	(0.732-2.650)	(1.334-36.44)	(1.411-39.43)	(1.354-38.82)	(1.089-33.41)	(0.923-31.04)

Part time worker		0.751	0.700	0.937	0.914		0.236**	0.253*	0.272*	0.260**
		(0.273-2.062)	(0.255-1.919)	(0.313-2.802)	(0.301-2.771)		(0.067-0.833)	(0.064-1.002)	(0.073-1.012)	(0.069-0.982)
Employed in a small or micro business			0.716	0.777	0.808			0.512	0.547	0.551
			(0.466-1.102)	(0.503-1.201)	(0.519-1.259)			(0.217-1.208)	(0.235-1.272)	(0.237-1.277)
Industry with high pension coverage				2.507***	2.555***				1.774	1.768
				(1.602-3.922)	(1.633-3.998)				(0.719-4.378)	(0.714-4.375)
Covered by union contract					3.375***					1.896
					(1.407-8.097)					(0.435-8.268)
Constant	7.243***	7.246***	8.293***	5.030***	4.235***	5.868***	6.151***	8.451***	6.442***	5.525***
	(5.099-10.29)	(5.100-10.30)	(5.586-12.31)	(3.245-7.795)	(2.635-6.808)	(2.559-13.45)	(2.631-14.38)	(3.076-23.22)	(2.343-17.71)	(2.141-14.26)
Observations	1 411	1 406	1 363	1 362	1 357	312	312	300	300	300
Pseudo R2	0.0508	0.0512	0.0567	0.0818	0.0967	0.0736	0.0940	0.0977	0.107	0.114

Note: Confidence intervals are reported in parentheses; *** p<0.01, ** p<0.05, * p<0.1. Cohort numbers refer to the following age groups: Cohort 1: All working age individuals (aged 15-64); Cohort 2: individuals aged 15-29; Cohort 3: individuals aged 30-44; Cohort 4: individuals aged 45-59; Cohort 5: individuals aged 60-64. The dependent variable is an indicator variable of whether the individual participates in occupational pension plan from their employer, if they are eligible for one. Independent variables are: female indicator; whether the individual attended college; whether the individual was in their current job for less than 1 year; whether the individual works for the federal, state or local government; whether the individual was employed on a part time basis (less than 30 hours per week); whether the individual was employed in a business that is classified as either micro or small (fewer than 10 employees or between 10 and 50 employees respectively); whether the individual works in an industry that overall has high occupational plan coverage (more than 60% of employees in that industry are covered by an occupational plan); and whether the individual's current job is covered by a union contract.
Source: OECD Secretariat calculations. Calculations were based on a sample of working age individuals (aged 15-64) from the 2017 PSID survey.

Annex Table 3.C.6. Results from logistic regressions: odds ratios predicting occupational pension plan coverage in Germany

	Cohort 1				Cohort 2				Cohort 3			
Female	0.736***	1.043	1.044	1.161*	0.601*	0.951	0.946	0.996	0.999	1.428*	1.416*	1.565**
	(0.631-0.859)	(0.874-1.243)	(0.877-1.242)	(0.976-1.380)	(0.342-1.055)	(0.513-1.764)	(0.508-1.764)	(0.540-1.838)	(0.756-1.320)	(0.989-2.062)	(0.978-2.049)	(1.089-2.249)
Interaction: Working as employee or self-employed * Hours working		1.019***	1.022***	1.036***		1.041***	1.042***	1.056***		1.013*	1.013*	1.026***
		(1.012-1.027)	(1.015-1.030)	(1.030-1.042)		(1.019-1.063)	(1.021-1.062)	(1.040-1.073)		(0.998-1.027)	(1.000-1.026)	(1.014-1.038)
Indicator: Has income from working (employee or self-employed)		3.023***				2.901				2.536**		
		(1.920-4.760)				(0.518-16.26)				(1.137-5.656)		
Indicator: Has employment income			2.979***				2.953				3.150***	
			(2.161-4.106)				(0.459-18.98)				(1.728-5.743)	
Indicator: Has self employment income				0.537***				1.137				0.569*
				(0.380-0.758)				(0.297-4.353)				(0.295-1.096)
Constant	0.323***	0.0596***	0.0584***	0.0949***	0.150***	0.0179***	0.0177***	0.0276***	0.320***	0.0784***	0.0683***	0.120***
	(0.288-0.362)	(0.041-0.087)	(0.042-0.082)	(0.074-0.121)	(0.109-0.207)	(0.004-0.082)	(0.003-0.095)	(0.014-0.056)	(0.262-0.390)	(0.039-0.160)	(0.034-0.138)	(0.072-0.200)
Observations	6 094	5 781	5 781	5 781	1 470	1 288	1 288	1 288	1 477	1 425	1 425	1 425
	Cohort 4				Cohort 5							
Female	0.650***	0.878	0.869	0.969	0.455***	0.528*	0.499*	0.545*				
	(0.503-0.839)	(0.656-1.174)	(0.648-1.166)	(0.726-1.294)	(0.251-0.826)	(0.263-1.062)	(0.248-1.003)	(0.274-1.084)				
Interaction: Working as employee or self-employed * Hours working		1.021***	1.023***	1.035***		1.004	1.006	1.024***				
		(1.009-1.033)	(1.012-1.035)	(1.025-1.045)		(0.984-1.024)	(0.990-1.023)	(1.009-1.040)				
Indicator: Has income from working (employee or self-employed)		2.496**				2.782*						
		(1.139-5.471)				(0.983-7.871)						
Indicator: Has employment income			2.823***				3.102***					
			(1.818-4.382)				(1.461-6.585)					
Indicator: Has self employment income				0.449***				0.318**				
				(0.292-0.689)				(0.109-0.929)				
Constant	0.456***	0.0883***	0.0793***	0.134***	0.427***	0.163***	0.155***	0.233***				
	(0.378-0.550)	(0.043-0.180)	(0.045-0.139)	(0.087-0.205)	(0.290-0.628)	(0.074-0.361)	(0.071-0.338)	(0.123-0.442)				
Observations	2 509	2 453	2 453	2 453	636	613	613	613				

Note: Confidence intervals are reported in parentheses; *** p<0.01, ** p<0.05, * p<0.1. Cohort numbers refer to the following age groups: Cohort 1: All working age individuals (aged 15-64); Cohort 2: individuals aged 15-29; Cohort 3: individuals aged 30-44; Cohort 4: individuals aged 45-59; Cohort 5: individuals aged 60-64. The dependent variable is an indicator variable of whether an individual is covered by an occupational pension plan from their employer. Independent variables are: female indicator; an interaction term between an indicator of whether a person was working and their hours worked; an indicator of whether person was working (either as an employee or self-employed); an indicator of whether a person was working as an employee; an indicator of whether a person was self-employed.
Source: OECD Secretariat calculations. Calculations were based on a sample of working age individuals (aged 15-64) from the HFCS Wave 2 data. Data relate to survey responses collected between 2013 and 2015.

Annex Table 3.C.7. Results from logistic regressions: odds ratios predicting occupational pension plan coverage in Finland

	Cohort 1				Cohort 2				Cohort 3			
Female	1.056	0.978	0.931	1.084	1.059	0.870*	0.893	1.065	0.944	1.137	0.957	0.963
	(0.960-1.162)	(0.876-1.093)	(0.838-1.035)	(0.984-1.193)	(0.921-1.218)	(0.738-1.025)	(0.760-1.049)	(0.925-1.226)	(0.669-1.332)	(0.777-1.663)	(0.664-1.377)	(0.682-1.358)
Indicator: Has income from working (employee or self-employed)		11.91***				10.82***				18.45***		
		(10.55-13.46)				(8.799-13.30)				(12.42-27.39)		
Indicator: Has employment income			9.012***				9.910***				14.60***	
			(8.031-10.11)				(8.124-12.09)				(9.931-21.45)	
Indicator: Has self employment income				1.971***				3.867***				1.396
				(1.631-2.382)				(1.746-8.564)				(0.715-2.728)
Constant	5.606***	1.008	1.412***	5.230***	3.446***	0.732***	0.790***	3.339***	18.34***	2.246***	3.434***	17.57***
	(5.284-5.948)	(0.911-1.116)	(1.293-1.542)	(4.913-5.569)	(3.145-3.776)	(0.614-0.873)	(0.666-0.936)	(3.042-3.666)	(14.09-23.89)	(1.553-3.250)	(2.478-4.761)	(13.35-23.13)
Observations	16 859	16 859	16 859	16 859	4 402	4 402	4 402	4 402	4 609	4 609	4 609	4 609
	Cohort 4				Cohort 5							
Female	1.149	1.000	0.945	1.194	1.042	0.992	0.933	1.067				
	(0.920-1.434)	(0.779-1.284)	(0.744-1.200)	(0.953-1.495)	(0.797-1.362)	(0.753-1.308)	(0.711-1.225)	(0.813-1.401)				
Indicator: Has income from working (employee or self-employed)		14.18***				4.946***						
		(10.95-18.38)				(3.620-6.759)						
Indicator: Has employment income			9.068***				3.869***					
			(7.107-11.57)				(2.926-5.115)					
Indicator: Has self employment income				2.141***				1.544**				
				(1.549-2.959)				(1.099-2.171)				
Constant	7.586***	1.246**	2.043***	6.839***	1.339***	0.454***	0.632***	1.240**				
	(6.584-8.740)	(1.001-1.551)	(1.694-2.463)	(5.871-7.967)	(1.112-1.611)	(0.342-0.604)	(0.501-0.796)	(1.011-1.520)				
Observations	6 358	6 358	6 358	6 358	1 490	1 490	1 490	1 490				

Note: Confidence intervals are reported in parentheses; *** p<0.01, ** p<0.05, * p<0.1. Cohort numbers refer to the following age groups: Cohort 1: All working age individuals (aged 15-64); Cohort 2: individuals aged 15-29; Cohort 3: individuals aged 30-44; Cohort 4: individuals aged 45-59; Cohort 5: individuals aged 60-64. The dependent variable is an indicator variable of whether an individual is covered by an occupational pension plan. Independent variables are: female indicator; an interaction term between an indicator of whether a person was working and their work income; an interaction term between an indicator of whether a person was working as an employee and their employment income; an interaction term between an indicator of whether a person was self-employed and their self-employment income.

Source: OECD Secretariat calculations. Calculations were based on a sample of working age individuals (aged 15-64) from the HFCS Wave 2 data. Data relate to survey responses collected between 2013 and 2015.

Annex Table 3.C.8. Drivers of gap in assets in defined contribution occupational plans in the United States

Cohort	Cohort 1				Cohort 2				Cohort 3			
Female indicator	-0.426***	-0.354***	-0.352***	0.0749	0.161	0.157	0.171	0.393	-0.340***	-0.301***	-0.301***	0.143
	(0.100)	(0.0851)	(0.0849)	(0.0774)	(0.266)	(0.252)	(0.251)	(0.245)	(0.127)	(0.103)	(0.104)	(0.0943)
Years participating in occupational plan		0.122***	0.119***	0.106***		0.244**	0.253**	0.224**		0.181***	0.181***	0.162***
		(0.00581)	(0.00576)	(0.00534)		(0.108)	(0.111)	(0.0892)		(0.0116)	(0.0116)	(0.0101)
Whether person has children			0.310***	0.266***			-0.282	-0.161			0.00169	0.0277
			(0.0910)	(0.0803)			(0.256)	(0.250)			(0.115)	(0.0971)
Log of income				1.072***				1.163***				1.177***
				(0.0781)				(0.198)				(0.0831)
Constant	11.09***	9.908***	9.708***	-2.195**	9.144***	8.597***	8.639***	-3.926*	10.77***	9.566***	9.565***	-3.595***
	(0.0689)	(0.0843)	(0.105)	(0.869)	(0.219)	(0.310)	(0.315)	(2.116)	(0.0909)	(0.107)	(0.131)	(0.941)
Observations	2 601	2 601	2 601	2 591	385	385	385	384	1 237	1 237	1 237	1 233
R-squared	0.0108	0.280	0.285	0.407	0.00156	0.129	0.132	0.240	0.00873	0.308	0.308	0.460
Cohort	Cohort 4				Cohort 5							
Female indicator	-0.522***	-0.479***	-0.478***	-0.0676	-0.791**	-0.765**	-0.777**	-0.294				
	(0.162)	(0.141)	(0.141)	(0.126)	(0.379)	(0.369)	(0.370)	(0.351)				
Years participating in occupational plan		0.0972***	0.0973***	0.0868***		0.0523***	0.0521***	0.0534***				
		(0.00698)	(0.00697)	(0.00635)		(0.0191)	(0.0192)	(0.0184)				
Whether person has children			0.0298	0.0681			0.132	0.110				
			(0.171)	(0.139)			(0.323)	(0.272)				
Log of income				0.874***				1.076***				
				(0.102)				(0.190)				
Constant	11.74***	10.48***	10.45***	0.641	11.80***	10.96***	10.86***	-1.324				
	(0.102)	(0.138)	(0.197)	(1.132)	(0.210)	(0.371)	(0.432)	(2.126)				

Observations	796	796	796	792	183	183	183	182			
R-squared	0.0189	0.243	0.243	0.358	0.0327	0.105	0.106	0.197			

Note: Standard errors are reported in parentheses; *** p<0.01, ** p<0.05, * p<0.1. Cohort numbers refer to the following age groups: Cohort 1: All working age individuals; Cohort 2: individuals aged 15-29; Cohort 3: individuals aged 30-44; Cohort 4: individuals aged 45-59; Cohort 5: individuals aged 60-64. The dependent variable is the log level of accumulated assets in an individual's occupational defined contribution account. Independent variables are: female indicator; the number of years an individual has participated in the pension plan; whether the individual has children; and the log of the individual's gross employee income over the 12 months prior to the interview.
Source: OECD Secretariat calculations. Calculations were based on a sample of working age individuals (aged 15-64) from the 2017 PSID survey.

Annex Table 3.C.9. Drivers of gap in expected income from defined benefit occupational plans in the United States

Cohort	Cohort 1				Cohort 3			
Female indicator	-0.417***	-0.408***	-0.407***	-0.197	-0.401***	-0.321**	-0.322**	-0.0651
	(0.150)	(0.145)	(0.145)	(0.181)	(0.145)	(0.143)	(0.144)	(0.103)
Years participating in occupational plan		0.0314***	0.0313***	0.0234**		0.0284**	0.0304***	0.0152*
		(0.00854)	(0.00858)	(0.0104)		(0.0112)	(0.0112)	(0.00812)
Whether person has children			0.0519	-0.00763			-0.243	-0.161
			(0.139)	(0.120)			(0.187)	(0.127)
Log of income				0.609***				0.905***
				(0.165)				(0.0888)
Constant	10.36***	9.828***	9.783***	3.064*	10.57***	10.20***	10.38***	0.268
	(0.0994)	(0.201)	(0.180)	(1.764)	(0.0944)	(0.165)	(0.211)	(1.016)
Observations	553	553	553	552	150	150	150	150
R-squared	0.0287	0.0892	0.0894	0.161	0.0721	0.124	0.140	0.519
Cohort	Cohort 4				Cohort 5			
Female indicator	-0.422*	-0.390*	-0.375*	-0.224	-0.326*	-0.365**	-0.375**	-0.107
	(0.231)	(0.219)	(0.221)	(0.267)	(0.193)	(0.167)	(0.169)	(0.170)
Years participating in occupational plan		0.0398***	0.0399***	0.0330**		0.0397***	0.0398***	0.0289***
		(0.0136)	(0.0137)	(0.0164)		(0.00675)	(0.00668)	(0.00615)
Whether person has children			0.207	0.117			0.108	0.0342
			(0.195)	(0.171)			(0.192)	(0.197)
Log of income				0.503**				0.539***
				(0.241)				(0.150)
Constant	10.29***	9.590***	9.402***	3.892	10.29***	9.434***	9.347***	3.530**

	(0.151)	(0.329)	(0.286)	(2.553)	(0.149)	(0.197)	(0.226)	(1.637)
Observations	317	317	317	317	86	86	86	85
R-squared	0.0217	0.0927	0.0950	0.132	0.0427	0.321	0.324	0.455

Note: Standard errors are reported in parentheses; *** p<0.01, ** p<0.05, * p<0.1. Cohort numbers refer to the following age groups: Cohort 1: All working age individuals; Cohort 2: individuals aged 15-29; Cohort 3: individuals aged 30-44; Cohort 4: individuals aged 45-59; Cohort 5: individuals aged 60-64. The results exclude cohort 2 because there were insufficient observations in that group to conduct the analysis. The dependent variable is the log expected annual income from an individual's defined benefit plan. Independent variables are: female indicator; the number of years an individual has participated in the pension plan; whether the individual has children; and the log of the individual's gross employee income over the 12 months prior to the interview.
Source: OECD Secretariat calculations. Calculations were based on a sample of working age individuals (aged 15-64) from the 2017 PSID survey.

Annex Table 3.C.10. Drivers of gap in employer contributions to occupational pensions in the United States

Cohort	Cohort 1				Cohort 2				Cohort 3			
Female indicator	-0.395***	-0.382***	-0.384***	-0.0179	-0.0964	-0.0943	-0.0755	0.0546	-0.359***	-0.352***	-0.352***	-0.00805
	(0.0774)	(0.0763)	(0.0762)	(0.0734)	(0.167)	(0.168)	(0.167)	(0.133)	(0.105)	(0.106)	(0.106)	(0.112)
Years participating in occupational plan		0.0225***	0.0237***	0.00719*		0.0288	0.0356	0.0154		0.0193	0.0204*	-0.00112
		(0.00465)	(0.00466)	(0.00394)		(0.0282)	(0.0293)	(0.0151)		(0.0118)	(0.0116)	(0.0103)
Whether person has children			-0.121	-0.136**			-0.262	-0.0653			-0.143	-0.119
			(0.0763)	(0.0653)			(0.180)	(0.147)			(0.111)	(0.0920)
Log of income				0.969***				1.019***				1.015***
				(0.0644)				(0.188)				(0.0754)
Constant	7.877***	7.671***	7.748***	-3.003***	7.399***	7.333***	7.372***	-3.643*	7.880***	7.756***	7.848***	-3.470***
	(0.0513)	(0.0646)	(0.0796)	(0.718)	(0.136)	(0.160)	(0.165)	(1.932)	(0.0624)	(0.101)	(0.140)	(0.911)
Observations	2 090	2 090	2 090	2 088	317	317	317	317	1 030	1 030	1 030	1 030
R-squared	0.0203	0.0389	0.0403	0.256	0.00134	0.00581	0.0127	0.216	0.0194	0.0257	0.0283	0.253
Cohort	Cohort 4				Cohort 5							
Female indicator	-0.470***	-0.461***	-0.486***	-0.0505	-0.564***	-0.558***	-0.616***	-0.109				
	(0.146)	(0.143)	(0.143)	(0.136)	(0.196)	(0.199)	(0.191)	(0.148)				
Years participating in occupational plan		0.0236***	0.0219***	0.00723		0.0146	0.0119	0.00945				
		(0.00792)	(0.00801)	(0.00671)		(0.00914)	(0.00863)	(0.00649)				
Whether person has children			-0.390***	-0.297**			0.606*	0.165				
			(0.137)	(0.136)			(0.360)	(0.255)				
Log of income				0.912***				1.033***				
				(0.113)				(0.105)				
Constant	7.948***	7.652***	8.022***	-2.234*	8.176***	7.960***	7.471***	-3.868***				
	(0.0995)	(0.143)	(0.181)	(1.269)	(0.108)	(0.173)	(0.385)	(1.160)				
Observations	616	616	616	615	127	127	127	126				
R-squared	0.0238	0.0442	0.0516	0.243	0.0761	0.0985	0.128	0.456				

Note: Standard errors are reported in parentheses; *** p<0.01, ** p<0.05, * p<0.1. Cohort numbers refer to the following age groups: Cohort 1: All working age individuals; Cohort 2: individuals aged 15-29; Cohort 3: individuals aged 30-44; Cohort 4: individuals aged 45-59; Cohort 5: individuals aged 60-64. The dependent variable is the log level of employer contributions to individuals' occupational pension plans, for individuals whose employers do make contributions. Independent variables are: female indicator; the number of years an individual has participated in the pension plan; whether the individual has children; and the log of the individual's gross employee income over the 12 months prior to the interview.
Source: OECD Secretariat calculations. Calculations were based on a sample of working age individuals (aged 15-64) from the 2017 PSID survey.

Annex Table 3.C.11. Drivers of gap in mandatory individual contributions to occupational pensions in the United States

Cohort	Cohort 1				Cohort 2				Cohort 3			
Female indicator	-0.132	-0.142	-0.141	0.117	-0.0123	0.00950	0.0149	0.0838	-0.224	-0.187	-0.186	0.0307
	(0.103)	(0.0968)	(0.0966)	(0.0797)	(0.243)	(0.242)	(0.242)	(0.217)	(0.137)	(0.136)	(0.136)	(0.118)
Years participating in occupational plan		0.0366***	0.0361***	0.0110***		0.0256	0.0280	0.0109		0.0402**	0.0406**	0.00762
		(0.00469)	(0.00479)	(0.00411)		(0.0181)	(0.0182)	(0.0103)		(0.0162)	(0.0162)	(0.0146)
Whether person has children			0.0898	0.0625			-0.169	0.0445			-0.0546	-0.0736
			(0.118)	(0.0913)			(0.225)	(0.188)			(0.142)	(0.109)
Log of income				1.026***				0.901***				0.931***
				(0.0801)				(0.158)				(0.0796)
Constant	7.899***	7.475***	7.409***	-3.572***	7.458***	7.370***	7.431***	-2.175	7.818***	7.484***	7.523***	-2.438***
	(0.0811)	(0.0908)	(0.132)	(0.878)	(0.206)	(0.223)	(0.232)	(1.710)	(0.102)	(0.144)	(0.180)	(0.883)
Observations	845	845	845	844	122	122	122	122	379	379	379	379
R-squared	0.00377	0.117	0.118	0.416	3.48e-05	0.0146	0.0215	0.355	0.0118	0.0637	0.0642	0.315
Cohort	Cohort 4				Cohort 5							
Female indicator	-0.134	-0.163	-0.158	0.181	0.0818	0.0654	-0.0407	0.146				
	(0.177)	(0.165)	(0.164)	(0.134)	(0.265)	(0.293)	(0.249)	(0.185)				
Years participating in occupational plan		0.0399***	0.0400***	0.0103*		0.0205	0.0288**	-0.000603				
		(0.00760)	(0.00765)	(0.00622)		(0.0127)	(0.0116)	(0.00904)				
Whether person has children			0.232	0.0978			0.764**	0.582**				
			(0.273)	(0.203)			(0.380)	(0.268)				
Log of income				1.154***				1.065***				
				(0.148)				(0.166)				
Constant	8.029***	7.446***	7.241***	-4.983***	8.031***	7.617***	6.855***	-4.237**				
	(0.141)	(0.184)	(0.339)	(1.638)	(0.191)	(0.306)	(0.490)	(1.806)				
Observations	280	280	280	280	64	64	64	63				
R-squared	0.00366	0.130	0.135	0.476	0.00187	0.0755	0.151	0.489				

Note: Standard errors are reported in parentheses; *** p<0.01, ** p<0.05, * p<0.1. Cohort numbers refer to the following age groups: Cohort 1: All working age individuals; Cohort 2: individuals aged 15-29; Cohort 3: individuals aged 30-44; Cohort 4: individuals aged 45-59; Cohort 5: individuals aged 60-64. The dependent variable is the log level of mandatory contributions by individuals to occupational pension plans, of individuals who are required to make mandatory contributions. Independent variables are: female indicator; the number of years an individual has participated in the pension plan; whether the individual has children; and the log of the individual's gross employee income over the 12 months prior to the interview.

Source: OECD Secretariat calculations. Calculations were based on a sample of working age individuals (aged 15-64) from the 2017 PSID survey.

Annex Table 3.C.12. Drivers of gap in voluntary individual contributions to occupational pensions in the United States

Cohort	Cohort 1				Cohort 2				Cohort 3			
Female indicator	-0.413***	-0.400***	-0.401***	0.0198	-0.401***	-0.421***	-0.397***	-0.196**	-0.353***	-0.333***	-0.333***	0.116*
	(0.0582)	(0.0573)	(0.0576)	(0.0437)	(0.132)	(0.130)	(0.125)	(0.0974)	(0.0824)	(0.0819)	(0.0821)	(0.0623)
Years participating in occupational plan		0.0177***	0.0179***	0.000915		0.0906***	0.135***	0.0487*		0.0270***	0.0278***	0.00303
		(0.00443)	(0.00474)	(0.00398)		(0.0300)	(0.0317)	(0.0264)		(0.00814)	(0.00840)	(0.00567)
Whether person has children			-0.0126	-0.0493			-0.753***	-0.552***			-0.0814	-0.0800
			(0.0749)	(0.0605)			(0.174)	(0.153)			(0.107)	(0.0774)
Log of income				1.198***				1.218***				1.296***
				(0.0321)				(0.0737)				(0.0419)
Constant	8.368***	8.198***	8.206***	-5.100***	7.915***	7.733***	7.819***	-5.260***	8.269***	8.079***	8.131***	-6.297***
	(0.0385)	(0.0496)	(0.0660)	(0.359)	(0.0888)	(0.111)	(0.106)	(0.800)	(0.0579)	(0.0825)	(0.115)	(0.489)
Observations	2 777	2 777	2 777	2 772	426	426	426	426	1 326	1 326	1 326	1 325
R-squared	0.0291	0.0455	0.0456	0.464	0.0284	0.0510	0.122	0.417	0.0223	0.0391	0.0401	0.503
Cohort	Cohort 4				Cohort 5							
Female indicator	-0.472***	-0.467***	-0.475***	-0.0203	-0.348	-0.378*	-0.369	0.0372				
	(0.0989)	(0.0977)	(0.0988)	(0.0728)	(0.238)	(0.222)	(0.227)	(0.174)				
Years participating in occupational plan		0.0122**	0.0117**	-0.00120		-0.0213	-0.0227	-0.0229				
		(0.00588)	(0.00583)	(0.00377)		(0.0155)	(0.0165)	(0.0169)				
Whether person has children			-0.205	-0.0795			0.383	0.334				
			(0.139)	(0.105)			(0.559)	(0.600)				
Log of income				1.118***				1.045***				
				(0.0515)				(0.178)				
Constant	8.558***	8.402***	8.587***	-4.046***	8.506***	8.836***	8.529***	-3.271*				
	(0.0591)	(0.0909)	(0.157)	(0.591)	(0.182)	(0.177)	(0.426)	(1.744)				
Observations	830	830	830	827	195	195	195	194				
R-squared	0.0428	0.0532	0.0574	0.525	0.0139	0.0406	0.0493	0.226				

Note: Standard errors are reported in parentheses; *** p<0.01, ** p<0.05, * p<0.1. Cohort numbers refer to the following age groups: Cohort 1: All working age individuals; Cohort 2: individuals aged 15-29; Cohort 3: individuals aged 30-44; Cohort 4: individuals aged 45-59; Cohort 5: individuals aged 60-64. The dependent variable is the log level of voluntary contributions by individuals to occupational pension plans, of individuals who do make voluntary contributions. Independent variables are: female indicator; the number of years an individual has participated in the pension plan; whether the individual has children; and the log of the individual's gross employee income over the 12 months prior to the interview.

Source: OECD Secretariat calculations. Calculations were based on a sample of working age individuals (aged 15-64) from the 2017 PSID survey.

Annex Table 3.C.13. Drivers of gap in occupational pension assets or entitlements in Germany

	Cohort 1				Cohort 2				Cohort 3			
Female	-0.540**	-0.474**	-0.525**	-0.510**	-1.305	-1.306	-1.191	-1.179	-0.480	-0.543	-0.446	-0.401
	(0.257)	(0.239)	(0.256)	(0.246)	(1.088)	(1.150)	(1.271)	(1.268)	(0.382)	(0.371)	(0.389)	(0.403)
Tertiary educated		0.790***	0.770***	0.753***		0.508	0.580	0.578		0.818**	0.703*	0.708*
		(0.214)	(0.223)	(0.234)		(0.709)	(0.787)	(0.786)		(0.394)	(0.415)	(0.415)
Log total time in employment		1.033***	1.019***	0.988***		0.783	0.497	0.512		0.816	0.882*	0.887*
		(0.195)	(0.202)	(0.209)		(0.570)	(0.803)	(0.801)		(0.512)	(0.466)	(0.468)
Coupled			0.317	0.338			-0.370	-0.383			0.746*	0.759*
			(0.243)	(0.242)			(1.163)	(1.159)			(0.400)	(0.400)
Interaction: Employee * Employment income			0.0233				0.135				0.148	
			(0.0628)				(0.442)				(0.0945)	
Interaction: Working (employee or self employed) * Total income				0.0703				0.125				0.184
				(0.0470)				(0.403)				(0.126)
Constant	8.823***	5.265***	4.915***	4.501***	7.279***	5.614***	4.838	4.907	8.609***	5.937***	3.754**	3.327*
	(0.134)	(0.604)	(0.825)	(0.717)	(0.353)	(1.125)	(4.202)	(3.800)	(0.210)	(1.523)	(1.658)	(1.911)
R-squared	0.0192	0.152	0.167	0.169	0.0924	0.145	0.175	0.173	0.0186	0.0760	0.134	0.138
	Cohort 4				Cohort 5							
Female	-0.447*	-0.401	-0.440	-0.400	-0.810	-0.426	-0.209	-0.203				
	(0.269)	(0.265)	(0.325)	(0.278)	(0.736)	(0.723)	(0.873)	(0.887)				
Tertiary educated		0.224	0.261	0.190		2.315***	2.033***	2.110***				
		(0.301)	(0.293)	(0.332)		(0.535)	(0.495)	(0.517)				
Log total time in employment		-0.959	-0.751	-0.875		1.035	0.545	0.547				
		(0.617)	(0.628)	(0.641)		(1.868)	(2.077)	(2.171)				
Coupled			-0.187	-0.151			1.138	1.154				
			(0.354)	(0.314)			(0.995)	(0.992)				
Interaction: Employee * Employment income			0.0390				-0.0553					
			(0.0964)				(0.0679)					
Interaction: Working (employee or self employed) * Total income				0.177**				-0.0505				
				(0.0893)				(0.106)				
Constant	9.218***	12.43***	11.49***	10.42***	9.432***	4.596	6.048	5.996				
	(0.213)	(2.049)	(2.430)	(2.615)	(0.459)	(6.974)	(7.690)	(7.954)				

R-squared	0.0155	0.0349	0.0461	0.0640	0.0291	0.342	0.416	0.411			

Note: Standard errors are reported in parentheses; *** p<0.01, ** p<0.05, * p<0.1. Cohort numbers refer to the following age groups: Cohort 1: All working age individuals; Cohort 2: individuals aged 15-29; Cohort 3: individuals aged 30-44; Cohort 4: individuals aged 45-59; Cohort 5: individuals aged 60-64. The dependent variable is the log current value of all occupational plans, for individuals for have occupational plans. Independent variables are: female indicator; whether an individual completed tertiary education; the log number of years an individuals has worked for all or most of the year; whether an individual is coupled; an interaction term between an indicator of whether a person was working as an employee and the log of the individual's gross employee income over the 12 months prior to the interview.
Source: OECD Secretariat calculations. Calculations were based on a sample of working age individuals (aged 15-64) from the HFCS Wave 2 data. Data relate to survey responses collected between 2013 and 2015.

Annex Table 3.C.14. Drivers of gap in occupational pension plan entitlements in Finland

	Cohort 1				Cohort 2				Cohort 3			
Female	-0.002	-0.126***	-0.135***	-0.102***	0.302***	0.242***	0.238***	0.221***	-0.121***	-0.198***	-0.209***	-0.0937***
	(0.0246)	(0.0188)	(0.0189)	(0.0174)	(0.0568)	(0.0488)	(0.0486)	(0.0397)	(0.0403)	(0.0351)	(0.0344)	(0.0342)
Tertiary educated		0.535***	0.515***	0.326***		0.185***	0.181***	-0.123***		0.426***	0.420***	0.219***
		(0.0182)	(0.0178)	(0.0163)		(0.0643)	(0.0643)	(0.0473)		(0.0352)	(0.0343)	(0.0275)
Log age		4.840***	4.712***	4.868***		8.552***	8.531***	7.956***		4.271***	4.173***	3.969***
		(0.0315)	(0.0397)	(0.0354)		(0.226)	(0.242)	(0.211)		(0.166)	(0.181)	(0.145)
Coupled			0.202***	0.106***			0.0835	0.144***			0.130***	0.0883***
			(0.0269)	(0.0233)			(0.0710)	(0.0522)			(0.0406)	(0.0329)
Previously coupled			0.126***	0.0927**			-0.762**	-0.0781			0.173*	0.180**
			(0.0410)	(0.0382)			(0.368)	(0.193)			(0.0962)	(0.0874)
Interaction: Working (employee or self employed) * Total income				0.105***				0.222***				0.141***
				(0.00395)				(0.0116)				(0.0123)
Constant	10.28***	-7.645***	-7.270***	-8.628***	7.487***	-19.53***	-19.46***	-19.41***	10.14***	-5.366***	-5.085***	-5.593***
	(0.0168)	(0.121)	(0.140)	(0.135)	(0.0429)	(0.705)	(0.751)	(0.639)	(0.0319)	(0.595)	(0.636)	(0.502)
R-squared	0.0000	0.777	0.779	0.814	0.00757	0.549	0.551	0.709	0.00298	0.290	0.294	0.453
	Cohort 4				Cohort 5							
Female	-0.168***	-0.251***	-0.263***	-0.263***	-0.105**	-0.134***	-0.156***	-0.152***				
	(0.0290)	(0.0273)	(0.0272)	(0.0255)	(0.0477)	(0.0459)	(0.0443)	-0.0439				
Tertiary educated		0.441***	0.422***	0.331***		0.543***	0.514***	0.468***				
		(0.0274)	(0.0269)	(0.0244)		(0.0425)	(0.0400)	-0.0387				
Log age		4.339***	4.224***	4.603***		4.374***	4.244***	5.613***				
		(0.171)	(0.171)	(0.170)		(1.008)	(0.962)	-0.985				
Coupled			0.232***	0.124***			0.397***	0.356***				

			(0.0441)	(0.0384)			(0.103)	-0.0995				
Previously coupled			0.206***	0.143***			0.332***	0.306***				
			(0.0525)	(0.0489)			(0.116)	-0.112				
Interaction: Working (employee or self employed) * Total income				0.0651***				0.0290***				
				(0.00643)				-0.00485				
Constant	11.63***	-5.607***	-5.316***	-7.276***	12.30***	-5.896	-5.664	-11.44***				
	(0.0196)	(0.677)	(0.674)	(0.694)	(0.0361)	(4.179)	(4.004)	-4.114				
R-squared	0.00923	0.239	0.252	0.323	0.00413	0.106	0.133	0.16				

Note: Standard errors are reported in parentheses; *** p<0.01, ** p<0.05, * p<0.1. Cohort numbers refer to the following age groups: Cohort 1: All working age individuals; Cohort 2: individuals aged 15-29; Cohort 3: individuals aged 30-44; Cohort 4: individuals aged 45-59; Cohort 5: individuals aged 60-64. The dependent variable is the log current value of all occupational plans, for individuals for have occupational plans. Independent variables are: female indicator; whether an individual completed tertiary education; the age of an individual (this was used because, unlike the case for Germany, the variable representing the number of years an individuals has worked for all or most of the year was not available in the data); whether an individual was coupled; whether an individual was previously coupled (divorced or widowed); an interaction term between an indicator of whether a person was working either as an employee or self-employed and the log of the individual's gross income over the 12 months prior to the interview.
Source: OECD Secretariat calculations. Calculations were based on a sample of working age individuals (aged 15-64) from the HFCS Wave 2 data. Data relate to survey responses collected between 2013 and 2015.

Annex Table 3.C.15. Drivers of gap in occupational pension plan entitlements for single individuals in Finland

	Cohort 1				Cohort 2				Cohort 3			
Female	0.0386	-0.166***	0.116***	0.084***	0.186***	0.0257	0.238***	0.196***	0.0918	0.0101	0.0113	-0.030
	(0.0543)	(0.0537)	(0.0365)	(0.0317)	(0.0555)	(0.0581)	(0.0459)	(0.0382)	(0.0688)	(0.0649)	(0.0616)	(0.0544)
Tertiary educated		1.386***	0.593***	0.261***		1.581***	0.325***	0.0206		0.170**	0.438***	0.318***
		(0.0625)	(0.0398)	(0.0354)		(0.0628)	(0.0592)	(0.0452)		(0.0707)	(0.0597)	(0.0536)
Log age			4.978***	5.157***			7.175***	6.716***			3.794***	3.564***
			(0.0584)	(0.0513)			(0.164)	(0.146)			(0.183)	(0.213)
Interaction: Working (employee or self employed) * Total income				0.167***				0.220***				0.0926***
				(0.00780)				(0.0113)				(0.0111)
Constant	9.076***	8.798***	-8.325***	-10.20***	7.810***	7.530***	-15.30***	-15.57***	10.88***	10.88***	-3.778***	-3.612***
	(0.0397)	(0.0457)	(0.204)	(0.188)	(0.0423)	(0.0470)	(0.520)	(0.446)	(0.0526)	(0.0575)	(0.726)	(0.905)
R-squared	7.74e-05	0.0811	0.722	0.795	0.00264	0.141	0.582	0.723	0.00137	0.00479	0.311	0.344

Note: The table shows regression results based on the single population, to explore whether career breaks in Finland could be a cause of a gender gap in occupational plan entitlements. Conducting the analysis on single people is a crude way to examine the effect of career breaks since the most common reason for a career break that differs between genders is taking time off for parenting. The single population, which excludes people in civil unions, married people, and divorced people, is an imperfect proxy for people who have not had children, but the results are still informative. Standard errors are reported in parentheses; *** p<0.01, ** p<0.05, * p<0.1. Cohort numbers refer to the following age groups: Cohort 1: All single working age individuals; Cohort 2: single individuals aged 15-29; Cohort 3: single individuals aged 30-44; Cohort 4: single individuals aged 45-59; Cohort 5: single individuals aged 60-64. The dependent variable is the log current value of all occupational plans, for individuals for have occupational plans. Independent variables are: female indicator; whether an individual completed tertiary education; the age of an individual; an interaction term between an indicator of whether a person was working either as an employee or self-employed and the log of the individual's gross income over the 12 months prior to the interview.
Source: OECD Secretariat calculations. Calculations were based on a sample of working age individuals (aged 15-64) from the HFCS Wave 2 data for Finland. Data relate to survey responses collected between 2013 and 2015.

Annex Table 3.C.16. Results from logistic regressions: odds ratios predicting personal pension plan coverage in Germany

	Cohort 1				Cohort 2				Cohort 3			
Female	0.926	1.057	0.955	1.182**	0.863	1.061	0.859	1.084	1.214	1.416**	1.196	1.672***
	(0.814-1.055)	(0.922-1.212)	(0.835-1.091)	(1.032-1.354)	(0.624-1.194)	(0.739-1.523)	(0.613-1.203)	(0.756-1.552)	(0.943-1.562)	(1.062-1.887)	(0.925-1.546)	(1.248-2.240)
Tertiary educated		1.860***	1.965***	1.550***		1.270	1.942**	1.255		1.584***	1.673***	1.399**
		(1.541-2.246)	(1.631-2.368)	(1.274-1.886)		(0.722-2.235)	(1.137-3.315)	(0.710-2.217)		(1.169-2.146)	(1.252-2.236)	(1.030-1.901)
Interaction: Employee * Employment income		1.117***				1.222***				1.111***		
		(1.097-1.138)				(1.156-1.292)				(1.071-1.153)		
Interaction: Self Employed * Self-employment income			1.044***				1.011				1.037	
			(1.015-1.074)				(0.903-1.131)				(0.981-1.095)	
Interaction: Working (employee or self employed) * Total income				1.175***				1.234***				1.178***
				(1.147-1.204)				(1.162-1.310)				(1.123-1.235)
Constant	0.886**	0.314***	0.700***	0.191***	0.419***	0.0927***	0.381***	0.0833***	1.116	0.385***	0.926	0.207***
	(0.792-0.992)	(0.258-0.382)	(0.609-0.803)	(0.149-0.245)	(0.334-0.526)	(0.055-0.155)	(0.296-0.489)	(0.0483-0.144)	(0.905-1.375)	(0.256-0.578)	(0.732-1.172)	(0.125-0.342)
Observations	6 355	6 300	6 291	6 298	1 470	1 459	1 458	1 459	1 481	1 465	1 462	1 465
	Cohort 4				Cohort 5							
Female	0.774**	0.843	0.823*	0.912	0.727	0.817	0.757	0.881				
	(0.630-0.950)	(0.677-1.050)	(0.666-1.018)	(0.730-1.141)	(0.482-1.096)	(0.519-1.287)	(0.489-1.172)	(0.553-1.404)				
Tertiary educated		1.873***	1.827***	1.613***		1.108	1.060	0.970				
		(1.418-2.476)	(1.372-2.432)	(1.212-2.145)		(0.670-1.833)	(0.610-1.842)	(0.572-1.644)				
Interaction: Employee * Employment income		1.062***				1.084***						
		(1.033-1.093)				(1.035-1.135)						
			1.035*				1.038					

Interaction: Self Employed * Self-employment income			(0.995-1.076)				(0.968-1.113)	
Interaction: Working (employee or self employed) * Total income				1.118***				1.101***
				(1.076-1.162)				(1.046-1.158)
Constant	1.345***	0.676**	1.044	0.411***	0.586***	0.337***	0.545***	0.287***
	(1.141-1.586)	(0.499-0.915)	(0.854-1.278)	(0.275-0.615)	(0.429-0.802)	(0.200-0.567)	(0.363-0.816)	(0.162-0.506)
Observations	2 545	2 521	2 517	2 520	859	855	854	854

Note: Confidence intervals are reported in parentheses; *** p<0.01, ** p<0.05, * p<0.1. Cohort numbers refer to the following age groups: Cohort 1: All working age individuals (aged 15-64); Cohort 2: individuals aged 15-29; Cohort 3: individuals aged 30-44; Cohort 4: individuals aged 45-59; Cohort 5: individuals aged 60-64. The dependent variable is an indicator variable of whether the individual is covered by a personal pension plan. Independent variables are: female indicator; whether the individual has a tertiary education; interaction terms of: log income from employment * indicator that the individual was employed; log income from self-employment * indicator that the individual was self-employed; log income from work (total of employment and self-employment income)* indicator that an individual was either employed or self-employed.
Source: OECD Secretariat calculations. Calculations were based on a sample of working age individuals (aged 15-64) from the HFCS Wave 2 data. Data relate to survey responses collected between 2013 and 2015.

Annex Table 3.C.17. Results from logistic regressions: odds ratios predicting personal pension plan coverage in Finland

	Cohort 1				Cohort 2				Cohort 3			
Female	1.228***	1.129***	1.179***	1.250***	1.325	1.243	1.336	1.365	1.140*	1.099	1.200**	1.250***
	(1.135-1.330)	(1.041-1.226)	(1.084-1.281)	(1.147-1.364)	(0.892-1.967)	(0.834-1.851)	(0.913-1.955)	(0.891-2.091)	(0.984-1.320)	(0.945-1.277)	(1.027-1.402)	(1.067-1.465)
Tertiary educated		2.003***	1.594***	1.256***		1.866***	0.950	0.551**		1.255***	1.082	0.968
		(1.824-2.199)	(1.439-1.765)	(1.134-1.391)		(1.200-2.902)	(0.574-1.572)	(0.344-0.883)		(1.057-1.490)	(0.905-1.294)	(0.807-1.159)
Interaction: Working (employee or self employed) * Total income			1.130***	1.088***			1.547**	1.006			1.105***	1.031
			(1.108-1.153)	(1.069-1.108)			(1.084-2.208)	(0.866-1.167)			(1.066-1.145)	(0.994-1.070)
Log occupational plan entitlements				1.440***				3.455***				1.527***
				(1.395-1.486)				(2.513-4.750)				(1.375-1.695)
Constant	0.226***	0.180***	0.0667***	0.00214***	0.0434***	0.0394***	0.000962***	1.51e-06***	0.310***	0.282***	0.115***	0.00307***
	(0.212-0.240)	(0.168-0.194)	(0.055-0.080)	(0.001-0.003)	(0.033-0.057)	(0.029-0.053)	(0.000-0.029)	(0.000-0.000)	(0.277-0.346)	(0.247-0.322)	(0.080-0.165)	(0.001-0.009)
Observations	17 602	17 602	17 602	4 402	4 402	4 402	4 609	4 609	4 609	17 602	17 602	17 602
	Cohort 4				Cohort 5							
Female	1.337***	1.252***	1.261***	1.331***	1.094	1.051	1.056	1.111				
	(1.187-1.506)	(1.109-1.414)	(1.115-1.425)	(1.177-1.505)	(0.865-1.384)	(0.827-1.335)	(0.830-1.343)	(0.870-1.418)				
Tertiary educated		1.708***	1.496***	1.386***		2.019***	1.814***	1.494***				
		(1.481-1.970)	(1.290-1.736)	(1.189-1.615)		(1.565-2.606)	(1.398-2.354)	(1.129-1.976)				
Interaction: Working (employee or self employed) * Total income			1.097***	1.078***			1.066***	1.055***				
			(1.066-1.128)	(1.048-1.109)			(1.036-1.096)	(1.025-1.085)				
Log occupational plan entitlements				1.277***				1.543***				
				(1.159-1.408)				(1.230-1.936)				
Constant	0.348***	0.290***	0.132***	0.00908***	0.227***	0.183***	0.127***	0.000675***				
	(0.316-0.383)	(0.258-0.325)	(0.010-0.173)	(0.003-0.028)	(0.193-0.267)	(0.151-0.222)	(0.097-0.168)	(0.000-0.011)				
Observations	6 410	6 410	6 410	6 379	2 181	2 181	2 181	2 171				

Note: Confidence intervals are reported in parentheses; *** p<0.01, ** p<0.05, * p<0.1. Cohort numbers refer to the following age groups: Cohort 1: All working age individuals (aged 15-64); Cohort 2: individuals aged 15-29; Cohort 3: individuals aged 30-44; Cohort 4: individuals aged 45-59; Cohort 5: individuals aged 60-64. The dependent variable is an indicator variable of whether the individual is covered by a personal pension plan. Independent variables are: female indicator; whether the individual has a tertiary education; an interaction terms of log income from work (total of employment and self-employment income) * indicator that an individual was either employed or self-employed; the log value of occupational pension plan entitlements.

Source: OECD Secretariat calculations. Calculations were based on a sample of working age individuals (aged 15-64) from the HFCS Wave 2 data. Data relate to survey responses collected between 2013 and 2015.

Annex Table 3.C.18. Drivers of gap in personal pension plan assets in Germany

	Cohort 1				Cohort 2				Cohort 3			
Female	-0.385***	-0.160**	-0.0844	-0.0849	-0.696**	-0.693***	-0.408	-0.402	-0.0680	0.0789	0.166	0.164
	(0.0880)	(0.0789)	(0.0852)	(0.0865)	(0.306)	(0.257)	(0.270)	(0.276)	(0.140)	(0.127)	(0.133)	(0.133)
Tertiary educated		0.838***	0.824***	0.806***		1.802***	1.733***	1.710***		0.909***	0.841***	0.821***
		(0.0943)	(0.0975)	(0.0985)		(0.471)	(0.436)	(0.473)		(0.154)	(0.157)	(0.152)
Log total time in employment		1.157***	1.236***	1.231***		0.986***	0.920***	0.913***		1.014***	1.023***	1.009***
		(0.0742)	(0.0770)	(0.0780)		(0.261)	(0.247)	(0.257)		(0.163)	(0.159)	(0.159)
Coupled			-0.292***	-0.290***			-0.622*	-0.628*			-0.207	-0.213
			(0.111)	(0.112)			(0.360)	(0.358)			(0.160)	(0.161)
Previously coupled			-0.543***	-0.551***			0.590**	0.485			-0.895***	-0.900***
			(0.151)	(0.156)			(0.269)	(0.424)			(0.261)	(0.264)
Interaction: Working (employee or self employed) * Total income			0.0353**	0.0345*			0.120**	0.118**			0.0554**	0.0535**
			(0.0177)	(0.0202)			(0.0583)	(0.0596)			(0.0249)	(0.0254)
Interaction: Value of occupational plan * has occupational plan				0.0174*				0.0163				0.0119
				(0.0103)				(0.0561)				(0.0166)
Constant	9.208***	5.362***	5.017***	5.018***	7.609***	5.418***	4.544***	4.561***	8.806***	5.642***	5.259***	5.308***
	(0.0704)	(0.248)	(0.311)	(0.316)	(0.201)	(0.549)	(0.706)	(0.726)	(0.103)	(0.494)	(0.521)	(0.520)
R-squared	0.0151	0.347	0.361	0.366	0.0424	0.330	0.410	0.410	0.000706	0.172	0.227	0.228
	Cohort 4				Cohort 5							
Female	-0.446***	-0.357***	-0.315**	-0.322**	-0.159	0.124	0.173	0.288				
	(0.124)	(0.132)	(0.133)	(0.135)	(0.251)	(0.252)	(0.314)	(0.347)				
Tertiary educated		0.481***	0.424***	0.436***		0.819***	0.789***	0.658***				
		(0.124)	(0.126)	(0.126)		(0.212)	(0.224)	(0.236)				
Log total time in employment		0.704***	0.623***	0.665***		0.887**	0.915**	1.005*				
		(0.211)	(0.227)	(0.228)		(0.429)	(0.465)	(0.543)				
Coupled			-0.415***	-0.381**			-0.227	-0.222				
			(0.151)	(0.153)			(0.493)	(0.714)				
Previously coupled			-0.562***	-0.540***			-0.322	-0.383				
			(0.192)	(0.200)			(0.574)	(0.744)				
Interaction: Working (employee or self employed) * Total income			0.0461	0.0360			-0.00406	0.000533				
			(0.0324)	(0.0342)			(0.0347)	(0.0523)				

Interaction: Value of occupational plan * has occupational plan				0.0146				0.00732				
				(0.0151)				(0.0294)				
Constant	0.0280	0.0751	0.0997	0.1000	0.00405	0.187	0.187	0.209				
	-0.446***	-0.357***	-0.315**	-0.322**	-0.159	0.124	0.173	0.288				
R-squared	(0.124)	(0.132)	(0.133)	(0.135)	(0.251)	(0.252)	(0.314)	(0.347)				

Note: Standard errors are reported in parentheses; *** p<0.01, ** p<0.05, * p<0.1. Cohort numbers refer to the following age groups: Cohort 1: All working age individuals (aged 15-64); Cohort 2: individuals aged 15-29; Cohort 3: individuals aged 30-44; Cohort 4: individuals aged 45-59; Cohort 5: individuals aged 60-64. The dependent variable is the log current value of personal plans, for individuals for have personal plans. Independent variables are: female indicator; whether an individual completed tertiary education; the log of the total time they spent in employment; whether an individual was coupled; whether an individual was previously coupled (divorced or widowed); an interaction term between an indicator of whether a person was working either as an employee or self-employed and the log of the individual's gross income over the 12 months prior to the interview; an interaction term between an indicator of whether a person had an occupational pension plan and the log value of that plan.
Source: OECD Secretariat calculations. Calculations were based on a sample of working age individuals (aged 15-64) from the HFCS Wave 2 data. Data relate to survey responses collected between 2013 and 2015.

Annex Table 3.C.19. Drivers of gap in contributions to personal pension plans in Germany

	Cohort 1				Cohort 2				Cohort 3			
Female	-0.423***	-0.330***	-0.309***	-0.262***	-0.643***	-0.712***	-0.669***	-0.634***	-0.291***	-0.218**	-0.195**	-0.119
	(0.0559)	(0.0535)	(0.0548)	(0.0604)	(0.163)	(0.157)	(0.170)	(0.177)	(0.0941)	(0.0913)	(0.0939)	(0.0939)
Tertiary educated		0.607***	0.614***	0.524***		0.825***	0.847***	0.739***		0.597***	0.594***	0.481***
		(0.0717)	(0.0717)	(0.0691)		(0.225)	(0.210)	(0.225)		(0.118)	(0.118)	(0.116)
Log total time in employment		0.437***	0.480***	0.420***		0.378***	0.406***	0.296**		0.321***	0.358***	0.239**
		(0.0520)	(0.0583)	(0.0553)		(0.104)	(0.112)	(0.121)		(0.123)	(0.128)	(0.120)
Coupled			-0.136	-0.0796			-0.229	-0.0969			-0.196*	-0.142
			(0.0950)	(0.0946)			(0.262)	(0.267)			(0.115)	(0.115)
Previously coupled			-0.227*	-0.163			0.215	-0.233			-0.350	-0.301
			(0.116)	(0.117)			(0.687)	(0.871)			(0.221)	(0.201)
Interaction: Working (employee or self employed) * Total income				0.0672***				0.0704				0.0787***
				(0.0149)				(0.0541)				(0.0226)
Interaction: Value of occupational plan * has occupational plan				0.0236***				0.0775***				0.00740
				(0.00900)				(0.0289)				(0.0149)
Constant	4.491***	2.962***	2.928***	2.419***	3.790***	2.977***	2.956***	2.434***	4.432***	3.311***	3.339***	2.880***
	(0.0452)	(0.179)	(0.181)	(0.217)	(0.125)	(0.252)	(0.245)	(0.450)	(0.0742)	(0.371)	(0.383)	(0.392)
R-squared	0.0339	0.169	0.172	0.212	0.0809	0.213	0.220	0.270	0.0181	0.0849	0.0945	0.138

	Cohort 4				Cohort 5			
Female	-0.503***	-0.418***	-0.404***	-0.386***	-0.204	-0.141	-0.152	0.0489
	(0.0938)	(0.101)	(0.104)	(0.103)	(0.174)	(0.231)	(0.253)	(0.324)
Tertiary educated		0.466***	0.470***	0.366***		0.558***	0.564***	0.419*
		(0.0951)	(0.0946)	(0.0948)		(0.209)	(0.219)	(0.228)
Log total time in employment		0.316*	0.325*	0.136		0.374	0.371	0.159
		(0.183)	(0.182)	(0.203)		(0.416)	(0.429)	(0.376)
Coupled			-0.148	-0.151			0.120	0.511
			(0.181)	(0.176)			(0.410)	(0.624)
Previously coupled			-0.236	-0.184			0.129	0.206
			(0.192)	(0.195)			(0.515)	(0.709)
Interaction: Working (employee or self employed) * Total income				0.0335***				-0.0173
				(0.0117)				(0.0298)
Interaction: Value of occupational plan * has occupational plan	4.759***	3.477***	3.580***	3.492***	4.511***	2.980*	2.883*	2.588
	(0.0665)	(0.662)	(0.650)	(0.702)	(0.140)	(1.596)	(1.613)	(1.662)
Constant	0.0509	0.0969	0.101	0.157	0.00833	0.0865	0.0873	0.146
	-0.503***	-0.418***	-0.404***	-0.386***	-0.204	-0.141	-0.152	0.0489
R-squared	(0.0938)	(0.101)	(0.104)	(0.103)	(0.174)	(0.231)	(0.253)	(0.324)

Note: Standard errors are reported in parentheses; *** p<0.01, ** p<0.05, * p<0.1. Cohort numbers refer to the following age groups: Cohort 1: All working age individuals (aged 15-64); Cohort 2: individuals aged 15-29; Cohort 3: individuals aged 30-44; Cohort 4: individuals aged 45-59; Cohort 5: individuals aged 60-64. The dependent variable is the log value of contributions to personal plans, for individuals for have personal plans. Independent variables are: female indicator; whether an individual completed tertiary education; the log of the total time they spent in employment; whether an individual was coupled; whether an individual was previously coupled (divorced or widowed); an interaction term between an indicator of whether a person was working either as an employee or self-employed and the log of the individual's gross income over the 12 months prior to the interview; an interaction term between an indicator of whether a person had an occupational pension plan and the log value of that plan.
Source: OECD Secretariat calculations. Calculations were based on a sample of working age individuals (aged 15-64) from the HFCS Wave 2 data. Data relate to survey responses collected between 2013 and 2015.

Annex Table 3.C.20. Drivers of gap in personal pension plan assets in Finland

	Cohort 1				Cohort 2				Cohort 3			
Female	-0.153**	-0.227***	-0.217***	-0.180***	-0.0287	0.0387	0.0859	0.0190	-0.304***	-0.394***	-0.384***	-0.327***
	(0.0609)	(0.0567)	(0.0561)	(0.0578)	(0.260)	(0.268)	(0.270)	(0.281)	(0.100)	(0.102)	(0.102)	(0.105)
Tertiary educated		0.545***	0.556***	0.492***		0.0822	0.0403	0.0881		0.544***	0.555***	0.499***
		(0.0640)	(0.0652)	(0.0654)		(0.289)	(0.289)	(0.289)		(0.115)	(0.117)	(0.119)
Log age		2.665***	2.785***	2.870***		3.579***	3.926***	3.692**		3.569***	3.645***	3.274***
		(0.133)	(0.137)	(0.144)		(1.331)	(1.415)	(1.869)		(0.441)	(0.427)	(0.438)
Coupled			-0.174**	-0.220***			-0.191	-0.206			-0.145	-0.133
			(0.0792)	(0.0803)			(0.269)	(0.287)			(0.119)	(0.117)
Previously coupled			-0.179*	-0.188*			-2.220***	-2.338**			-0.0721	-0.0236
			(0.105)	(0.106)			(0.374)	(1.112)			(0.210)	(0.213)
Interaction: Working (employee or self employed) * Total income				0.0463***				-0.0515				0.0373
				(0.0142)				(0.103)				(0.0239)
Constant	8.358***	-1.987***	-2.325***	-3.427***	6.527***	-5.233	-6.318	-5.338	8.037***	-5.109***	-5.308***	-5.001***
	(0.0471)	(0.506)	(0.512)	(0.532)	(0.212)	(4.343)	(4.599)	(5.535)	(0.0688)	(1.596)	(1.547)	(1.561)
R-squared	0.00221	0.194	0.196	0.219	0.000110	0.0559	0.0822	0.0863	0.0110	0.134	0.136	0.150
	Cohort 4				Cohort 5							
Female	-0.183**	-0.221***	-0.193***	-0.165**	0.259	0.296*	0.228	0.218				
	(0.0772)	(0.0758)	(0.0744)	(0.0756)	(0.180)	(0.173)	(0.169)	(0.203)				
Tertiary educated		0.449***	0.446***	0.418***		0.897***	0.902***	0.836***				
		(0.0826)	(0.0830)	(0.0836)		(0.179)	(0.182)	(0.223)				
Log age		2.920***	3.077***	3.103***		-12.03***	-11.64***	-9.408*				
		(0.481)	(0.474)	(0.468)		(4.214)	(4.179)	(5.317)				
Coupled			-0.268**	-0.331***			-0.104	-0.330				
			(0.112)	(0.115)			(0.283)	(0.379)				
Previously coupled			-0.454***	-0.471***			0.403	0.465				
			(0.137)	(0.139)			(0.312)	(0.423)				
Interaction: Working (employee or self employed) * Total income				0.0472**				0.0564				
				(0.0209)				(0.0427)				
Constant	8.819***	-2.889	-3.258*	-3.981**	8.615***	57.88***	56.29***	46.44**				

	(0.0595)	(1.898)	(1.873)	(1.848)	(0.151)	(17.39)	(17.24)	(22.00)				
R-squared	0.00379	0.0495	0.0582	0.0689	0.00500	0.0900	0.102	0.159				

Note:. Standard errors are reported in parentheses; *** p<0.01, ** p<0.05, * p<0.1. Cohort numbers refer to the following age groups: Cohort 1: All working age individuals (aged 15-64); Cohort 2: individuals aged 15-29; Cohort 3: individuals aged 30-44; Cohort 4: individuals aged 45-59; Cohort 5: individuals aged 60-64. The dependent variable is the log current value of all personal plans, for individuals for have personal plans. Independent variables are: female indicator; whether an individual completed tertiary education; the log of an individual's age (as time spent in employment was not available) ; whether an individual was coupled; whether an individual was previously coupled (divorced or widowed); an interaction term between an indicator of whether a person was working either as an employee or self-employed and the log of the individual's gross income over the 12 months prior to the interview.
Source: OECD Secretariat calculations. Calculations were based on a sample of working age individuals (aged 15-64) from the HFCS Wave 2 data. Data relate to survey responses collected between 2013 and 2015

Annex Table 3.C.21. Drivers of gap in contributions to personal pension plans assets in Finland

	Cohort 1				Cohort 2				Cohort 3			
Female	-0.144***	-0.188***	-0.182***	-0.162***	-0.349	-0.303	-0.287	-0.356	-0.151**	-0.219***	-0.211***	-0.192***
	(0.0464)	(0.0424)	(0.0429)	(0.0431)	(0.257)	(0.247)	(0.250)	(0.270)	(0.0621)	(0.0642)	(0.0646)	(0.0671)
Tertiary educated		0.188***	0.193***	0.172***		0.352	0.362	0.381		0.252***	0.264***	0.251***
		(0.0471)	(0.0470)	(0.0466)		(0.308)	(0.311)	(0.306)		(0.0747)	(0.0740)	(0.0758)
Log age		1.789***	1.863***	1.846***		2.783**	2.944**	1.956		1.633***	1.651***	1.550***
		(0.117)	(0.123)	(0.127)		(1.190)	(1.298)	(1.944)		(0.315)	(0.313)	(0.314)
Coupled			-0.0803	-0.0822			-0.218	-0.169			-0.120	-0.116
			(0.0571)	(0.0577)			(0.307)	(0.323)			(0.0762)	(0.0758)
Previously coupled			-0.137*	-0.145*							0.0226	0.0251
			(0.0828)	(0.0829)							(0.144)	(0.145)
Interaction: Working (employee or self employed) * Total income				0.0256*				-0.0379				0.0170
				(0.0135)				(0.144)				(0.0188)
Interaction: Value of occupational plan * has occupational plan				0.00598				0.108				0.0136
				(0.0108)				(0.185)				(0.0234)
Constant	4.086***	-2.720***	-2.941***	-3.194***	3.324***	-5.863	-6.350	-3.692	3.830***	-2.190*	-2.204*	-2.152*
	Cohort 4				Cohort 5							
Female	-0.144***	-0.129**	-0.126**	-0.116**	-0.181	-0.293	-0.285	-0.242				
	(0.0550)	(0.0553)	(0.0554)	(0.0543)	(0.195)	(0.201)	(0.196)	(0.219)				
Tertiary educated		0.110*	0.103*	0.0871		0.498**	0.542***	0.462**				
		(0.0623)	(0.0616)	(0.0606)		(0.201)	(0.208)	(0.216)				
Log age		2.541***	2.560***	2.562***		1.959	1.675	8.100				

		(0.369)	(0.367)	(0.376)		(4.541)	(4.464)	(5.053)				
Coupled			0.00690	-0.00324			0.0147	-0.284				
			(0.0895)	(0.0920)			(0.259)	(0.459)				
Previously coupled			-0.113	-0.119			-0.346	-0.759				
			(0.117)	(0.117)			(0.341)	(0.541)				
Interaction: Working (employee or self employed) * Total income				0.0382**				0.0336				
				(0.0173)				(0.0582)				
Interaction: Value of occupational plan * has occupational plan				0.00325				-0.0136				
				(0.0154)				(0.0226)				
Constant	4.390***	-5.672***	-5.726***	-6.147***	4.671***	-3.549	-2.301	-28.53				

Note:. Standard errors are reported in parentheses; *** p<0.01, ** p<0.05, * p<0.1. Cohort numbers refer to the following age groups: Cohort 1: All working age individuals (aged 15-64); Cohort 2: individuals aged 15-29; Cohort 3: individuals aged 30-44; Cohort 4: individuals aged 45-59; Cohort 5: individuals aged 60-64. The dependent variable is the log value of contributions to personal plans, for individuals for have personal plans. Independent variables are: female indicator; whether an individual completed tertiary education; the log of an individual's age (as time spent in employment was not available) ; whether an individual was coupled; whether an individual was previously coupled (divorced or widowed); an interaction term between an indicator of whether a person was working either as an employee or self-employed and the log of the individual's gross income over the 12 months prior to the interview; an interaction term between an indicator of whether a person had an occupational pension plan and the log value of that plan.

Source: OECD Secretariat calculations. Calculations were based on a sample of working age individuals (aged 15-64) from the HFCS Wave 2 data. Data relate to survey responses collected between 2013 and 2015

Notes

[1] While some countries have an earnings related pay-as-you-go system that is a significant component of retirement income, it is not considered in this case study whose scope is limited to funded pension arrangements.

[2] https://www.hoganlovells.com/~/media/hogan-lovells/pdf/2019/2019_08_14_german_pension_schemes__client_note.pdf?la=en

[3] In German, these are known as: *Pensionsfonds*, *Pensionskassen*, *Pensionsrückstellungen*, *Direkte Pensionszusagen*, and *Direktversicherungen*.

[4] The regression results available in Annex 3.C show that the gender variable loses statistical significance as a predictor of coverage and eligibility when part-time work is included in the model.

[5] Kobe (2010[1]) also finds that in 2006 a lower percentage of women took up occupational plans when their employer offered one.

[6] As identified in Section 3.2, people commonly under-report pension coverage, particularly regarding workplace plans, in survey responses. This is likely the case in Germany. Data from Bundesministerium für Arbeit und Soziales (2020[9]) finds that while a gender gap in occupational plan coverage exists, the reported proportions of covered individuals was higher (54.7% of men and 53.0% of women reported having occupational pensions). Readers should note that the results reported in this chapter for Germany rely on Wave 2 of the HFCS data, while the results in Chapter 1 rely on Wave 3 of the HFCS data, which leads to a slight difference in reported outcomes.

[7] See OECD.Stat, Labour force participation rate, by sex and age group.

[8] Gender split by industry is available at OECD.Stat, Employment by activities and status.

[9] See OECD gender wage gap statistics, available at OECD (2021[7]).

[10] While it is not possible to use the data to compare the outcomes between East and West Germany, the academic literature points to a significant difference in the gender pension gap. Bundesministerium für Familie, Senioren (2016[6]) finds that in 2011 the gender pension gap was 61.4% in West Germany and 35.7% in East Germany.

[11] Data provided to the OECD by the Finnish authorities show that in 2018, there was almost no difference in the average career lengths of between men and women born in 1980.

[12] Another data source, Bundesministerium für Arbeit und Soziales (2020[9]), finds a relatively different outcome to the HFCS data - when it comes to Reister pension plans, it finds that proportionally more women had personal plans than men (33.6% compared with 26.1%).

[13] See OECD.Stat, Educational attainment and labour-force status.

[14] For instance, in the United States, couples may jointly decide to save primarily through one retirement plan. As such, the 'true' effect of the gap in retirement assets may in some ways be overstated. In the United States, a qualified domestic relations order (QDRO) recognizes joint marital ownership interests in certain types of retirement plan assets (e.g. 401(k) plans), and grants an "alternative payee" the right to part of the retirement benefits a former spouse earned through occupational plans. Thus, assets in occupational plans can be divided at divorce. Similarly, most occupational plans in the United States provide a survivor benefit to a widowed spouse of plan participants. Since women tend to live longer and earn less than men, it benefits women more often than men. To the extent that these rights and benefits are not fully accounted for in the face value figures of assets or entitlements accumulated, studies such as this one may overstate the effects of gender gaps.

[15] Other studies follow this same approach. See, for example (Cooper, Dynan and Rhodenhiser, 2019[4]).

[16] According to the HFCS questionnaire, the value of entitlements from these schemes is "*the present value of all expected future pension payments corresponding to this pension plan, taking into account both mortality and an actualisation rate to be specified in the metadata, and based on some assumptions*".

4 Gender implications of the design of retirement savings plans

This chapter explores the extent to which the design of retirement savings plans may widen or narrow the gender pension gap. It examines the rules and parameters of retirement savings plans in OECD countries with respect to enrolment, contributions, financial incentives, the accumulation of assets, the pay-out phase, and communication and financial education, to see whether these rules and parameters may affect men and women differently. It also provides case studies illustrating the potential impact of different initiatives to reduce the gender pension gap in retirement savings systems.

The gender gap in pensions has multiple causes, as the previous chapters of this publication show. Chapter 1 confirms the well-documented gap in pension income between men and women. This gap exists when considering total pension income, as well as the income received from retirement savings arrangements only. Chapter 2 identifies behavioural and cultural elements that could contribute to the gender gap in retirement income through a literature review. Chapter 3 finds that, in three case study countries, while labour market factors are important drivers of the gender gaps in retirement savings plans, so are factors such as job sector, when it affects access to a pension plan, and behavioural biases.

This chapter contributes to this research by assessing the gender implications of the design of retirement savings plans. It explores the extent to which the design of retirement savings plans may widen or narrow the gender pension gap. It analyses the different design features of retirement savings plans in OECD countries using a gender lens to see whether the rules and parameters of these plans may affect men and women differently. It also provides case studies illustrating the potential impact of different initiatives to reduce the gender pension gap due to retirement savings arrangements.

Several design features of retirement savings plans are not gender neutral and tend to disadvantage women, while others help to reduce the gender gap. Some of the rules of these plans may reduce women's capacity to join a plan, to contribute or accrue rights during periods of maternity or parental leave, to earn good returns on their investments, to get recognition upon divorce for the time spent caring for the family, to protect their purchasing power during retirement, or to get longevity risk protection when surviving their spouse. By contrast, selected policy initiatives can contribute to narrowing the gender gap in pensions, such as introducing automatic enrolment, allowing spouses to contribute or transfer rights and assets to each other's retirement savings plan, letting employers pay higher contributions on behalf of women, making survivor pensions the default option for couples, disregarding women's longer average life expectancy when calculating retirement benefits, and having specific financial incentives, communication and financial education initiatives targeting women.

This chapter includes six sections assessing the extent to which the design of retirement savings plans affects men and women differently. It analyses the rules and parameters of retirement savings plans in OECD countries with respect to enrolment, contributions, financial incentives, the accumulation of assets, the pay-out phase, and communication and financial education. The last section concludes.

4.1. Enrolment

This section analyses how the design of retirement savings plans may affect the enrolment of men and women into these plans differently. It shows that women may have more limited access to retirement savings plans than men, but that periods of maternity and parental leave usually do not affect their eligibility to join plans. Policies such as automatic enrolment can help reduce the gender gap in the participation in retirement savings plans.

Although pension funds cannot discriminate based on gender when it comes to plan access, certain eligibility criteria may disadvantage women compared to men. Across the OECD, nearly 70% of people in part-time employment are women. The proportion of women over all part-time workers ranges from 54% in Turkey to 80% in Luxembourg.[1] Therefore, eligibility criteria based on a minimum number of working hours or on a minimum income threshold may restrict women's ability to join retirement savings plans more than men's. These criteria can be found for occupational pension plans in Australia, Canada, Japan, Switzerland and the United Kingdom (minimum income thresholds), as well as in Japan and Korea (minimum number of working hours) (OECD, 2019[1]).

Periods of maternity and parental leave usually do not delay women's eligibility to join retirement savings plans. Countries tend to consider periods of maternity and parental leave as normal employment periods for the purpose of calculating waiting and vesting periods. Women usually take time off work during pregnancy and after the birth or adoption of a child. In most countries, this time off work is included in the years of employment as normal working periods. Therefore, even if waiting or vesting periods apply, the maternity leave would not delay enrolment into the plan or prevent the acquisition of pension contributions. For example, in the Netherlands, when the waiting or vesting period ends during the period of maternity or parental leave, the pension accrual starts during the period of maternity or parental leave. In the case of the United States, for vesting and eligibility purposes, but not for benefit accrual, an employee who is absent from work due to pregnancy or the birth or adoption of a child is treated as having completed the number of hours that would normally have been credited for the period, up to 501 hours of service.[2] This credit for hours of service during the absence is only used to determine if a break in service has occurred.[3] In some countries, however, maternity and parental leave may not count as working periods. In Japan for example, it depends on plan rules whether the parental and maternity leave periods are included in the service period. In Ireland, there is no entitlement to continue to accrue retirement benefits during parental leave (i.e. beyond the statutory maternity leave), but service before and after this type of leave must be treated as continuous.

Policies aiming at reaching high participation levels in general may help close the gap in plan participation between men and women. Women tend to participate less in retirement savings plans than men do. Chapter 1 shows that the proportion of women being members of a personal or occupational pension plan is lower than that of men in most European countries. There are some exceptions, however, such as in Finland where men and women participate equally to the mandatory occupational pension system. In addition, in the United Kingdom, automatic enrolment helped close the workplace pension participation gap between men and women (Box 4.1). In Australia, women's participation in the mandatory superannuation system increased along with their increased participation in the labour market. The proportion of all superannuation accounts that belong to women increased from 37% in 2004 to 46% in 2018.[4]

Box 4.1. Automatic enrolment can help close the gender gap in participation

The United Kingdom introduced automatic enrolment in October 2012 for all workers who were not already covered by a workplace pension scheme. Employers are required to enrol automatically their eligible workers into a qualifying workplace pension. Eligible workers are all employees aged 22 to state pension age and earning over GBP 10 000 per year.

The policy reversed the previous downward trend in participation rates in the private sector (Figure 4.1). In 2012, 42% of eligible private-sector employees participated in a workplace pension. By 2018, this proportion had jumped to 85%.

Figure 4.1. Percentage of private-sector eligible employees participating in a workplace pension by gender, 2003-2018

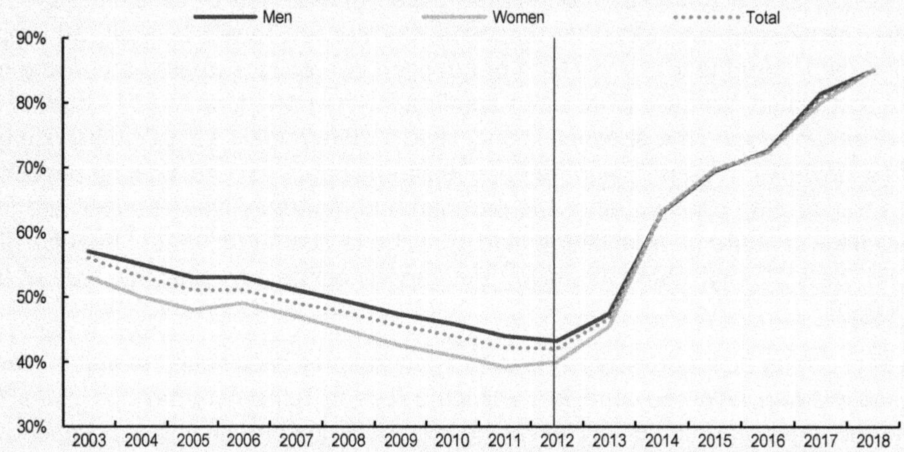

Source: DWP estimates derived from the ONS Annual Survey of Hours and Earnings.

StatLink https://doi.org/10.1787/888934230300

Automatic enrolment also closed the gap in participation between men and women. In 2012, there was a difference of three percentage points between eligible men and women working in the private sector in terms of participation. This difference fully disappeared by 2018.

The participation gap remains when looking at all employees, however. Because of the earnings threshold, women are less likely to be eligible for automatic enrolment than men. The gap between private-sector men and women in workplace pension participation barely changed between 2012 and 2018. In 2012, 26% of women and 36% of men were members of a workplace pension scheme. By 2018, participation rates had increased to 66% for women and 75% for men.[1] The difference between men and women has only declined by one percentage point. The earnings threshold prevents some part-time employees, most often women, from being enrolled automatically in a pension scheme by their employer.

1. ONS data, Annual Survey of Hours and Earnings, Table P2, "Pension type by industry and gross weekly earnings bands".

4.2. Contributions

This section explores the extent to which taking maternity or parental leave reduces women's contributions to retirement savings plans. It also looks at mechanisms to counter any negative impact on contributions for women, such as the possibility to contribute to a spouse's retirement savings plan, or to pay higher contributions on behalf of women to account for their higher life expectancy.

4.2.1. Contributions during maternity and parental leave

Contributions to retirement savings plans or pension right accruals may stop during periods of maternity or parental leave. This penalises women more than men, as fewer men take parental leave. Women would need to contribute more upon returning to work if they wish to compensate for the loss. Fortunately, in most countries with available information, contributions continue during maternity leave and/or parental leave. However, this is not the case in some countries (Table 4.1). In Australia, Austria, New Zealand and the United States, employers generally stop contributing on behalf of mothers on maternity leave. It depends on plan rules in Belgium, Denmark, Ireland and Slovenia.[5] In Australia, employers can pay superannuation contributions on parental leave payments on a voluntary basis. In New Zealand and the United States, only mothers benefiting from paid parental leave have their pension contributions paid during this period. In Austria, employees may contribute the employer's part, in addition to their own. In Belgium, when plan rules consider certain periods of inactivity as periods actually worked (such as maternity leave), the employer can either pay the contributions or take out a premium exemption insurance, in which case the insurance company pays the contributions during such periods.[6] In addition, in Lithuania, the social security institute stops collecting workers' contributions to the statutory voluntary personal pension system (second pillar) during periods of maternity leave.

Table 4.1. Pension contributions during maternity and parental leave in selected OECD countries

Country	Type of plan	Contributions continue	Financed by	Earnings base	Period covered
Australia	Mandatory occupational	No employer contribution (voluntary)			
Austria	Voluntary occupational	No employer contribution	Employee may pay the employer's part		
Belgium	Voluntary occupational	Depends on plan rules	Employer or insurance company		
Canada	Voluntary occupational	Yes	Employer and employee		Maternity leave
Chile	Mandatory personal	Yes	Employee	Average salary over previous 3 months up to 79.3 UF	24 weeks
Denmark	Quasi-mandatory occupational	Depends on plan rules			
Denmark	Mandatory personal	Yes	Employer and employee	Hourly rate × 2	Maternity, paternity, parental leave
Estonia	Mandatory personal	Yes	Government	Minimum wage	Up to 3 years /child
Finland	Mandatory occupational	No contributions paid but rights keep accruing	PAYG system	Parental allowance: 1.21 × previous year's earnings Child home care allowance: EUR 757.14 (2020)	Parental allowance: up to 10 months Chile home care allowance: until the child turns 3
Iceland	Mandatory occupational	Yes	Government	80% of salary up to ISK 520 000 /month	Maternity leave
Ireland	Voluntary occupational	Depends on plan rules	Employer and employee		Statutory maternity leave (26 weeks)
Japan	Voluntary occupational	Yes	Employer and employee		
Latvia	Mandatory personal	Yes	Government	Maternity or child care benefit	Up to 1.5 years
Lithuania	Automatic enrolment	No			
Luxembourg	Voluntary occupational	Yes	Employer and employee	Salary of the month before the leave	Maternity, parental leave

Country	Type of plan	Contributions continue	Financed by	Earnings base	Period covered
Mexico	Mandatory personal	Yes	Employer and employee		90 days
Netherlands	Quasi-mandatory occupational	Yes	Employer and employee		16 weeks
New Zealand	Automatic enrolment	No			
Norway	Mandatory occupational	Yes	Employer and employee	Salary	
Poland	Voluntary personal (OFE)	Yes	Social Security Institute	60% to 100% of salary	Maternity leave
Slovak Republic	Voluntary personal (second pillar)	Yes	Government	60% of the average wage in the economy	Maternity, parental leave
Slovenia	Voluntary occupational	Depends on plan rules			
Sweden	Quasi-mandatory occupational	Yes	Employer	Average earnings over previous 12 months	390 days
Sweden	Mandatory personal	Yes	Government	Parental benefit	Child's first 4 years
Switzerland	Mandatory occupational	Yes	Employer and employee		
United Kingdom	Automatic enrolment	Yes	Employer and employee		26 weeks
United States	Voluntary occupational	No			

Conditions for the payment of contributions during periods of maternity and parental leave may vary according to the type of retirement savings plan. For example, in the United Kingdom, in a defined benefit (DB) scheme, the member is entitled to have her benefits calculated for the period of paid maternity leave as if she had been working normally (which would include any increases to pensionable pay that would have applied to the member had she not been on maternity leave). By contrast, in a defined contribution (DC) scheme, the member's contributions are payable by reference to any reduced level of pay that the employer provides during the period of paid maternity leave, while the employer contributions are calculated by reference to what would have been the member's pensionable pay had she not been on maternity leave. This leads to a divergence of outcomes, as the period of paid maternity leave does not affect pension benefits in the DB scheme, while it reduces the level of contributions and thereby the future level of pension benefits in the DC scheme.

The government can subsidise contributions during periods of maternity and parental leave. In most countries, employees and employers keep contributing at the same rate during such periods. However, in several countries with mandatory or statutory personal pension systems (Estonia, Latvia, Poland, the Slovak Republic and Sweden) and in Iceland, the government or the social security institute pays contributions to the pension account of mothers on maternity or parental leave. In the case of Finland, individuals on parental leave are not liable for pension contributions, but pension rights continue to accrue and are financed jointly by the earnings-related pension system on a pay-as-you-go (PAYG) basis.

Even when contributions continue during maternity and parental leave, the earnings base used to calculate these contributions may be lower than past earnings, thereby reducing the level of contributions compared to a period of full activity. Some countries use the earnings just before the leave or an average of past earnings (e.g. 3 months in the case of Chile and 12 months in the case of Sweden for occupational pensions). However, some countries use a lower earnings base. For example, in Estonia, the government pays pension insurance contributions based on the minimum wage only. In Iceland 80% of the past salary is used up to a cap. In Poland, the proportion of past earnings varies with the length of the leave (on average 80% if someone uses the maximum length).

By contrast, pension contributions may be higher during periods of maternity and parental leave. This is the case in Denmark, Finland and Sweden for instance. In Denmark, individuals on maternity, paternity or parental leave get an ATP contribution of DKK 4.02 per hour, instead of DKK 2.01. In Finland, the pension accrues during the parental leave based on annual earnings in the previous year increased by 21%, which is the base for the family benefit.[7] In Sweden, the earnings base taken into account for the calculation of the parental benefit is the highest of:

- the earnings the year before the child was born, if income during the parental leave is zero or lower than previous earnings;
- 75% of economy-wide average earnings, for low-income workers or people who were not working before childcare responsibilities started;
- one income base amount, if income actually rises or does not decrease to a great extent as childcare responsibilities begin.

Finally, the length during which contributions are being paid varies greatly across countries. It may be during the maternity leave only, such as in Canada, Chile, Iceland, Mexico, the Netherlands, Poland and the United Kingdom. It is extended to the parental leave in Denmark (ATP), Luxembourg, the Slovak Republic and Sweden.[8]

Beyond periods of maternity and parental leave, women may also take time off work to care for relatives. These periods may be taken into account for pension contribution purposes. For example, in Chile, when a child under the age of one has a serious illness, the mother is entitled to take medical leave to take care of the child for a time deemed sufficient by a doctor. The medical leave allows the mother (or father, in case the mother agrees) to receive her wage and contribute to the pension system during this time.

4.2.2. Spouse contributions

One way to compensate for the periods that women spend off work without contributing to the funded pension system is to allow spouses to contribute to each other's retirement savings plans. Taking time off or cutting working hours to care for children or other relatives reduces the capacity to save for retirement and the level of contributions. Contributions from the working spouse in the retirement savings plan of the caring spouse could counterbalance this. Individuals can contribute to their spouse's retirement savings plan in several countries. In Chile, the Czech Republic, Latvia and New Zealand, anyone can contribute to an individual's voluntary personal pension plan, including the individual's spouse. The husband, wife or civil partner can also contribute to a spouse's retirement savings plan, usually a personal plan, in Australia, Hungary, Lithuania, Spain and the United Kingdom. The contribution limits applicable to the plan usually also include the spouse's own contributions.

Special retirement savings arrangements can be set up to allow an individual to contribute on behalf of his or her spouse. For example, Canada and the United States have dedicated spousal retirement savings plans. In Canada, a spousal registered retirement savings plan (RRSP) is a voluntary personal pension plan opened in the name of the contributor's spouse and controlled by the spouse. Contributions to a spousal RRSP are included in the contributor's RRSP contribution limit but do not affect the spouse's own contribution limit. Upon retirement, the spouse receives an income that is taxed at his or her marginal tax rate. However, if the spouse withdraws funds within three calendar years of the contributor's contribution, that amount will be added to the contributor's taxable income in the year of the withdrawal. In the United States, a spousal individual retirement account (IRA) is a voluntary personal pension plan that allows a working spouse to contribute to an IRA in the name of a non-working spouse.[9] The working spouse's income, however, must be equal to or exceed the total IRA contributions made on behalf of both spouses. The contribution limit for the spousal IRA is the same as for regular IRAs (USD 6 000 or USD 7 000 if the spouse is aged 50 or older due to the catch-up contribution provision in 2020) and does not limit any contribution by the working spouse to his or her own IRA.

Finally, special financial incentives may encourage individuals to contribute into a spouse's retirement savings plan. For example, in Australia, a tax credit (called Spouse Super Contribution Tax Offset) may apply to after-tax contributions made on behalf of non-working or low-income-earning spouses. It is payable to the contributor, not to the spouse. The tax credit is calculated as 18% of the lesser of AUD 3 000 (reduced by one dollar for every dollar that the sum of the spouse's income, total reportable fringe benefits and reportable employer superannuation contributions exceeds AUD 37 000) and the total amount of contributions paid.[10] However, few people make use of this option (Box 4.2). In Spain, an individual can deduct up to EUR 2 500 per year for contributions paid to his/her spouse's retirement savings plan when the spouse's net earned and business activities income is less than EUR 8 000. This deduction can be carried forward for five years. If the spouse is disabled, the individual can make an additional deductible annual contribution of up to EUR 10 000 to the spouse's retirement savings scheme.[11]

Box 4.2. Spouse super contribution tax offset in Australia

Few Australians make contributions to a non-working or low-earning spouse and claim the corresponding tax credit, according to data from the Australian Treasury. In the tax year 2019-20, only about 21 000 individuals claimed a tax credit for spouse contributions, which represents less than 0.1% of all the people having a superannuation account (13.8 million according to the Household Income and Wealth survey, 2017-18). That same year, total spouse contributions amounted to around AUD 100 million, while total contributions to the superannuation system are worth around AUD 120-130 billion every year.

Spouse contributions are mostly made by men, older people and high-income earners. In 2019-20, 85% of the individuals who claimed and received the tax credit for spouse contributions were men. Individuals aged 50 and above represented 72% of those who claimed the tax credit, and those aged 60 to 69 made 52% of all spouse contributions that year. Moreover, 46% of those who claimed the tax credit had a taxable income above AUD 120 000, with 24% earning more than AUD 180 000.

It is noteworthy that most people contribute more than the amount that would maximise the tax credit. The maximum tax credit is obtained with a contribution of AUD 3 000, provided that the spouse earns less than AUD 37 000. In 2019-20, the average spouse contribution by those claiming the tax credit was worth AUD 4 757. The average spouse contribution was particularly large for people aged 60 to 69 (AUD 7 265), those aged 70 to 79 (AUD 6 861) and those with a taxable income between AUD 20 000 and AUD 40 000 (AUD 6 392). Even though contributions above AUD 3 000 do not enjoy the tax credit, it may still be worthwhile for individuals to make spouse contributions, in particular when they have reached their concessional and non-concessional contributions caps (i.e. the limits above which they need to pay extra tax). This is because returns on investment in the superannuation system are taxed favourably at the rate of 15%, while they are taxed at the individual's marginal rate of income tax in other savings vehicles.

Source: Australian Treasury.

4.2.3. Higher contributions on behalf of women

Paying higher contributions on behalf of women could be a way to compensate for their longer life expectancy, but could have negative consequences on their employability. Women's longer life expectancy implies that they need to contribute more in DC plans to finance the same annual retirement income as men, everything else being equal. In all countries with mandatory or quasi-mandatory pension systems, contribution rates are set at the same level for both men and women. In occupational systems, mandating employers to pay higher contributions on behalf of women could provide a means to help close the retirement income gap. However, making it more costly to employ women could have negative consequences, as employers may refrain from employing them or reduce their base salary to compensate for the higher pension contribution. Still, some employers may be willing to make higher contributions on behalf of women on a voluntary basis to help their female employees, although non-discrimination rules may prevent them from doing so (Box 4.3).

Box 4.3. Voluntary initiatives from employers to pay higher contributions on behalf of women

Several employers in Australia voluntarily pay extra pension contributions to their female employees, on top of their mandatory contributions, to increase women's retirement savings. For example, ANZ and Rice Warner have introduced additional superannuation contributions to female employees to help address the fact that their retirement savings need to cover a longer pay-out period on average than for men.[1] As part of their submission to the inquiry into the economic security for women in retirement in 2015, these two companies described their measures in favour of their female staff (Senate Economics References Committee, 2016[3]).

In July 2015, ANZ began a programme to pay additional super contributions of AUD 500 per year for its eligible female staff. Eligible employees are every permanent and fixed-term female employee active on the payroll each January. This amount corresponds to 1% of earnings up to AUD 50 000 and would mean approximately AUD 30 000 in additional retirement savings over the lifetime of a 30-year-old woman.

As part of their "Valuing Females" package introduced in July 2013, Rice Warner pays its female staff an extra 2% contribution, up to a cap of twice the Adult Average Weekly Ordinary Time Earnings (AWOTE). This percentage was selected based on an analysis of the impact on retirement income of a 3-year life expectancy gap between women and men. The goal of the policy was both to improve the retirement savings of female employees, and to bring awareness to all staff of the challenges facing women in saving for a comfortable retirement. The response to the policy has been very positive. After two years of implementation, 95% of male employees believed the policy was a good initiative for female employees; 81% of males and 87% of females reported that the policy had increased their awareness of the challenges women face in saving adequately for retirement; 81% of females reported that the policy had encouraged them to make voluntary contributions; and 100% of females and 67% of males had told people outside Rice Warner about the policy.

However, both companies had to go through a complicated process to gain approval to ensure that they were not in breach of sex discrimination laws. Rice Warner secured approval of a special measure package under the Sex Discrimination Act, whereas ANZ secured an exemption under New South Wales law. However, a special measure can be challenged in Court. Based on these experiences, the Senate Economic References Committee (2016[3]) recommended to the Australian Government to amend the Sex Discrimination Act 1984 to ensure companies are able to make higher superannuation payments for their female employees when they wish to do so. Instead, the Government asked the Australian Human Rights Commission to prepare guidelines to provide greater certainty to employers about the lawfulness of any action they may wish to take to reduce the gender retirement savings gap (Australian Government, 2018[4]).

1. These two companies also pay the equivalent of superannuation guarantee contributions for all staff (men and women) on paid and unpaid parental leave for up to 24 months (ANZ) or 12 months (Rice Warner).

4.3. Financial incentives

Countries may also offer specific financial incentives to women. These incentives may be useful to encourage women, who tend to participate less in retirement savings plans, to join one. They may also help women to accumulate more retirement savings to compensate for periods off work or with reduced working hours. Other types of incentives may not target women specifically but may be particularly relevant to them.

Countries paying fixed nominal subsidies into the retirement savings plan of members having children usually do so in the account of mothers. Governments may pay these subsidies either once, such as in Chile, or regularly until the child reaches a certain age, such as in Estonia, Germany and Lithuania.

- In Chile, women aged 65 or older are entitled to a government subsidy for each child alive at birth. The subsidy is equivalent to 18 months of contributions (10%) over the minimum wage in place at the birth of the child, invested in fund type C since 2009 or since the birth of the child, whichever is later (Box 4.4).
- In Estonia, one of the parents is entitled to monthly contributions equal to 4% of the national average wage into the mandatory funded pension scheme for a maximum duration of three years per child (whether or not the parent has returned to work), for children born as of 1 January 2013.
- In Germany, the government pays a child subsidy into the *Riester* account of the parent receiving child allowances. The maximum subsidy amounts to EUR 185 per year and per child born before 1 January 2008 or EUR 300 per year and per child born on or after 1 January 2008. By default, the mother receives the subsidy, unless otherwise agreed.
- In Lithuania, the government pays a monthly contribution equal to 1.5% of the country's average wage of the year before last to the statutory personal pension accounts of people who have children up to three years old and who receive maternity benefits. For persons with more than one child under the age of three, the government pays contributions for all children to one of the parents.

Box 4.4. Chile bonus per child

The Chilean government has paid a subsidy to mothers for each live birth or adopted child since 2009. The main objective of this subsidy is to improve gender equality in the pension system. The subsidy is paid once the woman reaches the age of 65. Its amount corresponds to the mandatory contribution (10%) of a full-time average worker for 18 months. It is generated at the moment of birth (or adoption) and gets a return equivalent to the net yield of Fund C of the pension administrator until the woman reaches age 65.[1] This benefit is subject to residence requirements but not to income conditions.

The measure has been successful in a variety of dimensions. The subsidy has benefited 631 098 women between July 2009 and November 2020, representing 80.2% of the total number of retired women aged 65 or more as of November 2020. It increased female participation in the pension system, as only women affiliated to the system can receive the subsidy (Figure 4.2, left panel).[2] Most of the women newly affiliated after May 2009 did it to fulfil the requirements to get the subsidy. However, the measure did not translate into a kink in the trend of the number of women contributors (Figure 4.2, right panel).[3]

Figure 4.2. Chilean pension system's new voluntary affiliates (left panel) and contributors (right panel) by gender

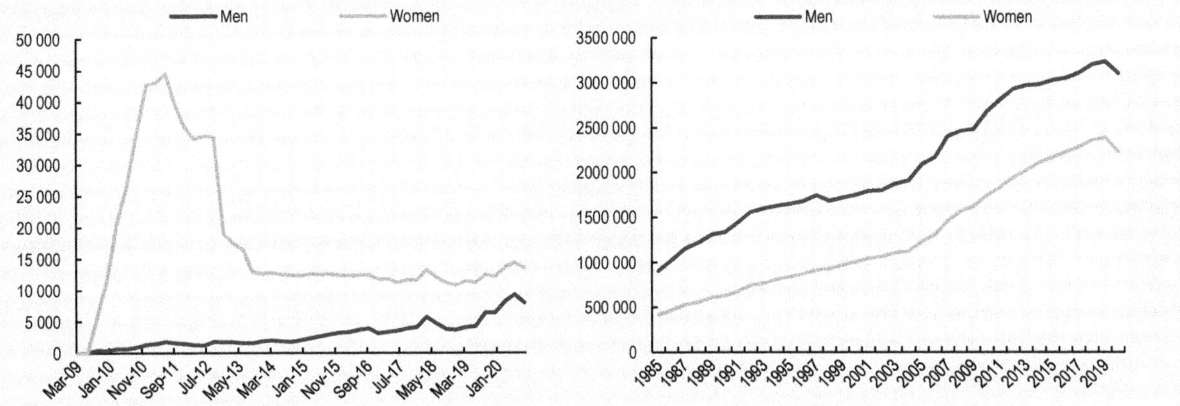

Source: Chilean Pension Superintendence.

StatLink https://doi.org/10.1787/888934230319

The subsidy is paid either as a monthly instalment if the woman is not a member of the contributory pension system and a beneficiary of the Solidarity Basic Pension (PBS), or as a single payment transferred to her individual account to increase the pension pot if she is a member of the contributory pension system. Although the type of payment is different, the present value of the total subsidy is the same in both cases. Around 34% of women receiving the subsidy are beneficiaries of the PBS. The grant has improved their monthly pensions by 9.5% on average for the period 2012-2020. For women affiliated to the AFP system, the monthly average transfer reached CLP 1 800 251 during 2020 (around 14% of average annual wages according to OECD data).

Notes: 1. Fund C is the default fund for members aged 36 to 55 for men (36 to 50 for women) in the multi-funds system. It carries an intermediate level of investment risk. 2. There is no age requirement to become an affiliate and receive the subsidy. 3. The Figure shows the number of members who contributed in December of each year (November for 2020) over their income from the previous month.

Financial incentives targeted at low earners may be particularly relevant for women, given that the proportion of women among low earners tends to be larger than that of men. Such incentives exist in Australia, Germany, Korea and the United States. In Australia, individuals earning up to AUD 37 000 are entitled to a tax credit (low-income super tax offset, LISTO) corresponding to 15% of concessional contributions paid, up to AUD 500. In addition, the government matches voluntary non-deducted contributions for individuals earning less than AUD 53 564. Individuals can get up to 50 cents for each dollar contributed, up to AUD 500. In Germany, employers contributing at least EUR 240 per year to an occupational pension scheme on behalf of an employee earning less than EUR 2 575 monthly, get a tax allowance of 30% of the contribution, up to a maximum contribution of EUR 960. In Korea, the tax credit received by individuals contributing to private pension plans is higher for individuals with an income lower than KRW 40 million (or KRW 55 million when the only income source is salary income). The tax credit is equal to 16.5% of the individual's contributions for low earners, instead of 13.2%. Finally, in the United States, middle and low income earners can receive a non-refundable tax credit for making eligible contributions to an IRA or occupational pension plan. The amount of the annual credit (so-called Saver's Credit) is 50%, 20% or 10% of the contribution up to USD 2 000 (USD 4 000 if married filing jointly), depending on the individual's adjusted gross income.

Government subsidies paid into retirement savings accounts are also attractive for low earners and therefore can potentially encourage women to save. Government subsidies are fixed nominal amounts and are therefore more valuable to low-income earners, as the fixed amount represents a higher share of their income. Beyond the child subsidies described earlier, Lithuania and Mexico pay government subsidies into the retirement savings accounts of contributing members. In addition, subsidies can also play a role in automatic enrolment schemes to reduce opt-out rates. In Poland and Turkey, the government pays a one-time contribution when the individual joins the plan (PLN 250 and TRY 1 000 respectively). A NZD 1 000 kick-start contribution was also available in the KiwiSaver system in New Zealand for contracts opened until May 2015.

Financial incentives may also aim to encourage people to compensate for a lack of, or lower contributions, during certain periods by contributing more later on. The possibility to make "catch-up" contributions aims to give flexibility to those who take time out of work, work part-time, or have irregular income and therefore have periods in which they make no or limited contributions to their retirement savings plan. This is particularly relevant for women who may not receive employer contributions during maternity leave and often work part-time to take care of the family. For example, in Australia, individuals with a total account balance of less than AUD 500 000 can carry forward up to 5 years their unused concessional cap space. Concessional contributions are taxed at 15% on amounts up to an annual cap of AUD 25 000. Someone with an account balance below AUD 500 000 and contributing AUD 10 000 in a year for example, will be able to contribute AUD 40 000 in the following year (AUD 25 000 of the current year cap plus AUD 15 000 from the unused cap of the previous year). The possibility to carry-forward unused contributions cap space is also available in Canada (in any future year for registered retirement savings plans), Italy (for the first five years of participation) and the United Kingdom (three years).

4.4. Factors affecting the level of assets accumulated

This section examines different design features of retirement savings plans that may affect the level of assets that men and women may build up during the accumulation phase. The first element is the investment strategy and this section therefore looks at the extent to which the design of default investment strategies helps to address differences in investment choices between men and women due to dissimilar levels of risk aversion. The section also discusses the possibility to have bespoke investment options for women. It then looks at the impact of divorce on pension rights and assets. Finally, one way to compensate for time taken off work for caring activities is to split or transfer pension rights and assets between spouses. The section describes this possibility in selected countries.

4.4.1. Investment strategies

The tendency to be more risk averse leads women to select more conservative investment choices. Women tend to be more risk averse than men in the allocation of their financial assets (Chapter 2) and are less likely to choose the high risk and high return option when offered investment choice (Garnick, 2016[5]; Watson and McNaughton, 2007[6]). This tendency may be against their best interest over the long term. Considering that women tend to contribute less to retirement savings plans and have a higher average life expectancy, it may be more optimal for them to invest in growth strategies in order to boost their retirement savings.

Conservative default investment strategies may reinforce women's natural biases against risk. In Italy, Latvia and New Zealand, the default investment strategy is a conservative fund (Table 4.2). Given that women already have a tendency to hold conservative investments, they are less likely to switch to an alternative investment option if the default already matches their risk aversion level. This may imply that women are less likely to reach high average returns over the entire accumulation phase.

Table 4.2. Default investment strategies in DC plans, selected OECD countries

No default	Conservative fund	Diversified fund	Life-cycle strategy
Czech Republic	Italy (auto-enrolment)	Australia (MySuper)	Australia (MySuper)
Estonia	Latvia (mandatory)	Canada (PRPP)[2]	Canada (PRPP)
Korea	New Zealand (KiwiSaver)[1]	Colombia	Chile
Slovak Republic		United States (QDIA)[3]	Israel
			Lithuania
			Mexico
			Poland (auto-enrolment)
			Slovenia
			Sweden (AP7)
			United Kingdom (Nest)
			United States (QDIA)[3]

1. The default fund will become a diversified (balanced) fund from June 2021. 2. PRPP means Pooled Registered Pension Plan. 3. QDIA means Qualified Default Investment Alternative.
Source: (OECD, 2020[7])

By contrast, life-cycle and diversified default investment strategies may help women achieve higher performance. Retirement savings plans in most countries with DC systems have to offer a life-cycle investment strategy as a default (Table 4.2). This allows members to have higher exposures to risky investments and higher potential performance when they are young, while reducing investment risk as they approach retirement and have less time to recover in case of losses. In the case of Australia, Canada (pooled registered pension plans, PRPP) and the United States (qualified default investment alternative, QDIA), pension providers can choose alternatively to offer a diversified investment option as a default.[12] Provided that inertia limits switching to a more conservative option, this type of default also helps members, and women in particular, to combat their natural tendency for conservatism and increases the potential long-term performance of their pension assets. Members, however, run a higher risk of a significant fall in their retirement savings account just before retirement because of a higher exposure to risky assets.

Bespoke investment strategies could also be designed for women. For example, the Pensions Policy Institute (2019[8]) argues that life-cycle investment strategies are not well suited for women as they tend not to have linear working and saving trajectories. Investing in risky assets during the early to middle years of the career and reducing risk during the years prior to retirement relies on stable careers and a relative predictability as to when the individual will start withdrawing assets. As women may leave and re-join the labour market several times during their life, they may not be able to contribute into their retirement savings plan steadily. In addition, some may want to delay retirement as a result of longer lives in good health, while others may withdraw their funds early because they need to provide care to a family member. Potential options to address these issues include investing in alternative assets to achieve stable long-term returns without the need to de-risk, or de-risking a portion of funds only, while continuing to invest the other part in risky assets to increase growth potential (Pensions Policy Institute, 2019[8]).[13]

4.4.2. Impact of divorce on pension rights and assets

Divorce may have detrimental effects on women depending on whether and how pension rights and assets accumulated during the period of marriage or partnership are split between former spouses upon break up. If women take time off work or reduce their working hours to take care of the family, they will accumulate less in their retirement savings account than their partner. If pension assets are considered as individual property, they cannot be split between former spouses upon divorce. Women who counted on their partner's retirement income to live on during retirement would therefore get no compensation. For example, the Pensions Policy Institute finds that divorce has a bigger impact on women's retirement savings than on men's in the United Kingdom, as the median pension wealth of a divorced man is a third less than the average man's, whereas the median pension wealth of a divorced woman is just half of the average woman's savings. One of the reasons is that 71% of divorce settlements do not take pensions into consideration.[14]

Pension rights and assets are usually considered as joint property during marriage or partnership but are not necessarily split equally upon divorce (Table 4.3). Pension entitlements are automatically split equally between former spouses upon divorce only in a few countries (e.g. Germany, the Netherlands, Poland and Switzerland).[15] However, even if joint property needs to be split equally upon divorce, it does not necessarily imply that pension assets will be split 50/50. For example, in New Zealand, partners can come to an agreement that their KiwiSaver plans will not be divided, but the proceeds of the sale of their house will be split 40/60 to favour the partner with the lower KiwiSaver value. Conversely, if partners decide to split the KiwiSaver plans, the portion of KiwiSaver assets that each partner gets may not be a 50/50 split depending on how the rest of joint property is divided. The exact split of pension assets therefore depends on total joint property split and is settled in a financial agreement between former spouses, or in a court order if former spouses cannot agree between themselves. In addition, when the split is not automatic, pension rights and assets may be overlooked in divorce settlements.

Table 4.3. Split of pension rights and assets upon divorce in selected OECD countries

	Split upon divorce	Split calculation
Australia	Yes	According to financial agreement or court order
Austria	No	
Belgium	Yes	According to financial agreement or court order
Canada	Yes	According to financial agreement or court order
Chile	Yes	According to financial agreement or court order, up to 50% of assets accumulated during marriage
Czech Republic	Yes	According to financial agreement or court order if the pension plan is part of the joint property of spouses
Denmark	No	Exceptions for occupational and voluntary personal pension savings in case of unfair pension payments, family work compensation and long marriage
Finland	No	
France	No	Compensation of 50% of contributions paid into the plan during marriage due to the ex-spouse if these contributions were done using common funds
Germany	Yes	Equalization of pension rights acquired by the spouses during marriage
Hungary	Yes	According to financial agreement or court order (civil law)
Iceland	No	
Ireland	Yes	According to financial agreement or court order
Japan	Yes	According to financial agreement or court order (civil law)
Latvia	No	
Lithuania	Yes	According to financial agreement or court order
Mexico	No	
Netherlands	Yes	50% of entitlements accrued during marriage
New Zealand	Yes	According to financial agreement or court order
Poland	Yes	50% of assets accumulated during marriage
Slovak Republic	No	
Slovenia	No	
Sweden	No	
Switzerland	Yes	50% of entitlements accrued during marriage
United Kingdom	Yes	According to financial agreement or court order
United States	Yes	According to financial agreement or court order

Several options may be available to split pension rights and assets between former spouses. For example, in the United Kingdom, three options are available: offsetting, pension sharing order and pension attachment order. Offsetting implies that pension assets can be offset against other assets of the divorcing parties. Under a pension sharing order, retirement assets are divided at the time of separation and the ex-spouse receives her share in her pension arrangement. Finally, a pension attachment order results in the pension provider of one party paying an agreed percentage of the member's pension directly to the former spouse when pension rights come into payment. There are several disadvantages with pension attachment orders: the ex-spouse has to wait until the member decides to retire and draw benefits before receiving anything; if the member dies before retirement, the ex-spouse does not receive anything; if the member dies during retirement, payments to the ex-spouse stop; if the member stops contributing, retires early or invests in poorly performing assets, the ex-spouse may receive less than expected. A pension attachment order may therefore be a riskier option for the former spouse unless the pension is already in payment. In addition, offsetting assets against each other may disadvantage one of the ex-partners, for example if one asset class (e.g. a retirement savings plan) has fallen in value more than another (e.g. the home). Pension sharing is therefore the favoured way to divide retirement assets.

Finally, a minority of countries do not split pension rights and assets upon divorce. Table 4.3 shows that this is the case in Austria, Denmark, Finland, France, Iceland, Latvia, Mexico, the Slovak Republic, Slovenia and Sweden. In the case of Finland, all earnings-related pension systems and plans are collective, which means that a person does not have her or his own ring-fenced assets. The rules upon divorce vary depending on the situation in Denmark and France. In Denmark, the general rule is that the individual keeps his/her own savings. However, a split of occupational and voluntary personal savings can be considered in three cases: i) one spouse gets much higher pension benefits than the other; ii) one spouse has saved less than usual during the marriage for the sake of the family (e.g. part-time work or parental leave); or iii) the marriage has lasted for more than 15 years and there is a large difference between the spouses' retirement savings.[16] In France, retirement savings plans are considered exclusive property of the individual member of the plan. However, if contributions paid into that plan during marriage were made using common funds from both spouses, the member must compensate his/her ex-spouse upon divorce with 50% of these contributions. In the other countries, pension rights and assets remain an exclusive property of an individual and therefore cannot be split in case of divorce.

4.4.3. Split or transfer of pension rights and assets between spouses

One way to compensate for lower pension rights accumulation for women is to allow spouses to split or transfer accrued pension rights and assets between themselves during the accumulation phase. This option is available in Iceland, the Netherlands and Sweden.

The split of pension rights between partners can result in a transfer from one spouse to the other or correspond to a mutual split of past and future rights. For example, in Iceland, pension fund members can decide that up to one-half of their retirement pension rights accrue to their spouse or former spouse. This results in a retirement pension paid directly to the spouse. Alternatively, spouses can mutually agree to split retirement benefit rights equally (50/50). This equal split can refer to benefit payments, accrued benefits or future accruals (Box 4.5).

Box 4.5. Iceland's mutual split of pension rights

Since 2002, couples in Iceland can mutually agree to split equally their retirement benefit rights in occupational plans. Spouses can agree to split:

- Retirement benefit payments when retiring;[1]
- Accrued benefits before the age of 65, in such a way that total liabilities remain unchanged to the pension fund;[2] or
- Future accruals, at any time.[3]

The number of contracts with such mutual split agreement is negligible, however, with only 73 contracts in 2019 compared to more than 200 000 active members under the age of 65 in the mandatory occupational pension system. Figure 4.3 still shows a significant increase in 2019, with most couples splitting both accrued and future accruals.

Figure 4.3. Number of contracts with mutual pension split agreement, 2010-2019

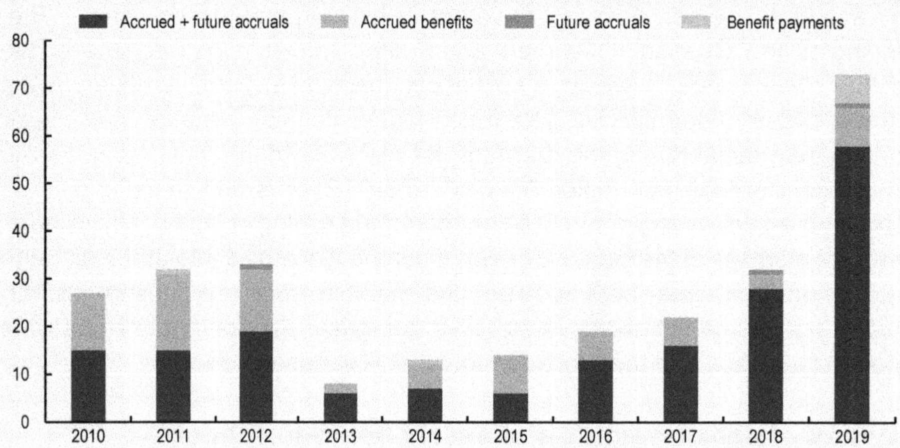

StatLink https://doi.org/10.1787/888934230338

Notes: 1. In case of death or termination of the agreement, the surviving partner receives back his/her benefits and loses the spouse's part. 2. In case of death, divorce or termination of the agreement, already transferred rights cannot be reversed back. 3. This agreement can be terminated by one party but already transferred rights cannot be reversed back.
Source: Icelandic Pension Fund Association.

The transfer could be the default option in case people do not make an active choice under certain conditions. In the Netherlands, a (former) member of a pension scheme who is married or has a registered partnership can partially exchange his or her retirement pension for a partner's pension.[17] This means that the (former) member will receive a lower retirement pension, while his or her partner will receive a higher survivor pension upon the death of the member. This option is available upon leaving the pension fund or in the last year before the payment of the retirement pension to the member. The level of the partner's pension cannot exceed 70% of the retirement pension that remains after the exchange.[18] In addition, the pension scheme will automatically exchange the retirement pension into a partner's pension if the (former) member has a partner but has only accrued a retirement pension (i.e. without a survivor option) and does not decide whether to exercise the exchange option within a certain period.

The transferred pension rights and assets may be reduced in order to reflect that transfers usually take place from men to women. In Sweden, it is possible to transfer entitlements to the premium pension between spouses. The transfer takes place annually and consists of the earned pension entitlement for the calendar year. To prevent unfair risk sharing, a charge of 6% of the assets transferred is levied. The charge is the same for men and women and reflects the fact that it is expected that there will be more transfers from men to women than vice versa, and that women have a longer life expectancy on average. Transfers can only start after the individual sends an application and stop when the individual notifies the end of the transfer.

Finally, options to withdraw the accumulated assets at retirement may include the transfer to a spouse's retirement savings plan. For example, in Portugal, members of the public voluntary funded pension scheme have several options to withdraw assets from the scheme upon retirement. Beyond the usual options of annuities and lump sums, they can also transfer part or all of the accumulated pension assets to a child or spouse's retirement savings plan.

4.5. Pay-out phase

As women live longer than men on average, the design of the pay-out phase may also affect the level of retirement income that men and women may receive during retirement. This section therefore describes the rules relating to the age of retirement, the mortality tables, the indexation of payments and the survivor benefits, and analyses how these rules interact with women's longer lives.

4.5.1. Age of retirement and mortality tables

Women are likely to draw their retirement income benefits for longer than men are. The age from which people can draw their retirement income is the same for men and women in most OECD countries. Women can withdraw their funded pension earlier than men do in Chile (60 for women / 65 for men), Israel (62/67), Poland (60/65), the Slovak Republic (women with children have a reduced age of retirement) and Switzerland (64/65). In Lithuania, withdrawal ages are currently different for men and women but are gradually converging to be equal as of 2026. Given women's longer average life expectancy, having the same age of retirement for men and women, or a lower age for women, implies that women will spend more time than men do in retirement.

In retirement savings plans where benefits are determined according to a formula based on past salaries and career length, women would be entitled to a higher pension wealth than men, *ceteris paribus*. For example, let us consider two individuals, one man and one woman, with the same number of years of participation in a DB plan and at the same level of salary over their career. If they both retire at the same age, they will receive the same level of retirement income benefits every year from the DB plan. As the woman is likely to survive the man, however, she would receive benefits for longer. Women are therefore advantaged in DB systems.

Similarly, women have an advantage over men when annuity providers have to use unisex mortality tables for the calculation of annuity payments. In all European countries, insurance companies have to use unisex mortality tables for pricing, meaning that, for a given level of assets accumulated in a DC plan, a man and a woman retiring at the same age will get the same level of annuity payments every year. Given their longer life expectancy, women are likely to receive these payments for longer. In most countries outside Europe, annuity providers use differentiated mortality tables for men and women. For these countries, for a given level of assets accumulated at retirement, a woman would therefore receive lower annual annuity payments, although for longer, thereby equalising the pension wealth between men and women. In the United States, qualified occupational pension plans under ERISA regulation are not allowed to distinguish mortality tables between genders. The consequence is that occupational plans use women mortality tables and men have an incentive to roll over their funds to a non-ERISA plan (e.g. an IRA), where different tables across genders can be used.

Finally, women are more exposed to longevity risk when they select programmed withdrawals. If a woman withdraws her assets at the same rate as a man does, for a given level of assets accumulated at retirement, she is more likely to deplete her account before passing away. To make sure that assets can finance a longer retirement period, a woman would need to withdraw less each year.

4.5.2. Indexation of benefit payments

As women tend to live longer than men on average, the extent to which benefit payments are indexed during the retirement phase matters even more to them. Indexation is important to make sure that women's retirement incomes do not lose purchasing power and women do not fall in the income distribution over time. However, Table 4.4 shows that there is no legal requirement for the indexation of funded pensions in most OECD countries. Pension providers (e.g. insurance companies) may index benefit payments on a discretionary basis. Indexation may also depend on the financial position of the pension funds, such as in the Netherlands and Switzerland. Indexation in line with inflation (Consumer Price Index, CPI) is the most common.

Table 4.4. Indexation of pensions in payment in selected OECD countries

Mandatory indexation (index)	Discretionary basis	No indexation
Austria (book reserves: social security benefits), Chile (inflation), Finland (80% CPI and 20% wage growth), Germany (CPI, wage growth, 1% a year), Hungary (CPI), Iceland (CPI), Latvia (if assets transferred to the NDC system: inflation + part of the real growth of the wage sum, up to a threshold), Mexico (CPI)	Australia, Belgium, Canada, Czech Republic, Germany (depends on financial situation of the fund or of the employer), Japan (depends on plan rules), Korea, Netherlands (depends on financial position of the fund, CPI ambition), Portugal (usually CPI), Spain, Sweden (depends on returns achieved), Switzerland (depends on financial position of the fund), United States	Denmark, Estonia, Ireland, Israel, Italy, Lithuania, Luxembourg, New Zealand, Norway, Slovak Republic, Slovenia, Turkey, United Kingdom

The indexation of annuity payments comes at the cost of lower initial payments. Annuity providers indeed adjust the initial payment downward to account for later increases in line with the index. This keeps the total pension wealth equal to the case of an annuity with fixed payments in nominal terms. In the case of DB plans, such downward adjustment is embedded in the formula to calculate the initial payment (e.g. lower accrual rates).

4.5.3. Survivor benefits

Finally, women may be entitled to survivor benefits at the death of their partner. A survivor pension may be granted to a surviving spouse or relatives as part of the deceased's pension to help maintain material living standards after the death of a partner or parent. The retirement income of the surviving spouse may be much lower than the one of the deceased person, as is often the case for women, especially among older generations. Relying on the pension entitlements accrued by the surviving woman alone may reduce her standard of living.

In most DC retirement savings systems, survivor risk is covered through the inheritance of unspent pension capital. Table 4.5 shows that eligible survivors or designated beneficiaries receive the remaining assets in the account upon the death of the deceased member in most DC retirement savings arrangements. This implies that the survivor does not get protection against longevity risk, unless he or she buys a lifetime annuity with the inherited lump sum. Exceptions include Chile, Denmark and Mexico, where the funded DC pension system is mandatory or quasi-mandatory and requires the payment of survivor pensions. In DB systems, survivors tend to receive a survivor pension.

Table 4.5. Survivor benefits in selected OECD countries

	Mandatory survivor benefits	Formula	Other types of benefits upon death of the member
Australia	No		
Austria	Yes (pension funds only)	Usually 60% of the deceased's actual or projected benefit	
Belgium	No but usually provided	Depends on plan rules	
Canada	Yes	60% of the deceased's benefit	
Chile	Yes	50% or 60% of the reference pension (70% of the real average covered earnings of the member in the last 10 years before death) for spouses with or without children	
Czech Republic	No		Assets paid as a lump sum to designated beneficiaries
Denmark	No but usually provided	60% of the deceased's benefit	
Estonia	No		Pension fund units are inheritable Annuity contracts may provide for a guaranteed period
Finland	Yes	50% of the deceased's benefit for spouses with no or one child (lower rate if more children)	
Germany	No but usually provided		
Hungary	No	Full survivor pension from the social security scheme if the eligible survivor chooses to transfer the accumulated capital to that scheme, 75% otherwise	The eligible survivor can choose to receive the accumulated capital as a lump sum Annuity contracts may include a survivor option
Iceland	Yes	The full spouse's pension is at least 50% of the disability pension to which the deceased member would have been entitled in the case of full disability. It is paid for at least 24 months	
Ireland	No	Depends on plan rules	
Israel	Yes (new pension funds only)	Depends on plan rules If an old-age pensioner dies before having received 60 monthly pension payments, the fund must pay 100% of the member's old-age pension to the eligible survivors for the remainder of the 60 months. If the old-age pensioner dies after having received 60 but before 120 monthly pension payments, or after 120 but before 180 monthly pension payments, the full pension continues to be paid for the remainder of the 120 months or 180 months respectively.	If the total survivor pension is less than the minimum pension stipulated in the plan rules, survivors receive the cash value of the deceased member's accrued rights or accumulated capital as a lump sum
Italy	No		Assets paid as a lump sum to designated beneficiaries
Japan	No		Assets in corporate DC plans paid as a lump sum to designated beneficiaries
Korea	No		
Latvia	Yes if assets transferred to NDC	A lump sum of two months of the deceased's NDC old-age, disability, or work injury pension is paid	Annuity contracts may include a survivor option
Lithuania	No		Assets are inheritable

	Mandatory survivor benefits	Formula	Other types of benefits upon death of the member
Luxembourg	No but usually provided with group insurance	Between 60% and 80% of the deceased's projected or actual retirement benefit	
Mexico	Yes	90% of the disability pension paid or payable (IMSS scheme)	
Netherlands	No but usually provided		
New Zealand	No		Assets are inheritable
Norway	No but can be provided	DB schemes: a percentage of the deceased member's projected or actual old-age pension, or a percentage of the deceased member's salary	
Poland	No		OFE: 50% of the balance transferred to the spouse's account upon death of the member before retirement. The rest is paid in equal parts to the designated beneficiaries
Portugal	No	DB plans: Usually 60% of the deceased's accrued old-age pension	DC plans: Assets paid as a lump sum to designated beneficiaries
Slovak Republic	No		Assets paid as a lump sum to designated beneficiaries
Slovenia	No		Assets paid as a lump sum to designated beneficiaries
Spain	No		
Sweden	No	Optional for the member	
Switzerland	Yes	60% of the full invalidity pension that the member would have received in the case of invalidity or of the last monthly retirement or invalidity pension paid to the deceased	Surviving spouses may opt to commute the pension to a lump sum payment if the surviving spouse's pension is lower than 6% of the minimum old-age retirement pension under the basic insurance scheme
Turkey	No		Assets paid as a lump sum to designated beneficiaries Annuity contracts may include a survivor option
United Kingdom	No		
United States	Yes (default option)	DB plans: 50% to 100% of the deceased's benefit or accrued pension at the time of death	DC plans: Assets paid as a lump sum to designated beneficiaries

Among countries where retirement savings arrangements pay survivor pensions, the survivor usually receives a fraction of the deceased member's actual pension (if death occurs after retirement) or projected pension (if death occurs before retirement). This fraction varies from 50% in Chile and Finland, to 60% in Austria, Canada, Denmark, Portugal and Switzerland, and to 90% in Mexico. In the case of Iceland, Mexico and Switzerland, the survivor pension is actually expressed as a fraction of the disability pension rather than the old-age pension. In Chile, the survivor pension is calculated as a percentage of a reference pension, which is 70% of the real average covered earnings of the member in the last 10 years before death.[19] Finally, in Chile and Finland, the survivor pension of the surviving spouse is reduced for each additional dependent child because an orphan pension is paid to children.

The survivor may receive benefits until his/her own death or just for a fixed period. For example, in Israel, survivor benefits are only paid for a maximum period of 60 months. The lifelong or temporary nature of survivor pensions may also depend on whether the member dies before or after retirement. For example, in Norway, if a member of a DC savings plan dies before retirement, the accumulated capital must be used first to buy an insured annuity for each orphan up to the age of 21 and then, if there is excess capital available, a fixed term annuity must be bought for the spouse.

Survivor pensions can be set up as a default option for couples. In the United States, federal law encourages survivor protection by requiring employers that sponsor DB plans to offer joint and survivor annuities as the default pay-out option (Box 4.6).[20] Members can choose a single life annuity only if both spouses submit their written consent to the plan within 90 days of when annuity payments will begin. In addition, plans must require a plan representative or notary to witness the spouse's consent.

Box 4.6. Default joint and survivor annuity for married couples in the United States

In the United States, the Employee Retirement Income Security Act (ERISA) of 1974 requires employers that sponsor DB pension plans to offer joint and survivor annuities as the default pay-out option for married members. The Retirement Equity Act (REA) of 1984 further requires members to obtain the written consent of their spouse before they can decline survivor benefits. Married members who select the joint and survivor option typically accept lower monthly payments than with a single life annuity, in return for protection for their spouse, should they live longer. The amount paid to the surviving spouse must be no less than 50% and no greater than 100% of the amount of the annuity paid during the member's life.

These laws appear to have improved access to retirement benefits for surviving spouses. Holden and Nicholson (1998[9]) show that the proportion of men choosing a joint and survivor annuity increased from 48% to 64% after the passage of ERISA in 1974. It is not possible to know, however, how much of this increase is due to the introduction of the default option, and how much is due to the increased availability of joint and survivor annuities among plans that were not offering them previously. The introduction of the REA appears to have raised the take-up of joint and survivor annuities even further. Aura (2001[10]) finds an increase of 5% to 10% in the take-up of joint and survivor annuities following the requirement to get explicit spousal consent to opt out of the default.

In addition, most married members choosing a single life annuity instead of the default joint and survivor annuity seem to rationally balance the costs and benefits of each type of annuity. Johnson, Uccello and Goldwyn (2005[11]) find that 28% of married men and 69% of married women choose a single life annuity. Individuals are more likely to reject the default option when their spouse has alternative sources of survivor protection, they have limited pension wealth, they expect to outlive their spouse, and the relationship with the spouse is weak. Only 7% of married men and 3% of married women opt out of joint and survivor annuities without evidence of potentially compelling reasons.

4.6. Communicating and educating about the design of retirement savings plans

This section provides selected case studies showing how communication and financial education initiatives can be targeted at women to increase their financial awareness and help them take action to improve their retirement readiness. It complements the examples provided in Chapter 2, looking at the potential impact of calculators, personalised videos, and communication and financial education strategies by pension providers. These initiatives are in line with the *OECD/INFE Policy Guidance on Addressing Women's and Girls' Needs for Financial Awareness and Education* endorsed by the G20 in 2013 (OECD/INFE, 2013[12]). They are also in line with the recently approved *OECD Recommendation on Financial Literacy* (OECD, 2020[13]).

Calculators can help individuals, in particular women, to assess the impact of family leave on their pension. In Finland for example, people who are planning to use family leave can use a calculator to assess how family leave periods of different lengths would affect their future pension and to compare their pension accrual during family leave with what they would earn as pension if they worked the same period. Finnish parents earn pension benefits during their maternity, paternity or parental leave almost the same way as when they are working, but long periods of child home care allowance have a negative impact on pensions. This is because the earnings base for pension accrual is the previous years' income raised by 21% during maternity, paternity or parental leave, as opposed to a fixed amount of EUR 757.14 per month (in 2020) during the period of child home care allowance. Figure 4.4 shows the calculator's output for a person born in 1990, earning EUR 2 000 per month in the previous year, and taking 10 months of maternity, paternity or parental leave, plus 26 months of child home care allowance. While the pension accrual during the parental leave (first 10 months) is slightly higher than the pension accrual had the person worked (EUR 24 vs. EUR 22 per month), pension accrual from working is 72% higher at the end of the child home care allowance period (EUR 79 vs. EUR 46 per month).

Figure 4.4. Illustration of the calculator's output

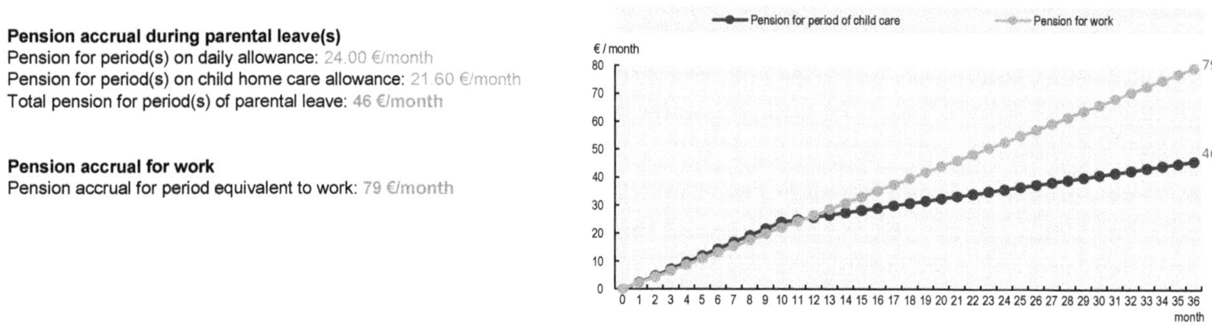

Note: Results based on a person born in 1990, earning EUR 2 000 per month in the previous year, and taking 10 months of maternity, paternity or parental leave, plus 26 months of child home care allowance.
Source: https://www.tyoelake.fi/en/how-much-pension/pension-for-family-leaves/.

StatLink https://doi.org/10.1787/888934230357

Communication and financial education initiatives targeting women can succeed in making them join a retirement savings plan. For example, the Italian pension fund Laborfonds has managed to attract more women than men recently.[21] Since 2017, the number of women in the plan has even exceeded that of men (Figure 4.5), in particular in the 40 to 60 age group. This is the result of several initiatives put in place by Laborfonds in the last few years to increase individual awareness about pensions and develop a retirement culture, in particular among women and young workers:

- Organisation of or participation in the general assemblies of firms having a pension plan with them. During these meetings, experts explain to the firms' employees the main characteristics of the pension fund, the benefits, costs and incentives (i.e. contributions of the employer, tax benefits, lower cost compared to with-profit pension funds). Laborfonds targets firms where a small portion of employees are already members of the fund, or with a large representation of women or young people. In particular, the significant increase in the participation of women in the fund is related to the fact that several firms are in the agricultural sector and employ a lot of women.
- Organisation of special events, some of them together with Pensplan, to reduce the pension gap between women and men (e.g. "Equal pension days", "Equal pay day").
- New communication approach via a periodic newsletter and social media (Facebook, Instagram).
- New agreements signed with local info-points in order to explain the characteristics of the pension fund and attract new members.
- Participation in specific events during the Financial Education Month (every year in October since 2018) promoted by the Italian Committee for the Planning and Coordination of Financial Education Activities (www.quellocheconta.gov.it).

Figure 4.5. Evolution of the number of male and female members in Laborfonds, 2010-2019

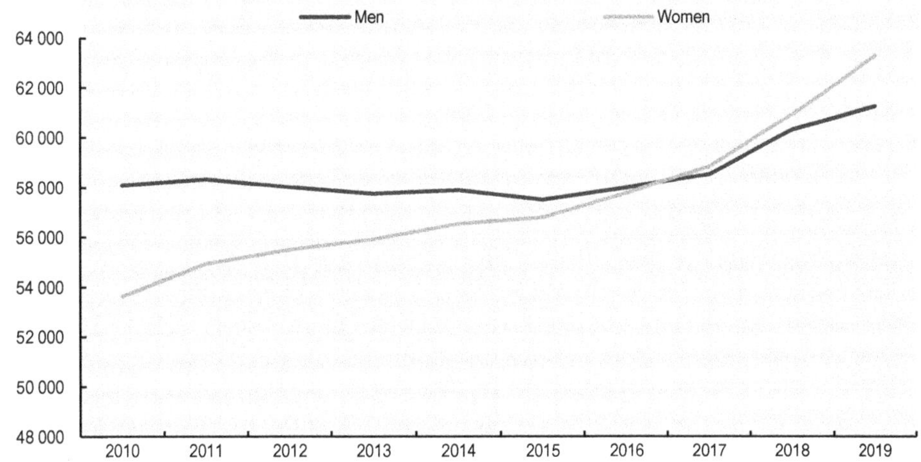

Source: Laborfonds' annual reports, 2010-2019, available at http://www.laborfonds.it/it/documentazione/74-0.html.

StatLink https://doi.org/10.1787/888934230376

Finally, personalised pension videos can successfully engage women with their pension once they are members of a plan. For instance, Mercer works with several employers to develop personalised videos for each of their employees who are members of their DC retirement savings scheme. The short video highlights the figures members need to know about their pension (e.g. contributions made, total assets already accumulated), including an estimate of their income at retirement. Using insights from behavioural economics, it encourages members to take actions. It keeps the messaging clear and simple, and reduces the gap between intention and action by including an on-video link that members can click on to improve their retirement readiness (e.g. increase contributions).[22] Whilst videos are aimed at all genders, anecdotal evidence from some employers suggests that women may be more likely to watch the video until the end and to click to increase their contributions (Read, 2017[14]). This could be due to the imagery and messaging in the video, although the fact that women are more likely than men to fall short of expectations in terms of their pension could also be a factor explaining why more women take action after viewing their video.

4.7. Conclusion

This chapter has assessed the gender implications of the design of retirement savings plans. It reviewed the rules and parameters of these plans in OECD countries using a gender lens, assessing whether they may affect men and women differently.

Several design features of retirement savings plans are not gender neutral and tend to disadvantage women:

- Although pension funds cannot discriminate plan access based on gender, some countries still have eligibility criteria based on a minimum number of working hours or on a minimum income threshold that may restrict women's ability to join retirement savings plans more than men's.
- While periods of maternity and parental leave usually do not delay women's eligibility to join retirement savings plans, in some OECD countries, they lead to a break in contributions or pension

right accruals. This penalises women, who would need to contribute more upon return to work to compensate for the loss.

- Conservative default investment strategies may reinforce women's natural biases against risk. Given that women tend to contribute less to retirement savings plans and have a higher average life expectancy, it may be better for them over the long term to invest in growth strategies in order to boost their retirement savings.
- Some OECD countries do not consider pension rights and assets as joint property built up during marriage or partnership. This implies that women who took time off work or reduced their working hours to take care of the family, would not get compensation for accumulating less in their own retirement savings account in case of divorce. In other countries, pension rights and assets built up during marriage or partnership are considered as joint property, but the split between the ex-spouses is not automatic and pensions risk not being accounted for in divorce settlements.
- There is no legal requirement for the indexation of benefits received from retirement savings plans in most OECD countries. As women tend to live longer than men on average, the lack of indexation puts them at higher risk of falling in the income distribution at the end of their life.
- In most DC plans, survivors do not get protection against longevity risk as survivor risk is covered through the inheritance of unspent pension capital. By contrast, in DB plans, survivors tend to receive a lifelong pension upon the death of the spouse. Making survivor pensions the default option for couples can improve access to retirement benefits for surviving spouses.

By contrast, other design features of retirement savings plans are gender neutral or favour women and may help to reduce the gender pension gap:

- Policies aiming at reaching high participation levels in general, e.g. automatic enrolment, can help close the gap in plan participation between men and women.
- Options to offset contributions gaps for women include the possibility for spouses to contribute to each other's retirement savings plans, the possibility to split or transfer pension rights or assets between spouses, or the possibility for employers to contribute more on behalf of women. For the latter, however, making it more costly to employ women could have negative consequences, as employers may refrain from employing them or reduce their base salary to compensate for the higher pension contribution. There may be also legal barriers preventing contribution discrimination between men and women.
- Specific financial incentives for women may be useful to encourage them to join retirement savings plans. They may also help women to build larger pension accumulations to compensate for periods off work or with reduced working hours. Incentives targeted at low earners or allowing catch-up contributions can also be particularly relevant for women.
- Women are likely to spend more years than men in retirement due to their longer average life expectancy. Everything else equal, this translates into a higher pension wealth for women than for men when retirement benefits are determined according to a formula based on past salaries and career length, or when annuity providers have to use unisex mortality tables for the calculation of annuity payments. By contrast, women are more exposed to longevity risk when they select programmed withdrawals if unisex tables are referenced.
- Communication and financial education initiatives targeted at women (e.g. calculators, seminars, communication through social media, or personalised videos) can successfully increase their financial awareness and help them take action to improve their retirement readiness.

References

Aura, S. (2001), "Does the balance of power within a family matter? The case of the Retirement Equity Act", *Innocenzo Gasparini Institute for Economic Research Working Paper* 202. [10]

Australian Government (2018), *Australian Government response to the Senate Economics References Committee Report: "A husband is not a retirement plan: Achieving economic security for women in retirement"*, https://www.pmc.gov.au/sites/default/files/publications/govt-response-inquiry-husband-not-retirement-plan.pdf. [4]

Garnick, D. (2016), *Income Insights: Gender Retirement Gap*. [5]

Holden, K. and S. Nicholson (1998), "Selection of a joint-and-survivor pension", *Institute for Research on Poverty Discussion Paper* 1175-98. [9]

Johnson, R., C. Uccello and J. Goldwyn (2005), "Who foregoes survivor protection in employer-sponsored pension annuities?", *The Gerontologist*, Vol. 45/1, pp. 26-35, http://dx.doi.org/10.1093/geront/45.1.26. [11]

OECD (2020), *Recommendation of the Council on Financial Literacy*, https://legalinstruments.oecd.org/en/instruments/OECD-LEGAL-0461. [13]

OECD (2020), "Selecting default investment strategies", in *OECD Pensions Outlook 2020*, OECD Publishing, Paris, https://dx.doi.org/10.1787/1c7381db-en. [7]

OECD (2019), "Are funded pensions well designed to adapt to non-standard forms of work?", in *Pensions at a Glance 2019: OECD and G20 Indicators*, OECD Publishing, Paris, https://dx.doi.org/10.1787/1231a36d-en. [1]

OECD (2019), *Pension Markets in Focus*, http://www.oecd.org/daf/fin/private-pensions/Pension-Markets-in-Focus-2019.pdf. [2]

OECD/INFE (2013), *OECD/INFE Policy Guidance on Addressing Women's and Girls' Needs for Financial Awareness and Education*, https://www.oecd.org/daf/fin/financial-education/G20-Women-Girls-Fin-Ed-Policy-Guidance-2013.pdf. [12]

Pensions Policy Institute (2019), "The gender pension gap: can it be closed?", *PPI Briefing Note* 114, https://www.pensionspolicyinstitute.org.uk/media/3185/20190604-the-gender-pensions-gap-can-it-be-closedpub.pdf. [8]

Read, E. (2017), *Pension Gender Gap: How can we respond?*, https://www.slideshare.net/OECD-DAF/eve-read-pension-gender-gap-how-can-we-respond. [14]

Senate Economics References Committee (2016), *A husband is not a retirement plan: Achieving economic security for women in retirement*, https://www.aph.gov.au/Parliamentary_Business/Committees/Senate/Economics/Economic_security_for_women_in_retirement/Report. [3]

Watson, J. and M. McNaughton (2007), "Gender differences in risk aversion and expected retirement benefits", *Financial Analysts Journal*, Vol. 63/4, pp. 52-62, http://dx.doi.org/10.2469/faj.v63.n4.4749. [6]

Notes

[1] OECD Labour Force Statistics 2020.

[2] This credit applies regardless of whether the employees' leave of absence during this period was paid or unpaid, and whether their leave was approved.

[3] If individuals leave an employer for whom they have worked for several years and later return, they may be able to count those earlier years towards vesting. Generally, a plan must preserve the service credit individuals have accumulated if they leave their employer and then return within five years. Service credit refers to the years of service that count towards vesting.

[4] Source: APRA Annual Superannuation Bulletin, June 2018.

[5] In Slovenia, employer contributions to voluntary occupational schemes during maternity and parental leave are not mandatory. However, employer contributions must continue during maternity and parental leave for mandatory occupational schemes covering civil servants and workers in arduous and hazardous conditions.

[6] Employers may also include a social component to their occupational pension plan. Employers pay additional contributions to a solidarity fund, which can finance the continuation of the pension right accumulation (or the payment of contributions) during periods of inactivity, including maternity leave. See https://www.fsma.be/fr/faq/quelles-autres-couvertures-est-il-possible-de-proposer, sections C and D.

[7] For someone with no earnings in the previous year, pension benefits accrue as if the person had earnings worth EUR 757.14 per month (in 2020). The same earnings base is used while receiving the child home care allowance.

[8] In some countries, the term parental leave is used distinctively from the terms maternity leave and paternity leave to describe a separate family leave available to either parent to care for small children.

[9] A spousal IRA can be a traditional or Roth IRA. They are subject to the same income limits, annual contribution limits and catch-up contribution provisions as traditional and Roth IRA.

[10] It is also possible to split the compulsory superannuation contributions from one's employer and have these paid into a spouse's account.

[11] Contributions to protect a person with disabilities applies if the contributor has a relationship of kinship in direct or collateral to the third degree with the member, as well as the spouse or for those who have the disabled person in custody or foster care.

[12] A qualified default investment alternative (QDIA) must be diversified. It may be (i) a life cycle (or target date) fund; (ii) a balanced fund; or (iii) a professionally managed account.

[13] The authors acknowledge, however, that there are difficulties associated with investing in alternatives, which tend to be more expensive and require more resources to manage.

[14] https://www.nowpensions.com/press-release/divorced-women-half-of-average-savings/

[15] In the Netherlands, a new law on pension distribution after divorce will enter into force on 1 January 2022. Pensions accrued during marriage will be automatically split in half and distributed, without any action required from the ex-partners. Today, even if the ex-partner is entitled to receive half of their former spouse's pension built up during the marriage, pensions are often overlooked in a divorce (see https://apg.nl/en/publication/what-does-divorce-mean-for-your-pension/).

[16] These exceptions do not apply to ATP plans, which cannot be split upon divorce.

[17] The exchange may also go in the other direction, exchanging a partner's pension (i.e. a survivor pension) for a higher retirement pension. This requires the consent of the partner.

[18] The exchange takes place on the basis of collective actuarial equivalence, which means that the collective actuarial value of the partner's pension is at least equivalent to the collective actuarial value of the retirement pension calculated on the same basis. This implies that the same exchange factors apply to men and women. The pension scheme can determine the exchange factors on the basis of actual percentages of male and female participants, as well as on the basis of an expected exchange pattern.

[19] This is only for members currently insured (i.e. contributing and paying the insurance premium), not all members of the system.

[20] If a DB participant survives until retirement age, the Retirement Equity Act (REA) of 1984 requires that the participant's annuity be a qualified joint and survivor annuity (QJSA), under which payments continue for the lives of both the employee and their spouse. However, if a DB participant dies before retirement and is vested, a qualified pre-retirement survivor annuity (QPSA) is paid to offer compensation to the surviving spouse for the loss of retirement benefits that would have otherwise been paid to the employee.

[21] Laborfonds is an occupational pension fund for people working in the public and private sectors in the Trentino-Alto Adige region. It is connected with Pensplan, a public company aiming at developing the private pension sector in the Trentino-Alto Adige region. Pensplan provides operational support (e.g. administrative service) to regional pension funds (Laborfonds and three other open pension funds) and organises local info-points to provide free advice to citizens with reference to the public and private pensions.

[22] See https://www.uk.mercer.com/what-we-do/wealth-and-investments/personalised-pension-videos.html for an example of a personalised video.

5 Policy options for funded retirement savings arrangements to tackle the gender gap

This chapter discusses policy options available to address the gender gap in retirement savings arrangements. While the pension system itself cannot correct for all of the factors driving the gender pension gap, its overall design should not put women at a further disadvantage. After summarising the various drivers that directly contribute to the gender pension gap within retirement savings arrangements, the chapter looks at various policy options that can address gender gaps at each stage of preparing financially for retirement.

The gender pension gap is the result of many interconnected and complicated factors relating to society, employment, childcare, education, and individual bias. Therefore, fixing the gender pension gap will necessarily require measures to address these other areas, in particular those relating to the labour market and its inequalities with respect to participation, pay, and the cost of care.

While the pension system itself cannot correct for all of these factors, its design should at least not increase inequalities, and at best should reduce the impact that existing inequalities can have on the retirement benefits that women will receive. Public pensions can incorporate various progressive formulas and subsidies in their design to offset some of these inequalities. However, the importance of retirement savings arrangements is growing around the world, so their potential contribution to the gender pension gap – currently at 26% in OECD countries – can be expected to increase going forward. Policy makers must therefore consider how these arrangements may contribute to the gap both today and in the future, and ensure that their design does not increase the gap, especially given the close relation of the retirement income from these arrangements to employment and income patterns.

This chapter first summarises the various drivers that directly contribute to the gender pension gap within retirement savings arrangements that previous chapters have identified, and how each of these drivers affects the retirement income that women can expect to receive. It then looks at various policy options to address each of these impacts. It concludes with a reflection on the current challenges facing policy makers to close the gender pension gap.

5.1. The female affliction: drivers of the gender pension gap

The gender pension gap is reinforced at every stage of preparing financially for retirement:

- Women have less access to retirement savings arrangements.
- Women less often participate in retirement savings arrangements.
- Women contribute lower amounts and less frequently.
- Women earn lower investment returns.
- Women have lower benefit entitlements of their own.
- Women have lower retirement income and need it to last longer.

There are two biological drivers that impact the amount of retirement income that a women can expect to receive. First, women give birth to children, and take time off work around the birth of their child, during which they may not have income to contribute to their retirement savings plans. Second, women on average tend to live longer than men, and so their retirement savings must finance a longer period.

However, the majority of characteristics of being a woman that contribute to the gender pension gap relate to social constructs and institutional factors. These have a large impact on how women participate in the labour market and their patterns of employment and pay. In addition, they also have other subtle influences on the choices that women themselves make with respect to the types of careers they pursue, their financial education, and attitudes towards saving and investing. All of these factors play a role in determining the amount of retirement income that women will be able to obtain.

Women's role as caretaker of children and/or family members is often the source of the determinants of the gender pension gap that relate to the labour market. Women's higher involvement in carrying out this unpaid work compared to men may lead to lower participation in the labour market, more breaks in their employment history, higher rates of part-time work, and lower salaries. This means that they are less likely to have access to a retirement savings arrangement, are less likely to contribute even if they do have access, and are likely to have lower and less frequent contributions. Furthermore, even if their spouse accumulates sufficient retirement entitlements to finance both partners' retirement, women may still have fewer entitlements of their own, leaving them in a more vulnerable position in case of divorce or the death of their spouse.

Career patterns are a major factor in the gender pension gap. Women in the OECD have a career length just two-thirds that of men. Women also make up 70% of part-time workers in the OECD (OECD, 2019[1]). Career patterns are the largest contributor to the gender pension gap in the United Kingdom (Jethwa, 2019[2]). The OECD analysis of Germany and the United States indicates the likely influence of the caretaking role and career breaks on the gender pension gap, as gaps in entitlements do not emerge until women are in their 30s – the age when they are most likely to take a break from full-time employment to care for children (Chapter 3).

Lower incomes are another leading driver of the gender pension gap. The average gender pay gap for full-time employees in the OECD currently stands at around 13% (OECD, 2020[3]). Chapter 3 shows that income differences are a main driver of the gender pension gap in Finland and the United States.

The fact that women tend to earn less than men, increases their likelihood to leave full-time employment to be caretakers, and the link between pay and employment patterns becomes a circular problem. The lack of affordable childcare in many jurisdictions means that women may not see much financial benefit in returning to work full-time after maternity leave. An example calculated in the context of the Australian system shows that 90% of the additional income of working a fourth day a week on a AUD 60 000 annual salary (around 20% less than the average salary) would be lost to care costs, taxes, and lost welfare payments, and there would be zero financial gain from working a fifth day (Dale and St John, 2020[4]). Low salaries therefore lead women to take more part-time work or career breaks to be caretakers, which in turn leads them to earn lower salaries. Caretaking also increases a woman's reliance on the salary of the spouse, ultimately leading to a lack of her own entitlements to retirement income.

The lack of their own retirement income entitlements puts women in a much more vulnerable position in the case of divorce, and the reduction in retirement income is larger for women than for men following divorce. The financial impact of divorce on retirement income in the United Kingdom is 50% for women, compared to 33% for men (Jethwa, 2019[2]).

While factors linked to participation in the labour market are the main drivers of the gender pension gap, other secondary factors come into play and are also worth recognising. Lower levels of financial education and literacy may lead women to engage less in retirement planning. Women demonstrate lower levels of financial knowledge in the majority of OECD countries (OECD/INFE, 2016[5]). Women are also underrepresented in the fields of science, technology, engineering, and mathematics (STEM). This trend seems to be driven by stereotyping and expected gender roles rather than actual interest and ability, as the educational paths of boys and girls only start to diverge around age 15 (OECD, 2017[6]). Nevertheless, this divergence ultimately leads females to industries where employers are less likely to offer an occupational retirement savings arrangement, with one exception being the public sector where women are highly represented and have access to an occupational plan. Chapter 3 shows that lack of access is a significant driver of the difference in coverage of these types of arrangement in the United States, and therefore also for the gender pension gap.

Women also frequently demonstrate higher levels of risk aversion than men, which can translate into a preference for lower-risk investments and therefore lower returns on their retirement savings. Chapter 2 presents evidence that this is linked to differences in attitudes towards risk and competition that are shaped by societal factors and expectations rather than an inherent difference in preferences (Croson and Gneezy, 2009[7]; Gneezy, Leonard and List, 2008[8]). This bias can be reinforced by financial advisors who may be influenced by gender stereotypes (Roszkowski and Grable, 2005[9]).

Nevertheless, some of these societal constructs do seem to be changing over time, leading to a gradual reduction in the gender pension gap in a number of countries. Women are participating in the labour market at higher rates. The proportion of working-age women having a job in the OECD has increased from 46%

in the 1990s to 52% in 2017 (OECD, 2019[10]). Changing attitudes towards the role of women has aided this trend. The proportion of the UK population supporting the idea that women should stay home and care for children has decreased by 35 percentage points since the 1980s (Government Equalities Office, 2019[11]). Women's education is also improving, with 57% of bachelor's and master's degrees across the OECD obtained by women in 2014 (OECD, 2017[6]). These trends have contributed to higher participation of women in occupational retirement savings arrangements. The gap in coverage for occupational arrangements is shrinking in Germany, and females aged 30-40 now have higher participation in occupational arrangements in the United Kingdom than men (Now Pensions, 2019[12]).

Despite these positive developments, the gender pension gap remains significant and needs to be reduced. The following section discusses some of the options available to address the drivers of this gap within the funded pension system.

5.2. Policy options to reduce the gender pension gap in retirement savings arrangements

There are numerous options for retirement savings arrangements to avoid exacerbating the negative impact on retirement income from the drivers of the gender pension gap summarised in the previous section. While they cannot address the drivers themselves in all cases, the design of the plans should at least account for and accommodate gender differences that can lead to lower eligibility, lower participation, lower and less frequent contributions, less regular career patterns, lower returns, lower individual rights, and lower retirement income. As such, they should aim to have a gender neutral design.

5.2.1. Options to increase women's access

Women have less opportunity to access retirement savings arrangements. This is largely because women are more likely to work in industries that do not provide access to an arrangement and are more likely not to meet eligibility requirements defined in terms of minimum salary or hours worked.

Increase the availability of retirement savings arrangements in industries employing women

The proportion of women covered by an occupational arrangement is lower than for men in many countries. One reason for this is that employers are less likely to offer such arrangements in the private sector industries where women tend to work.

Mandating employers to establish an occupational arrangement is one way to improve access for women, even if participation is not mandatory for the employee. Several countries demonstrate a negative relationship between the proportion of women in a sector and the availability of occupational plans in that sector (Chapter 1). Chapter 3 shows that one of the main drivers of the lack of participation in occupational arrangements by women in the United States – where employers are not required to set up a plan – is that the industries in which women are more likely to be employed are less likely to offer an occupational arrangement.

As an alternative to mandating the offer of an occupational plan, the government could provide incentives for employers to establish occupational arrangements for their employees. The SECURE Act in the United States, for example, offers a tax credit for small employers to help cover the costs of setting up a plan and educating their employees about it, and encourages them to establish Multiple Employer Plans with other small employers to mitigate the administrative expenses.

Increasing the availability of personal arrangements could also improve the participation of women. The coverage gap for personal plans is much lower than that for occupational arrangements, and participation by women in personal plans is equal to or higher than by men in several countries. This indicates that the availability of personal plans allows women who would like to save for retirement, but may not otherwise have access to an alternative arrangement, to do so.

Relax eligibility requirements for occupational arrangements

Eligibility requirements to participate in occupational arrangements should be relaxed in order to be more inclusive of women. Many countries impose criteria for employees to be eligible to participate in the retirement savings arrangement offered by the employer that disproportionally impact women. Such requirements are usually expressed as a minimum income threshold or a minimum number of hours worked (OECD, 2019[11]). As such, they are more likely to exclude women from participating, as women tend to earn lower salaries and more often hold part-time jobs. The impact of income thresholds is evident in the United Kingdom, where automatic enrolment has succeeded in increasing the participation of eligible employees, but had little impact on the 10 percentage point gap in participation between men and women among all employees (Chapter 4).

5.2.2. Options to increase women's participation

Measures should also be in place to encourage women who have access to a retirement savings arrangement to participate in and contribute to it. This can be done by nudging and providing incentives to participate, as well as engaging women in retirement planning with targeted educational workshops and communication that convey the importance of having their own savings for retirement.

Encourage participation through hard or soft compulsion

Mandatory participation for employees is effective at reducing the coverage gap and furthermore automates the link between women's increased participation in the labour market and their participation in a retirement savings arrangement. For example, women are not underrepresented in occupational arrangements in Finland, where participation in an earnings-related arrangement is mandatory for most types of workers, even the self-employed. In the United States, female participation is higher in plans where contributions are mandatory (Chapter 3). Women's participation in the mandatory superannuation in Australia has increased along with their participation in the labour market.

As an alternative to mandates, automatic enrolment into a retirement savings arrangement can also increase women's participation. The requirement in the United Kingdom to automatically enrol eligible employees in a workplace pension scheme succeeded in eliminating the participation gap between eligible males and females, which stood at three percentage points when the policy was introduced. Where automatic enrolment is not required, governments can provide incentives to encourage employers to adopt it. In the United States, the SECURE Act provides small businesses with a tax credit for implementing automatic enrolment of employees into their occupational scheme, on top of the tax credit for establishing a plan.

Provide financial incentives to join the plan

Subsidies to new members of retirement savings schemes can be helpful to encourage low-income individuals – and therefore also women – to have an account and start saving for retirement. Several countries, in particular those having automatic enrolment (e.g. New Zealand, Poland, Turkey) have introduced an initial one-off subsidy that individuals receive if they do not opt out of the retirement savings scheme. While the initial "kick-start" subsidy for the KiwiSaver in New Zealand has been discontinued, it contributed to the initial take-up and popularity of the plan, even for those who were not automatically enrolled. The scheme has also been successful among women, with over 50% of participants being women (Inland Revenue, 2019[13]). Nevertheless, their participation cannot be attributed solely to the kick-start subsidy, as the proportion of women participants has not significantly dropped since it was eliminated, and matching contributions also likely contribute to the KiwiSaver's popularity.

Chile also pays a subsidy to new low-income members of their defined contribution system, but rather than a one-off payment, the subsidy is for workers who join the system in their early working years. Individuals between the ages of 18 and 35 having a wage lower than 1.5 times the minimum monthly wage are eligible for the subsidy for each contribution that they make during the first 24 months. As such, it intends to encourage low-income individuals to start to contribute at a young age, thereby having a larger long-term impact on retirement savings. When the subsidy was introduced in 2011, more than half of the recipients were women (Hinz et al., 2013[14]).

Tailor financial education to women

Improvement in women's financial literacy and knowledge of the retirement system is needed to overcome their reluctance to deal with financial matters and to close the gap in financial knowledge relative to men. In line with the OECD Recommendation on Financial Literacy, programmes to improve women's financial literacy should be modified to be relevant for women. Chapter 2 shows that several jurisdictions have developed financial education programmes that specifically target women to help them to understand the importance of saving and preparing for retirement (OECD, 2013[15]). New Zealand has a *Women in Super* programme that organises meetings and events to educate women on the superannuation system and their specific retirement needs. Singapore's programme *Financial Education for Mature Women* targets middle aged women to help them prepare to be financially independent in older age.

Educational efforts will also need to help women to overcome their lower levels of confidence with respect to financial matters. Education involving peer groups and providing financial advice can help women to overcome their lack of confidence (OECD/INFE, 2013[16]). A successful example of a financial education campaign is the EMPOWER (Embracing and Promoting Options for Women to Enhance Retirement) programme in Wisconsin (Chapter 2). The programme developed communication materials targeted specifically at women and organised educational sessions for women only. The programme succeeded at increasing women's participation in the occupational plan by 2.6%, having a significant impact on the participation gap, and was particularly successful among younger women and those with lower earnings (Anderson and Collins, 2017[17]). Another example is Laborfonds, an occupational pension fund in Italy, which organises educational sessions to explain the benefits of the fund and how it works (Chapter 4). They have succeeded in increasing women's participation by targeting industries with a large representation of women. Other organisations focus more on the provision of advice, such as the women's group Frauenzentrale Zurich in Switzerland, which has set up a popular pension advice session for women (Leybold-Johnson, 2017[18]).

The way in which the importance of saving for retirement is communicated can also have a large influence on how successful the messages will be in encouraging women to save. One study showed that messages framed in a positive way to emphasise the benefits of saving for retirement were much better received by participants than negative messages emphasising the risks of not saving. For those not yet saving, negative messaging was particularly ineffective. Interestingly, this was the case for both women and men, even though women used more negative language when discussing saving for retirement (Behave London, 2019[19]).

5.2.3. Options to increase the level and frequency of contributions for women

Women contribute less to their retirement savings plans due to lower wages and a higher likelihood of being in part-time work. Career breaks linked to caretaking can also lead to contribution gaps and shorter contribution periods for women compared to men. This can be addressed through higher contributions from employers, employees, and/or spouses; financial incentives to contribute; subsidies for caretaking activities; allowance for catch-up contributions; tailored fee structures; and targeted communication efforts.

Encourage contributions from employers

A lack of employer contributions to employee's retirement savings schemes can contribute to lower retirement savings for women. For example, Chapter 3 shows that in the United States women are less likely to be members of plans into which employers contribute.

Eligibility requirements for employees to receive employer contributions to their retirement savings plans should not penalise low-income women. Australia, for example, has a minimum income threshold under which employers are not required to make the mandatory superannuation contributions for their employees on top of their paid wages. Total remuneration across multiple employers is not taken into account. Low-income women therefore miss out on this additional compensation.

A total remuneration approach to employee compensation could help to ensure that low-income women in particular are not completely excluded from employer-provided retirement income benefits and miss out on this compensation that they would otherwise receive. This could be a problem, for example, where the scheme has voluntary employer contributions and the employee is not eligible to participate (Dale and St John, 2020[4]). With a total remuneration approach, compensation takes into account the total monetary value of all benefits received. Any contributions to a retirement savings scheme would be deducted from this amount, so ineligible individuals would still be entitled to the compensation even if it is not paid to the retirement savings scheme.

Employer contributions can also be encouraged through financial incentives. In Germany, for example, employers making contributions on behalf of low-income employees receive a tax allowance.

Allow additional contributions from spouses

An additional source to increase contributions levels for women is their spouse. Permitting spousal contributions would allow the spouse to make contributions to their partner's retirement savings to compensate for lower salaries or for any time out of work to perform caretaking responsibilities. Many countries allow for such contributions, either to the partner's account directly (e.g. Australia, Hungary, Lithuania, Spain, the United Kingdom) or to a separate account set up by the spouse (e.g. Canada, the United States). The same contribution limits typically apply, that is the spousal contributions count against the contribution limits for the recipient spouse, including any contributions they have made themselves. As such, the same financial incentives in place to contribute to one's own plan also apply for the spouse's plan (e.g. tax deductibility).

Where there are financial incentives to contribute to a plan, allowing for spousal contributions may lead to this option being used solely to optimise taxes at the household level. Indeed, the few individuals making use of this option in Australia tend to earn higher incomes, and therefore likely benefit more from the tax concessions provided. As such, the benefit for the majority of women is likely to be minimal.

Spousal contributions have the large benefit of allowing women to accrue their own individual rights rather than rely solely on the entitlements accrued by their spouse on behalf of the household. In this way the receiving spouse is less penalised by the service she provides for the household through unpaid activities such as caretaking.

Provide financial incentives to increase contributions for those with low income

As women are more likely to have low incomes, they are also more likely to be able to benefit from financial incentives targeted directly at those with low incomes. Such incentives can encourage them to contribute more and more regularly. They most often take the form of tax credits – either for the low-income earner or their spouse – or matching contributions and subsidies.

Tax credits targeting low-income earners allow women with lower incomes to contribute higher amounts, all else equal. Several countries (e.g. Australia, Korea, the United States) provide larger tax credits specifically for low-income contributors.

Financial incentives can also encourage spouses to make additional contributions towards the retirement savings of their low-income partner. For example, the Spouse Super Contribution Tax Offset in Australia provides a tax credit to the spouse contributing on behalf of their non-working or low-income partner.

Matching contributions or subsidies can also target low earners, providing an additional incentive for them to contribute regularly to their retirement savings plan and increasing the amount that they can accumulate. For example, in Australia the government matches voluntary contributions by low-income earners, which seems to be effective at increasing contributions for this group. A reduction in the match rate and maximum benefit corresponded with a reduction in contributions, and while low-income groups are less likely to make voluntary contributions, those that do have higher contribution rates than other income groups (OECD, 2018[20]). Another example is in Germany, where the government provides subsidies for savers in the Riester plans that provide higher relative benefits for those with low-income, and as such have been effective at attracting low-income earners (OECD, 2018[20]). Furthermore, over the period 2008 to 2013, women received the majority of these subsidies (Klammer, 2017[21]).[1]

Provide subsidies for maternity and caretaking

Subsidies for having children and caretaking leave can help to counter the negative impact on retirement income for women who have children. These can take the form of contributions paid during maternity leave, potentially extended for a longer period of parental leave, to those who work part-time to care for children, or per-child subsidies.

Ideally, contributions for women on maternity leave would continue at the same rate as when they were working. In practice, the benefit to women varies depending on who pays the contribution and the earnings base on which contributions are made. In most countries, contributions to mandatory, quasi-mandatory, or occupational pension arrangements can continue during maternity and parental leave (Chapter 4). Often, contributions towards mandatory plans are taken over by the government. However, in some countries the contribution is voluntary, paid by the plan sponsor, or the employees themselves. Furthermore, contributions are not always based on the woman's full salary, but rather a percentage of salary or a flat amount, though in some cases contributions can be even higher than when women were working. Some benefits are only for the period of maternity leave, while others continue during parental leave and/or up to a maximum duration.

Contributions may also continue during time off of work for caretaking that does not necessarily follow the birth of a child, though this is less common. In Chile, for example, parents are entitled to take medical leave with their full salary to care for a child with a serious illness. A study in the United Kingdom showed that a policy to top up pension contributions for carers – including both those working part-time and those caring full-time – had a significant impact on the gender pension gap, as women are typically the ones working less to care for children (Jethwa, 2019[2]).

Per-child subsidies paid by the government, usually over a fixed period of time, are another way of compensating for the child penalty on retirement savings regardless of the time taken off of work, and is an approach found in several countries. However, if offered unconditionally, this type of subsidy may be less effective in promoting retirement savings over the long term. While the child subsidy in Chile has been effective at increasing the number of women with a retirement savings account, it has not led to increased contributions (Chapter 4). Similarly, the balances in retirement savings accounts for women in Korea who received a child subsidy remained low because they did not make additional contributions afterward (Hinz et al., 2013[14]). In contrast, Germany requires a minimum level of contributions to the Riester plan in order to receive the child subsidy, which encourages regular savings behaviour.

Allow contribution limits to be carried forward

Allowing any contribution limits to be carried forward to future years would allow women to be able to make up any lost contributions during time off work for maternity leave or caretaking. Several jurisdictions allow for this, with the period that can be carried forward ranging from three years (the United Kingdom) to indefinitely (Canadian registered retirement savings plans).

Target communication to educate women on the importance of regular contributions

Communication and education for financial matters is more effective if it is personalised, and if made in a timely manner corresponding to specific life events and "teachable moments" (OECD, 2019[22]). Communication to encourage women to contribute to their retirement savings plan should therefore be tailored to their specific situation and period of life.

Personalisation of communication can go a long way to better capture the attention of the individual and help them to understand what action they could or should take given their situation. In one example carried out by Mercer, employees were sent short, personalised videos about the impact that additional contributions could have on their retirement savings and income in retirement (Chapter 4). The videos also linked the level of contribution and retirement income with the expected quality of life that they could provide in retirement. Women were particularly receptive to this type of communication, and were significantly more likely to watch the video to the end, as well as more likely to increase their pension contributions after they watched it (Read, 2017[23]).

The timing of the communication also matters, and can be more effective if provided at the relevant moment in a woman's life, such as around the birth of a child. Nationwide Pension Fund in the United Kingdom provides a link on their website with specific information for new parents, explaining under what conditions pension contributions and insurance coverage will continue. It also takes advantage of this moment to encourage new parents to review their beneficiary information in case of death (Nationwide Pension Fund, 2020[24]). The Finnish Centre for Pensions provides a calculator for new parents to understand the financial impact of the length of the parental leave that they take, showing at which point their benefit accrual will start to suffer if they take a longer period of leave. Verve Super, a pension fund for women in Australia, offers free coaching and guidance, and helps women with decisions relating to specific questions, such as contributions during parental leave.

5.2.4. Options to better accommodate the career patterns of women

Women are more likely to have shorter careers and career breaks, as well as low and irregular contributions to their retirement savings plans. This is driven by lower incomes on average and taking time off from full-time work for caretaking. The design of retirement savings arrangements could better accommodate the career patterns of women by being more flexible with respect to contribution levels, improving the portability of occupational arrangements and adapting the fee structure to accommodate lower balances.

Allow for flexible contribution levels

Given the career pattern of women is not always constant, contribution rates should be able to vary over time to allow women the flexibility to balance immediate needs with long-term savings goals, and to contribute more when they are better able to. This could be done by allowing women to choose from a range of contribution levels, as is the case for the KiwiSaver plan in New Zealand. Allowing for contribution holidays could also be helpful to allow a temporary break in contributions during periods of greater financial difficulty, particularly for low-income caretakers.

Improve the portability of plans

Women are more likely to move in and out of the labour market to accommodate the caretaking needs of their family. This means that they may not have access to a plan during these periods, and when going back to work they may have to contribute to a different scheme with the new employer.

Being able to contribute to the same plan regardless of whether they are employed or not would facilitate more continuity in retirement savings for women who take time off from working. Nevertheless, this would need to be accompanied with the allowance for flexible contributions in order to be most effective. Requirements around the frequency and level of contributions seem to be a barrier for individuals to make use of such arrangements in practice (OECD, 2020[25]).

For women changing employers, it is also important to avoid the accumulation of several accounts linked to each employer to help women build up more retirement savings in total. Having several small accounts could result in higher overall fees, unnecessarily deteriorating women's retirement savings. Furthermore, having several accounts impedes active engagement with retirement planning as it reduces the visibility of the future retirement income potential that the retirement savings will be able to provide.

Ensuring that people are able to contribute to the same plan even when changing employers is one way to avoid several small accounts. This could be done by having a centralised institution managing the collection and payment of contributions, so that they can direct all contributions on behalf of a given member to the pension fund of her choice. This is the approach taken for the KiwiSaver in New Zealand and the Premium Pension in Sweden. Another approach is to de-link the choice of provider from employment, so the individual can choose to which account all of her contributions are paid, as is done in Mexico.

An alternative to having a single account would be to facilitate the transfer of the existing account when changing employment. This would be more effective if done automatically, as employees do not always take the necessary steps to make the transfer. In Australia, the tax office plays a central role in facilitating the consolidation of small accounts and preventing individuals from opening new accounts unnecessarily. It can track small inactive accounts to consolidate them into the current active account, and now automatically provides new employers with the employees' active account details. Their website also includes a "consolidate my accounts" button which automates the consolidation for savers.

Adapt the fee structure for small balances

Smaller and less regular contributions due to lower incomes and periods away from work can mean that the balance in women's retirement savings accounts starts very low and grows slowly. As such, fixed fees that the provider charges can have a relatively large impact on the balance of the account, and be a barrier for women to accumulate retirement savings.

Fee structures for retirement savings accounts could adapt to help small savings accounts to grow and be more forgiving to lower contributions during time off of work for caretaking. In particular, fee structures should avoid charging fixed fees, particularly for small balances.

5.2.5. Options to improve investment returns for women

Women tend to demonstrate more risk-aversion than men – a bias which is often reinforced by financial advisors – leading them to invest in more conservative strategies that offer potentially lower returns. Appropriate default investment strategies and objective assessments of individual risk tolerance can help women overcome their conservative bias.

Implement a non-conservative default option

Nudging women towards more balanced-risk investment options would help to overcome their tendency to select a more conservative strategy and take on a reasonable level of risk for the long-term horizon when saving for retirement. Numerous studies have shown that most retirement savers will remain in the default investment option that their savings plan offers, and offering an appropriate default investment option is a key recommendation of the *OECD Roadmap for the Good Design of Defined Contribution Pension Plans*. The default strategy should therefore be one that appropriately balances risk with the need to protect the retirement savings from severe market downturns. Indeed, there is some evidence that the introduction of qualified default investment alternatives in the United States, has reduced the difference in investment returns between men and women (Garnick, 2016[26]).

The appropriate default option should aim to be the optimal strategy for the typical career of women participating in the plan. Lifecycle default strategies are common in most OECD jurisdictions. Such strategies balance risk-taking with protection by gradually reducing the exposure to risky assets as the individual approaches retirement. However, other strategies could be considered that better account for women with low-income or those who take more career breaks. For example, alternative assets could potentially provide stable returns in the long term without the need to de-risk, offering a better solution for those having less regular contributions and an uncertain retirement date (Pensions Policy Institute, 2019[27]). Other options could aim to optimise the risk of the default strategy taking into account the expected importance of other sources of retirement income, namely the public system.

Offer objective assessments of risk tolerance

Objective assessments of risk tolerance could help women to avoid biased investment recommendations that are more conservative than appropriate for their actual risk appetite. According to the OECD Recommendation on Financial Literacy, women should have access to appropriate, independent and adequate financial advice. Financial advisors may be influenced by gender bias and reinforce women's tendency towards risk aversion by advising them to invest more conservatively regardless of their demonstrated risk tolerance. To overcome this bias, assessments of risk tolerance could be automated to provide an objective view of risk appetite. Numerous robo-advisors already implement such assessments on their platforms to determine the range of investment options and vehicles that would be appropriate for the saver (e.g. Yomoni in France). As digital investment platforms become more prevalent, such assessments could be more easily implemented for retirement savings.

5.2.6. Options to increase the individual retirement benefit entitlements of women

Not having sufficient benefit entitlements of their own puts women at increased risk of poverty in old age. While income resources are usually shared between spouses, which compensates for women having lower incomes and taking time off of work to care for children, this is not always the case for retirement benefits and savings. As a result, many women may lose access to or part of those retirement benefits if they divorce or upon the death of their spouse. To ensure that women share a part of their spouse's retirement benefit accrual as well as their income, entitlements can be split either while the spouse accumulates them or upon the divorce of the couple. Communication around the options available should increase women's awareness of the possibility and importance of splitting retirement assets upon divorce.

Split the retirement benefit entitlement of the spouse

Individual benefit entitlements could be increased for women by allowing members to transfer part of their own retirement income benefit entitlements to their spouse. The split can be made at any point in time, from the initial contribution to the accrued benefits to the withdrawal of assets or payment of benefits at retirement.

Allowing for a split of entitlements as they are accrued ensures that spouses will have their own entitlements throughout the accumulation period. Australia allows individuals to divert a portion of their mandatory contribution to the superannuation system to a spouse's account. Sweden allows a portion of entitlements earned over the last calendar year to be transferred to a spouse's account once per year, though a charge is levied on the transfer to recognise that they most often are transfers from men to women, who can expect to receive retirement income benefits over a longer period of time. Iceland offers significant flexibility to share benefit entitlements with spouses. The split can be done during accumulation for past and/or future benefits in accrual, or alternatively the split can apply to retirement income based on current and/or future accruals. However, the take-up of this option remains very low, with less than 0.1% of accounts splitting their entitlements (Chapter 4).

Alternatively, the split can be executed upon termination of the accumulation of entitlements, whether this is due to leaving the plan or to retirement, though protections to the spouse in case of death may still be in place before that. The transfer of assets accumulated at retirement to a spouse's account is one withdrawal option available in Portugal. The Netherlands allows accumulated entitlements to be split either when a member leaves the arrangement or up to a year before the arrangement pays a retirement income. If the member does not request a transfer within a certain time period, benefits will automatically be paid to a partner upon the death of the member when the partner reaches pensionable age.

Facilitate the split of retirement benefit entitlements upon divorce

Facilitating the split of benefit entitlements upon divorce will help to protect women who have relied on the income of their spouse and therefore accumulated fewer of their own entitlements, and allow them to have a higher retirement income than they could have on their own. Most countries allow for the split of entitlements upon divorce, and view retirement benefits as the joint property of the couple.

Explicitly requiring a split of retirement assets upon divorce, not only total assets, would better contribute to women's financial security in retirement. Making the split automatic, as the Netherlands is planning to do, would further facilitate the transfer of entitlements to women and ensure that they receive the retirement benefits that they should be entitled to. Alternatively, certain criteria could determine whether the split is justified. In Denmark the split of benefits is considered when there is a large difference in retirement benefits accrued by the spouses or if one spouse has saved less for the sake of the family.

Relying solely on court orders to split retirement assets at divorce – the approach taken in a majority of countries – does not often result in a split. Oftentimes women are not aware that this is a possibility, and lawyers may be reluctant to promote this option due to the complexities involved in splitting some types of benefit entitlements. Less than 4% of divorce orders in 2018 in the United Kingdom included an attachment order to divide the pension entitlements accumulated during marriage once they are in payment (Now Pensions, 2019[12]). Nevertheless, this rate is higher when considering all types of pension split orders. In 2011-2012, a sample of cases indicated that 14% of cases accounted for a split of pension assets in some manner (Woodward and Sefton, 2014[28]).

Splitting accumulated entitlements at the time of divorce rather than splitting future benefits when they will be paid may better ensure that women receive the benefits they should be entitled to. This allows for a clearer split based on entitlements accumulated during marriage, and avoids complications relating to age differences and the timing of retirement income payments as well as the risk of losing benefits altogether in case of the death of the ex-spouse. Nevertheless, for entitlements that are more difficult to split during accumulation due to a lack of individual rights, the law should allow for adjustment of the retirement income to be paid to accommodate age differences.

Practical considerations as to how the split is made for non-defined contribution (DC)-type arrangements should also be taken into account. In theory the split can either be done by splitting entitlements within a plan, thereby adding the spouse as a member of the scheme, or by transferring entitlement to another plan. The former solution may present some logistical challenges that could increase the cost of the split, reducing the benefit for the spouse (Serenelli, 2020[29]).

Increase women's awareness of the possibility to share their ex-spouse's retirement benefits

Information on the possibility and the process of splitting retirement assets upon divorce should be available to women at the time of their divorce. Women need to be more aware of the possibility of splitting retirement assets, as well as the impact that not splitting these assets can have on their retirement security. As with communicating on the financial impact of taking time off to care for children, providing this information at a time that corresponds with relevant life events – both at marriage and at divorce – could improve the impact that this information has on the financial decisions of women. Nationwide Pension Fund provides a good example of communication with their Pensions and Divorce Leaflet, which describes the options available and the procedure to follow in simple terms (Nationwide Pension Fund, 2020[24]). It also includes a reminder to update beneficiary information, which could change following divorce.

5.2.7. Options to increase the level of retirement income that women receive

Women can expect to spend a longer period of time in retirement, putting them at a disadvantage relative to men as to how long their retirement savings have to last. For defined contribution-type arrangements, this often translates into a lower monthly retirement income for the same account value, and an increased risk of a loss in purchasing power. Options for the design of the system that could help to address this inequality include equalising retirement ages, basing retirement income on unisex mortality rates, providing an explicit subsidy to women, promoting survivor income benefits, and encouraging the availability of pay-out options that increase retirement income over time.

Equalise retirement ages between genders

Women should not systematically retire earlier than men given that they can already expect to spend a longer time in retirement if retiring at the same age. Retiring earlier than men can put women at a disadvantage by shortening the amount of time they have to accumulate benefit entitlements and increasing the length of time that benefits are paid. While most OECD countries have the same retirement age for both genders, several still have an earlier retirement age for women or reduce the retirement age for women who have children.

While the targeted retirement ages should not be different between men and women, there should still be some flexibility around the allowed retirement age to allow women to accommodate potential caring responsibilities. Women nearing retirement age can often have caretaking responsibilities for elderly parents, an older husband or grandchildren. Flexibility around the age at which they retire can therefore be valuable to them to be able to balance their financial and family needs.

Calculate retirement income based on unisex mortality

Calculating retirement income based on unisex mortality rates would equalise the amount of income that women and men receive, all else equal. Nevertheless, this solution cannot be effectively applied in all retirement schemes. First, unisex mortality will only be effective in collective arrangements that can benefit from longevity risk pooling. Using unisex mortality rates for the purpose of calculating programmed withdrawals would simply increase the risk that women would run out of assets in retirement. Second, unisex mortality rates are not likely to be effective at increasing women's retirement income where annuitisation is voluntary within the scheme. In the United States, annuitisation by men within occupational DC schemes – where unisex rates are obligatory – is rare because males can simply transfer their assets out of the scheme and purchase an annuity offering a higher income priced with gender-distinct rates. This effectively results in the calculation of retirement income using female mortality rates, with no additional benefit to women from the requirement for unisex rates (OECD, 2016[30]).

Where annuitisation is mandatory, an additional benefit of requiring a retirement income based on unisex mortality rates is that it may also encourage women to save more for retirement. Following the introduction of unisex pricing in Germany, women seem to save in Riester plans – which require the annuitisation of the accumulated balance at retirement – beyond their normal savings behaviour (Jusufovic, 2015[31]).

Provide a subsidy to compensate women for higher life expectancies

Direct subsidies, either during accumulation or at the point of retirement, could compensate women for having higher life expectancies and increase the level of retirement income that they receive. However, such subsidies could potentially have a negative impact on women's wages and employment depending on how they are financed. Some employers in Australia voluntarily pay an additional contribution to the retirement savings plan of female employees as a way of promoting gender equality and positioning themselves as an attractive employer for women. As the additional contribution is voluntary, there is no negative impact on the employability of women. Nevertheless, gender discrimination laws that prohibit offering different compensation depending on gender could be a barrier to such subsidies in many countries. As an alternative, the government could provide a subsidy. A recent reform proposal in Chile included a subsidy to women at the point of retirement to increase the amount of retirement income that they would receive.

Promote pay-out options with survivor income

Having pay-out options that include the payment of an income to a surviving spouse can protect women having a partner from the risk of poverty in old age. A pay-out option offering survivor income may not always be available, particularly in less developed retirement markets that are not yet mature. In contrast with inheriting assets as a lump sum, survivor incomes will also protect the surviving women from the risk of outliving those assets. Nevertheless, survivor income is typically lower than the retirement income paid while the primary beneficiary is alive, so this solution is not a substitute for increasing women's own benefit entitlements.

Where joint benefits are available, take-up can be encouraged through the use of hard or soft compulsion. Several OECD countries with DC arrangements require survivor income benefits for spouses. For example, married men choosing an annuity option in Chile are required to take a joint-and-survivor annuity rather than an individual annuity. Behavioural nudges can also be effective at increasing the take-up of joint and survivor annuities. The United States significantly increased the proportion of retirees taking survivor benefits through their occupational defined benefit plan by imposing this option as a default for married individuals and requiring the additional administrative step of the agreement of both spouses to opt out of this option (Chapter 4). Part of this increase, however, may also be attributed to an increase in the availability of this option.

Encourage the availability of pay-out solutions that increase payments over time

Pay-out solutions that offer increasing payments over time can protect individuals from a loss of purchasing power over time. Because of their longer lives, women are more exposed to the risk of losing purchasing power due to the compounding effects of inflation. Options that provide indexation to an inflation measure are the most effective solution to protect women from inflation risk. Most jurisdictions allow for this option at least on a discretionary basis, if not a mandatory one. Nevertheless, indexation to inflation may not necessarily be the most efficient option for individuals to hedge the risk of a loss of purchasing power in retirement. Where inflation risk is not easily hedged, such options can entail significant risk to the providers and therefore involve substantial cost to the individual (OECD, 2016[30]).

As an alternative to full indexation to inflation, arrangements relying on risk sharing, where retirement income is not fully guaranteed, can aim to increase payments over time depending on investment and longevity experience. Such arrangements are likely to be able to pay higher retirement incomes as well due to the lower risk exposure for the provider (OECD, 2020[25]). Numerous countries have retirement income arrangements that aim to keep up with inflation. The bonus policy for the ATP in Denmark includes this objective. Another example are conditional indexation arrangements in Canada, which tie the indexation of retirement income payments to the financial strength of the scheme.

5.3. Looking forward

Much progress has been made in societies over the last decades in reducing the gender differences driving the gender pension gap. Societal attitudes about the role of women as homemakers and caretakers have been evolving. This has contributed to an increase in female participation in the workforce, leading to increased access to retirement savings schemes. This has also enabled women to accumulate retirement savings and entitlements of their own rather than relying solely on those of their spouse. Furthermore, there is a downward trend in the gender pay gap, providing women with more resources to put aside for their retirement. Women are also more often completing higher education, giving them access to higher paying jobs and leaving them in a better position to effectively plan and manage their financial future.

The ongoing COVID-19 crisis is threatening this progress, and is exacerbating many of the drivers of the gender pension gap. Women face an increased risk of unemployment, as they are more likely to work in sectors that have been heavily affected by restrictions, namely hospitality, tourism and retail sectors. Women also make up the majority of part-time workers, who are at higher risk of being laid off in times of crisis. When schools close, women are taking the burden of ensuring the education of their children. Physical distancing norms mean that women may also have to take over the caretaking responsibilities from grandparents who were contributing to caring for grandchildren in order to protect their elderly parents from the virus. These pressures may cause women to reduce their working hours to be able to fulfil the additional caretaking responsibilities, or prevent them from returning to the labour market. They may also lead women to reduce or suspend their contributions to their retirement savings plans.

Women are also less likely to be in a position to fully participate in the post-COVID recovery phase and to be able to overcome the detriment that the pandemic has had on their retirement preparedness. Their risk aversion in investment may make them less likely to invest in the stock market and benefit from the economic recovery. Women will also be more adversely affected by policies allowing the withdrawal of retirement savings during this period. Their lower balances on average mean that it will be even harder to make up these losses as they will miss out on the compound returns. The increase in divorce rates following lockdown measures will leave women in a more vulnerable position as they could lose the retirement benefits of their spouse.

In the wake of the pandemic, policy makers are therefore facing an even greater challenge to reduce the gender pension gap and improve gender equality. Fixing this problem will necessarily have to go beyond improving the design of retirement savings arrangements, and will need to target the major drivers behind the gender pension gap, particularly gaps in labour market participation and pay.

To target the drivers of the gender pension gap, pension funds themselves can make a difference with the way they choose to invest their members' assets, provided their investment decisions remain in the best interest of members. They can invest in projects that promote social infrastructure that address the sources of the gender gap, such as childcare and financial education. They can also actively engage as shareholders to ensure that the companies they are investing in are also working towards gender equality in terms of pay and executive-level representation, and can sanction those who fall short with their voting decisions. Such investment behaviour will eventually have a real impact on how companies address gender gaps in their employment practices, and the benefits will translate into higher salaries and higher retirement savings for women.

The current situation calls for more drastic measures to reduce existing gaps linked to employment and to help women return to work in the recovery from this crisis so that they may continue to effectively plan for a secure financial future. The gender pay gap, disincentives linked to the cost of care, and low financial capabilities all need to be tackled – in addition to the design of retirement savings arrangements– if we are to continue to progress in closing the gender pension gap.

References

Anderson, D. and J. Collins (2017), *Can knowledge empower women to save more for retirement?*, https://crr.bc.edu/wp-content/uploads/2017/09/wp_2017-12.pdf (accessed on 25 February 2019). [17]

Behave London (2019), *Gender, Age & Pension Savings: New research for the pension industry into communication biases.* [19]

Croson, R. and U. Gneezy (2009), "Gender differences in preferences", *Journal of Economic Literature*, Vol. 47/2, pp. 448-474, http://dx.doi.org/10.1257/jel.47.2.448. [7]

Dale, M. and S. St John (2020), *Women and Retirement in a post COVID-19 world*, https://cdn.auckland.ac.nz/assets/business/about/our-research/research-institutes-and-centres/RPRC/OtherPapers/Women%20in%20Super%20September%202020.pdf. [4]

Garnick, D. (2016), *Income Insights: Gender Retirement Gap.* [26]

Gneezy, U., K. Leonard and J. List (2008), *Gender differences in competition: Evidence from a matrilineal and patriarchal society*, NBER Working Paper Series, http://www.nber.org/papers/w13727. [8]

Government Equalities Office (2019), *Gender Equality Monitor*, HM Government. [11]

Hinz, R. et al. (eds.) (2013), *Matching Contributions for Pensions: A review of international experience.* [14]

Inland Revenue (2019), *Annual Kiwisaver Statistics*, https://www.ird.govt.nz/about-us/tax-statistics/kiwisaver/datasets. [13]

Jethwa, C. (2019), *Understanding the Gender Pension Gap.* [2]

Jusufovic, K. (2015), *To Riester or not to Riester: A matter of pension regulations in Germany.* [31]

Klammer, U. (2017), *The family and gender dimension in German pension reforms.* [21]

Leybold-Johnson, I. (2017), *Pensions - what women need to know*, https://www.swissinfo.ch/eng/gender-pension-gap_pensions-what-women-need-to-know/42970284. [18]

Nationwide Pension Fund (2020), *Change in Circumstance*, https://nationwidepensionfund.co.uk/active/benefits/change-in-circumstance (accessed on September 2020). [24]

Now Pensions (2019), *Facing an unequal future Closing the gender pensions gap*, https://www.nowpensions.com/wp-content/uploads/2019/07/NP-gender-pensions-gap-report.pdf. [12]

OECD (2020), *OECD Employment Outlook 2020: Worker Security and the COVID-19 Crisis*, OECD Publishing, Paris, https://dx.doi.org/10.1787/1686c758-en. [3]

OECD (2020), *OECD Pensions Outlook 2020*, OECD Publishing, Paris, http://dx.doi.org/10.1787/67ede41b-en. [25]

OECD (2019), "Are funded pensions well designed to adapt to non-standard forms of work?", in *OECD Pensions at a Glance 2019: OECD and G20 Indicators*, OECD Publishing, Paris, https://doi.org/10.1787/1231a36d-en. [1]

OECD (2019), *Pension Markets in Focus*. [10]

OECD (2019), *Smarter financial education: key lessons from behavioural insights for financial literacy initiatives*. [22]

OECD (2018), *Financial Incentives and Retirement Savings*, OECD Publishing, Paris, https://doi.org/10.1787/9789264306929-en. [20]

OECD (2017), *The Pursuit of Gender Equality: An Uphill Battle*, OECD Publishing, Paris, http://dx.doi.org/10.1787/9789264281318-en. [6]

OECD (2016), *Life Annuity Products and their Guarantees*, OECD Publishing, Paris, https://doi.org/10.1787/9789264265318-en. [30]

OECD (2013), *Women and Financial Education: Evidence, Policy Responses and Guidance*, OECD Publishing, Paris, https://dx.doi.org/10.1787/9789264202733-en. [15]

OECD/INFE (2016), *International Survey of Adult Financial Literacy Competencies*. [5]

OECD/INFE (2013), *OECD/INFE Policy guidence on addressing women's and girls'needs for financial awareness and education*. [16]

Pensions Policy Institute (2019), "The gender pension gap: can it be closed?", *PPI Briefing Note* 114, https://www.pensionspolicyinstitute.org.uk/media/3185/20190604-the-gender-pensions-gap-can-it-be-closedpub.pdf. [27]

Read, E. (2017), *Pension gender gap, how can we respond?*, https://www.slideshare.net/OECD-DAF/eve-read-pension-gender-gap-how-can-we-respond. [23]

Roszkowski, M. and J. Grable (2005), "Gender Stereotypes in Advisors' Clinical Judgments of Financial Risk Tolerance: Objects in the Mirror Are Closer than They Appear", *Journal of Behavioral Finance*, Vol. 6/4, pp. 181-191, http://dx.doi.org/10.1207/s15427579jpfm0604_2. [9]

Serenelli, L. (2020), "German pension equalisation changes likely to hinder providers", *IPE*, https://www.ipe.com/news/german-pension-equalisation-changes-likely-to-hinder-providers/10047767.article?utm_campaign=107549_11.9.20%20ipe%20daily%20news&utm_medium=email&utm_source=IPE&dm_i=5KVE,2AZH,C5K8L,8U0R,1. [29]

Woodward, H. and M. Sefton (2014), *Pensions on divorce: an empirical study*, Cardiff University. [28]

Notes

[1] However, this also includes women receiving the per-child subsidy, which go to the mother by default.

www.ingramcontent.com/pod-product-compliance
Ingram Content Group UK Ltd.
Pitfield, Milton Keynes, MK11 3LW, UK
UKHW051504290926
15471UKWH00008B/1399

9 789264 334533